Cruising Culture

TENDENCIES: IDENTITIES, TEXTS, CULTURES

Series Editor: Peter Brooker

Other titles in the series are:

Cruising Culture

Promiscuity, Desire and American Gay Literature

Ben Gove

Edinburgh University Press

© Ben Gove, 2000

Edinburgh University Press Ltd
22 George Square, Edinburgh

Typeset in Melior
by Pioneer Associates, Perthshire, and
printed and bound in Great Britain by
MPG Books Ltd, Bodmin

A CIP Record for this book is available from the British Library

ISBN 0 7486 1361 7 (paperback)

The right of Ben Gove
to be identified as author of this work
has been asserted in accordance with
the Copyright, Designs and Patents Act 1988.

Contents

*For Alex, who brightens everything
and for my parents, Phyllis and Peter*

Acknowledgements

Like most things in life, my experience of writing this book is best summed up by a lyric from The Smiths: 'Oh I can smile about it now, but at the time it was terrible.' My love and thanks go to these people, who variously cheered me up, helped me out and taught me all sorts of things:

Alex, Rachel Bowlby, Elaine Cade, Chris Clegg, Jonathan Dollimore, Alexander Doty, Angela Dress, Jan Fergus, Cory Gnazzo, Peter Gove, Liz Lewin, Stephen Maddison, Ellen McNeilly, Gwyn Metz, Peter Nicholls, Rachael Philipps, Lucy Robinson, Phyllis SantaMaria, Simon Shepherd, Alan Sinfield and Chris West.

Many thanks as well to the following: the British Academy for funding my Ph.D. research at Sussex University, where this book began; Pandora Press/Rivers Oram Press for permission to reprint a diagram from Gayle Rubin's 'Thinking Sex: Notes for a Radical Theory of the Politics of Sexuality,' in Carole D. Vance (ed.), *Pleasure and Danger: Exploring Female Sexuality*; and Peter Brooker, Nicola Carr and James Dale, my refreshingly human editors at Edinburgh University Press.

This book is also dedicated to the memory of David Wojnarowicz, with whom I had no personal connection, but whose absence as a public figure feels like a personal loss.

Series Editor's Introduction

Contemporary history continues to witness a series of momentous changes, altering what was only recently familiar ideological, political and economic terrain. These changes have prompted a new awareness of subjective, sexual, ethnic, racial, religious and cultural identities and of the ways these are constructed in metropolitan centres, regions and nations at a time when these spheres are themselves undergoing a period of critical transition. Recent theory has simultaneously encouraged a scepticism towards the supposed authenticity of personal or common histories, making identity the site of textualised narrative constructions and reconstructions rather than of transparent record. In addition, new developments in communication and information technology appear to be altering our fundamental perceptions of knowledge, of time and space, of relations between the real and the virtual, and of the local and the global.

The varied discourses of literature and media culture have sought to explore these changes, presenting life as it is negotiated on the borderlines of new, hybridised, performative, migrant and marginalised identities, with all the mixed potential and tensions these involve. What emerges are new, sometimes contradictory perceptions of subjectivity or of relations between individuals, social groups, ideologies and nations, as the inner and public life are rewritten in a cultural environment caught up in religious and political conflict and the networks of global consumption, control and communication.

The series *Tendencies: Identities, Texts, Cultures* follows these debates and shows how the formations of identity are being articulated in contemporary literary and cultural texts, often as significantly in their hybridised language and modes as in their manifest content.

Volumes in the series concentrate upon tendencies in contemporary writing and cultural forms, principally in the work of writers, artists and cultural producers over the last two decades. Throughout, its consistent interest lies in the making and unmaking of individual, social and national identities. Each volume draws on relevant theory and critical debate in its discussion *inter alia* of questions of gender and sexuality, race and ethnicity, class, creed and nation, in the structuring of contemporary subjectivities.

The kinds of text selected for study vary from volume to volume, but most often comprise written or visual texts available in English or widely distributed in English translation. Since identities are most often confirmed or redefined within the structures of story and narrative, the series is especially interested in the use of narrative forms, including fiction, autobiography, travel and historical writing, journalism, film and television.

Authors are encouraged to pursue intertextual relations between these forms, to examine the relations between cultural texts and relevant theoretical or political discourse, and to consider cross-generic and intermedia forms where these too bear upon the main concerns of the series.

Peter Brooker
University College, Northampton

Passing Pleasures:
Gay Men and Promiscuity

. . . a girl ought to celebrate what passes by.
Stephen Sondheim, A Little Night Music

I'll begin with two fictional moments. The first takes place on a mid-summer's night in late nineteenth-century Sweden, and comes from Stephen Sondheim and Hugh Wheeler's musical, *A Little Night Music* (1973; music and lyrics by Sondheim, book by Wheeler). As the upper-class central characters run amorously astray on the grounds of a country house, Petra, a maid, sings 'The Miller's Son'. Her words oscillate between fantasies of future married life, and her present youthful concern to promiscuously 'seize the day' before drab routine sets in:

It's a very short road
From the pinch and the punch
To the paunch and the pouch and the pension. . . .
In the meanwhile,
There are mouths to be kissed
Before mouths to be fed,
And a lot in between
In the meanwhile.
And a girl ought to celebrate what passes by. . . .

It's a very short day
'Til you're stuck with just one
Or it has to be done on the sly.
In the meanwhile,
There are mouths to be kissed
Before mouths to be fed,
And there's many a tryst
And there's many a bed.

There's a lot I'll have missed
But I'll not have been dead when I die!
And a person should celebrate everything
Passing by.
And I shall marry the miller's son.[1]

The second fictional moment also takes place on a summer's night, this
time in a park in New York's East Village in the 1970s, and comes from
Andrew Holleran's *Dancer from the Dance* (1978), considered by many
to be the quintessential gay male novel of that decade. Shortly before
hosting their final summer party on Fire Island, the novel's two central
characters – the promiscuous romantic Malone and the scandalous
socialite Sutherland – sit cooling off in that 'perfect place to rub the
itchy sore of lust':[2]

'Ah,' . . . [Sutherland] said, as a boy staggered out of the bushes zipping up
his leather pants, 'it is so good to get back to the original source, the Ur-text,
of it all,' he said, looking around at the dark figures bobbing at crotches, 'to
refresh ourselves with the original mysteries and rites around which, really,
our whole lives revolve. It is just this,' he said sitting back to regard the life
of our lagoon.[3]

Taken together, these two promiscuity espousing scenes from prominent gay male writers express one of the key gay cultural concerns
during what Holleran elsewhere calls 'the Age of Promiscuity', which
spanned roughly from the 1970s to the mid-1980s: namely, gay male
culture's concern with its right to – and with the perceived psycho-
social benefits of – multiple forms of sexual pleasure with multiple,
often unknown, partners.[4] Taken separately, however, these textual
fragments can also serve to illustrate two distinct (though sometimes
overlapping) recurring approaches to representing sexual 'promiscuity'
in contemporary American gay male writing.
    In the first scene, Sondheim's focus on Petra's attitude towards sexual
pleasure may be seen to follow on from several other highly influential,
and now canonical, American gay male theatre texts in the postwar
period that include iconic representations of *heterosexual* promiscuity
(adulterous or otherwise): Tennessee Williams's Blanche DuBois in *A
Streetcar Named Desire* (1947) and Reverend Shannon in *The Night of
the Iguana* (1962); Edward Albee's Martha in *Who's Afraid of Virginia
Woolf?* (1962); and – the most consistently foregrounded as 'promiscuous' of them all – Sondheim's own Robert/Bobby in *Company* (1970;
music and lyrics by Sondheim, book by George Furth). In all of these
performance texts, the gay male writer implicitly problematises the
dominant culture's frequent projection of promiscuous sexuality on to

gay men (amongst other groups) by focusing instead upon conflicting heterosexual experiences of, and attitudes towards, promiscuous sexuality and desire.

In the second scene, Sutherland's joyful declaration of the primary social importance and fascination of sexual pleasure – 'around which, really, our whole lives revolve' – partly reiterates the point I have just made: that gay male writers have often countered dominant culture's anxious projection of its own sexual diversity, in pathologised form, on to gay men by underlining the ubiquity of non-monogamous desires and practices in all sexual cultures; or in other words, by universalising promiscuity.[5] Yet at the same time, Sutherland's unabashed promiscuity – and his belief that romantic monogamous 'love is, after all, my dears, all anticipation and imagination'[6] – expresses a perspective openly espoused by many (though by no means all) gay men, both during the sexually prolific 'Age of Promiscuity', and also, in various forms, before and since the mythologised 1970s–early 1980s. It is this avowedly promiscuous gay male perspective – or rather, competing manifestations of it – that I want to examine in this study, alongside some of the innumerable (gay and straight) cultural objections to it.

As the commercial and critical success of *Dancer from the Dance* (and the lesser success of Larry Kramer's contemporaneous novel, *Faggots*) exemplifies, gay male fiction writers have played a crucial role in these complex gay cultural debates about the visible rise, and social effects, of non-monogamous sexual practice amongst gay men, particularly since the late 1970s. In one sense, the performance texts I have already cited, while addressing straight sexuality, can also be seen to comment upon gay male promiscuity under the guise of manifestly heterosexual narratives. Hence the *double entendre* for 'feminine'-identified gay male audiences of Petra's 'a girl ought to celebrate what passes by' in *A Little Night Music*; hence the symbolic significance of Blanche becoming promiscuous only *after* learning of her late husband's homosexuality in *Streetcar*; and hence the continuing speculation that Bobby in *Company* is a promiscuous 'gay man in straight drag', surrounded by fascinated, yet judgemental, married heterosexual couples.[7]

Alongside these Broadway-bound heterosexual narratives by and partly about gay men, however, Mart Crowley's 1968 off-Broadway play, *The Boys in the Band* (film version 1970), offered an explicit representation of opposing gay male attitudes to sex, crystallized in the tensions – and tentative resolution – between a long-term couple where one partner seeks monogamous stability, while the other craves multiple partners.[8] More recently, the mainstream American theatre and its audiences have become somewhat more receptive to openly gay male-themed works which comment upon gay sexual promiscuity, with varying degrees of success: Harvey Fierstein's *Torch Song Trilogy*

(1978; film version 1988); Tony Kushner's epic 'gay fantasia on national themes', *Angels in America* (1991–2; film version currently in production); Terrence McNally's 1990s variation on *Boys in the Band*, *Love! Valour! Compassion!* (1994; film version 1997); and the late heterosexual composer/lyricist Jonathan Larson's East Village rock musical, *Rent* (1995; film version currently in production), have all had highly successful Broadway productions, and all received Tony awards for best play or musical.[9]

But while the American commercial theatre has – like dominant culture generally – been slow to accommodate the range of gay sex-related material that frequently appears (off-)off-Broadway, or in other queer and 'alternative' small venues across the country,[10] gay male writers have more often turned to the novel, or to autobiography or poetry, to explore issues of sexual practice that are specific to gay culture through a less expensively produced and rarefied medium.[11] On the one hand, as Sarah Schulman notes, 'for those of us [particularly lesbians] who have decided to write about gay people in the same manner that heterosexual writers write about heterosexual people, for the most part even our best work will not be reviewed in the most prestigious publications nor sold in most American bookstores.'[12] On the other hand, though, both a handful of 'cross-over' authors (including James Baldwin, Michael Cunningham, David Leavitt, Armistead Maupin and Edmund White) and a wide range of other gay male writers have made important contributions to contemporary cultural understandings, and retrospective appraisals, of the spectrum of gay sexual practice – and particularly promiscuous sex, which is, unsurprisingly, most often foregrounded and treated seriously by the more marginalised writers (Bruce Benderson, Dennis Cooper, Samuel R. Delany, Gary Fisher, Robert Glück, Brad Gooch, Bo Huston, Gary Indiana, Kevin Killian, Michael Rumaker, David Wojnarowicz, and so on).[13] Moreover, many of these authors – and not only those with cross-over sales – tend to reach a far wider gay (and bisexual, and sometimes heterosexual) audience than the most commercially successful gay male playwright who directly addresses gay issues in his work.

Equally influential upon the sexual viewpoints of large numbers of gay readers, and upon many literary gay writers as well, are the less culturally sanctioned – and hence, frequently anonymous or pseudonymous – gay male writers of 'pulp' and porn fiction. (Most famously associated with promiscuous sexual narratives are the late John Preston, and Sam Steward, writing porn under the name of Phil Andros.) Since a decade before Gay Liberation, literally countless pulp and/or pornographic paperback novels have circulated amongst gay readers, shaping their fantasies and understandings of promiscuous sex (alongside and together with filmic and photographic porn).[14] As an article in the 1984 inaugural issue of *Advocate Men* recalled, 'for many an older gay man, Phil Andros, in the early 1960s, was his first encounter with a writer who dealt with the taboo subject of sex between men in a positive, guilt-free way... [f]rom first encounter under the counter to when in the early '70s he was more openly available.'[15] More generally, John Preston has noted that 'for myself and many other gay men, *pornographic writings were how we learned the parameters of our sexual life*. ... Pornography was how we developed our fantasies, both sexual and emotional.'[16] In the late 1970s and early 1980s, Preston writes, 'explicit erotic material ... was especially important to gay men because we were all in open rebellion over the way our sexuality had been repressed. We were breaking out in our lives, and people were looking for a literature to reflect that breakout.'[17] Responding to this cultural shift, an increasing range of large-circulation magazines like *Advocate Men* and *Mandate* – and 'alternative' queer 'zines like *Holy Titclamps* – have juxtaposed explicit images with written narratives, offering up (often subliminally) influential competing representations of sexual pleasure.

Of course, our sexual fantasies also frequently exceed the most widely available pornographic repertoire. Perhaps more interestingly, then, popular 'zines like *18 Wheeler, Straight to Hell* and *T.R.A.S.H (True Revelations and Strange Happenings)* consist almost entirely of readers' accounts of their sexual experiences and fantasies. These narratives therefore provide rich documents of gay male sexual diversity that extend back at least through the history of Gay Liberation (*Straight to Hell* has been published since 1969), and exceed the fairly narrow representational parameters of more commercial magazines: as one early editorial statement declared, 'if [*Straight to Hell*] doesn't reflect your experience and opinions send them to us and it will. We will publish articles by all homosexuals except women-haters ... and homosexual-haters.'[18] Many of these ephemeral 'zines have been reprinted in anthologies sold in gay/alternative bookstores as well as sex shops, making them more widely and lastingly available. Like the professional pulp and porn writers gestured towards above, these non-professional writers are of central importance to gay cultural understandings of sex and sexuality – not least for their largely uncensored public articulation of sexual fantasies and attitudes, in comparison with the greater caution of much mainstream gay male literature and mass media representation.

Although these porn/pulp writers are beyond the scope of this study, their explicitness in addressing gay male sexual practice and fantasy is shared by all three of the gay male writers of autobiography and fiction on whom I will be focusing, whose work narrativises gay promiscuity in contrasting, and interrelated, ways: John Rechy's cross-over best-seller, and now classic, *City of Night* (1963), and his ensuing gay-themed texts of the late 1960s and 1970s; Larry Kramer's contentious bestseller, *Faggots* (1978), and internationally produced AIDS play, *The Normal Heart* (1985); and the late David Wojnarowicz's more determinedly marginal, but nevertheless widely influential, *Close to the Knives: A Memoir of Disintegration* (1991) and other writings.

Defining 'Promiscuity': Dominant Meanings

Before proceeding, though, I should clarify my own understanding and use of that perennially vexed term, 'promiscuity'.

Notoriously vague, the word derives partly from the Latin *miscere*, meaning 'to mix', which is subsumed within *promiscuus*, meaning 'mixed' or 'indiscriminate'.[19] True to the multiple connotations of 'mixing' and 'indiscriminacy', the term has, throughout its history, contained both derogatory and more unassuming meanings. The Oxford English Dictionary's earliest citations, for example – from the seventeenth century – include Hobbes's 'To forbid the promiscuous Use of Women' in *Human Nature* (1650), which foreshadows the now common disparaging sexual meaning of 'promiscuous'; but there is also Milton's reference to 'the promiscuous crowd' in *Paradise Lost* (1667), which exemplifies the then-popular notion of the 'promiscuous' as 'consisting of members or elements of different kinds grouped or massed together without order . . .; [r]arely of a single thing.'[20] Hence, if this disorderly mixture – whether sexual or otherwise – has most frequently been interpreted as being detrimentally 'without discrimination or method; done or applied without respect for kind, order, number . . .; confusedly mingled,'[21] then these anxiously negative connotations are nevertheless not *intrinsic* to the notion of 'promiscuity'.

The more judgemental uses of the term have, however, always been predominant – as befits a modern Western history overwhelmingly characterised by fear and punishment of hybridity, plurality and change. Nowhere has this been more the case than in the primarily eroticised deployment of the term within late nineteenth and twentieth-century sexological, legal, literary and popular discourses: 'promiscuity' now conventionally connotes 'excessive', 'indiscriminate', and often 'insatiable' sexual practice. The question of just how much sex is required to render the participant(s) and event promiscuous is, of course, extremely nebulous and contextually specific. Yet as Michael Schofield, the British author of *Promiscuity* – one of many (pseudo-) sociological works on the subject published during the 1960s and 1970s – summarises, 'although the word means different things to different people, most people regard promiscuity as undesirable behaviour to be avoided if at all possible.'[22]

As Schofield himself later acknowledges, however, such a general statement about derogatory cultural understandings of 'promiscuity' effaces the crucial issue of who exactly is constructing the definition, and in relation to whose sexual practices. A brief look at Gayle Rubin's highly influential essay, 'Thinking sex: notes for a radical theory of the politics of sexuality' (1982), can help us to begin specifying the various prevalent cultural forces which deploy the notion of promiscuity in this derogatory way. Rubin writes:

Popular culture [and most other forms of sexual discourse are] permeated with ideas that erotic variety is dangerous, unhealthy, depraved, and a menace to everything from small children to social security. . . . All these hierarchies of sexual value – religious, psychiatric, and popular – function in much the same ways as do ideological systems of racism, ethnocentrism, and religious chauvinism. They rationalize the well-being of the sexually privileged and the adversity of the sexual rabble.[23]

She goes on to define the dominant 'sex hierarchy' more precisely as a binarised struggle between sex that is seen as '"good," "normal" and "natural" – ideally heterosexual, marital, monogamous, reproductive, and non-commercial – [and] "bad," "abnormal" or "unnatural" [sex, which] may be homosexual, unmarried, promiscuous, non-procreative, or commercial. It may be masturbatory or take place at orgies, may be casual, may cross generational lines, and may take place in "public", or at least in the bushes or the baths,' and so on.[24] In fact, most of the practices listed in this latter category ('non-procreative . . . commercial . . . orgies . . . casual . . . "public" . . . bushes or the baths') are regularly placed in the category of the 'promiscuous'.

Rubin then elaborates on 'the sexual hierarchy['s] . . . need to draw and maintain an imaginary line between good and bad sex.' She emphasises that most sexual discourses, 'be they religious, psychiatric, popular, or political . . . assume a domino theory of sexual peril. The line appears to stand between sexual order and sexual chaos. It expresses the fear that if anything is permitted to cross . . ., the barrier against scary sex will crumble and something unspeakable will skitter across.' In order to maintain this division (albeit unevenly),

Only sex acts on the good side are accorded moral complexity. . . . In contrast, all sex acts on the bad side of the line are considered utterly repulsive and devoid of all emotional nuance. The further from the line a sex act is, the more it is depicted as a uniformly bad experience.[25]

Rubin complicates her description of the dominant 'sex hierarchy', however, by situating different marginalised and/or denigrated sexual practices at varying distances from that conceptual line between 'good' and 'bad' sex, according to the degree of cultural hostility that

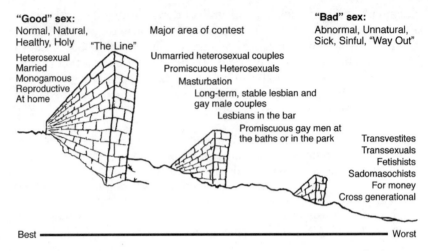

Figure 1.1 The sex hierarchy: the struggle over where to draw the line.
(Source: Pandora Press)

each receives (see Figure 1.1). In particular, her observation that both 'promiscuous heterosexuals' and 'long-term, stable lesbian and gay male couples' have become increasingly tolerated in the middle ground between 'good' and utterly 'bad' underlines that it is not 'promiscuity' *per se* that is usually condemned within normative discourses, but rather, the promiscuous sexuality of specific cultural groups – particularly, for example, promiscuous gay men.[26]

Who, then, defines who else is 'promiscuous'? On the one hand, the morally normative division between 'good' monogamy and 'bad' promiscuity is never solely traceable to blatant political conservatism: as we will see later, those who actively defend progressive social values – whether queer or otherwise – may well denounce or dismiss the sexual activities of others. Rubin writes that 'although its content varies, the format of a single sexual standard' – or a narrowly defined range of standards – 'is continually reconstituted within other rhetorical frameworks' outside of the more obvious institutions such as religion, right-wing politics or conventional psychiatry – frameworks 'including feminism and socialism.'[27] This common disparity between a progressive social perspective and an overly simplified and judgemental understanding of sex/uality reminds us that while sexual desire and activity are produced in and through social relations, they are also marked by the contradictions and opacities of the subconscious and unconscious, and as such, raise complex anxieties and resistances across all social groups – especially towards the supposed sexual 'excesses' of promiscuous forms of sex.

On the other hand, though, the denigration or demonisation of specific cultural groups as 'promiscuous' *can* also be broadly traced to the
conservative factions of dominant social groups; factions which at present have more cultural prominence and power than the range of anti-
promiscuous 'progressives' I have just mentioned. Crucially, although
Rubin's diagram distinguishes between heterosexual and homosexual
forms of promiscuity, we also need to add the further dominant distinction (amongst several others) between male and female sexualities.
The patriarchal cultural double standard that condones or encourages
male sexual adventuring, yet denigrates or punishes female non-
monogamy (or female sexual pleasure in general) as 'promiscuous',
remains all too pervasive. In their landmark study, *Re-Making Love:
The Feminization of Sex*, Barbara Ehrenreich, Elizabeth Hess and Gloria
Jacobs note that 'whether in 1950 or 1980, casual sex had always been
the macho symbol, and very few men were complaining as long as they
controlled the action.'[28] Hence, after a period of significant (if also
compromised) gains for female sexual autonomy in the late 1960s and
the 1970s:

By the early 1980s a backlash was brewing against what was pejoratively
called female 'promiscuity'. The media began to metamorphize the modern
woman, who had been practicing her sexual negotiating skills throughout
the 1970s, into an old-fashioned girl looking for moonlight, flowers, and
commitment. Women who didn't fit this stereotype were portrayed as
hopelessly misdirected. . . . Despite the enthusiasm women brought to the sexual revolution, this new revisionism inevitably began to feed on their doubts,
undermining the positive feelings of many who had enjoyed the freedom of
casual sex.[29]

These circumstances are frequently heightened for lesbians, and for
bisexual women who have sex with other women. For even though
promiscuous sexual practice is decidedly alive and well in lesbian
culture (as elsewhere), the prevailing dominant cultural representation
of lesbian sexuality – and of sex between women in general – as
intrinsically monogamous, domestic, or else predominantly desexu-
alised, serves to trivialise and condemn those forms of sexual pleasure
that men have no access to, or control over. (At the same time, though,
Tamsin Wilton has argued that even as 'the feminist politicisation of
lesbianism . . . set the stage for the construction of a proud, assertive
lesbian identity and . . . communities,' some feminists – particularly
some types of radical feminist – have, for various reasons, insisted that
lesbianism is 'an *escape*, not just from sex with men but from sexuality
per se.'[30])
     But there is another double standard at work in relation to promiscuity

which is central to the parameters of this study, based not on sexual difference, but on the related gender binarism: namely, the dominant presumed distinction between the appropriately (and for many, naturally) 'masculine' promiscuity of the heterosexual man, and the inappropriate (and for many, unnatural) promiscuity of the gay man, who is conventionally associated in dominant culture, of course, with the supposedly monogamous and domestic realm of 'femininity'. The profound influence of gender ideology upon different forms of gay male promiscuity is the subject of Chapter 1. Suffice it for now to point out the incoherence between this normative straight male = 'masculine'/gay male = 'feminine' binary, and dominant culture's concurrent partial awareness (and fear) of the hypermasculinised promiscuous butch gay man. Dominant discourse usually tries to get around this contradiction by positing gay men's identifications with 'masculinity' as ultimately unsuccessful attempts to mask their 'essential femininity'.

Yet the dominant negative deployment of the term 'promiscuous' does not only take place in patriarchal discourses and material practices – although other manifestations often intersect with patriarchal interests. As John D'Emilio and Estelle B. Freedman comment in their historical overview of sexuality in America, even though it is generally true that 'public expressions of and commerce in sexuality did not pose serious difficulties'[31] for the working class in the nineteenth century, nevertheless, dominant 'portrayals of workers as promiscuous and depraved helped define middle-class moral superiority' during that period.[32]

If we return to *A Little Night Music* for a moment, we find an example of the common association between promiscuity and the working class which is more favourable to its subjects. Immediately before Petra sings 'The Miller's Son', she has sex in the gardens of the country house with Frid, a butler, who tells her he is 'in the mood' for sex 'twenty-four hours a day', and contrasts their shared openness about casual sex with the apparent restraint of their employers:

FRID: You saw them all at dinner, dressed up like waxworks, jabbering away to prove how clever they are. And never knowing what they miss. . . . Catch one of them having the sense to grab the first pretty girl that comes along – and do her on the soft grass, with the summer night just smiling down.[33]

However, Sondheim and Wheeler are careful to situate Frid's words within the context of multiple upper-class sexual infidelities and confusions occurring on the same night.[34] This similarity between the employers' and employees' sex lives suggests the precariousness of generalising about the sexual proclivities of a social class, or even a sample from that class (although Frid and Petra's verbal and physical erotic directness does stand in direct contrast with the *secretive* promiscuity of most of their upper-class counterparts).

Despite Frid's attempt to position himself as the 'active' sexual figure in this brief seduction, Petra also connects with a long history of dominant cultural representations specifically of the young working-class woman as signifier of 'low' licentious sexuality: Susan J. Douglas notes in relation to postwar America that:

In pop culture iconography [as in various other forms of cultural discourse], the 'bad' girl . . . [has been] easily identified by class and ethnicity. She came from the 'wrong side of the tracks,' had dark hair and was not fair-skinned, wore spit curls and skirts with slits, and was the the kind of girl boys were urged to sow their 'wild oats' with before marrying. . . In other words, her willingness or desire to be sexually active could be dismissed as the allegedly hypersexualised, unrestrained behavior of the lower classes.[35]

In the case of Petra, though, Sondheim and Wheeler highlight her confident sexual agency favourably, as opposed to the more conventional trope of the ever-available working class 'slut' as mere receptacle for male virility. (PETRA: Who needs a haystack? Anything you've got to show, you can show me right here.[36])

Douglas's reference to normative links between 'bad' promiscuous sexuality and certain forms of ethnicity also points to another central aspect of prevailing notions of 'promiscuity' that Rubin's diagram omits. This is the widely documented dominant white cultural conversion of its own erotic anxieties and desires into fantasies of hypersexualised racial and ethnic 'others'. Such fantasies of the sexual prowess and voraciousness of 'non-whites' – perceived either as an open invitation, or a dire threat, to the white subject – generally increase in direct proportion to the darkness of skin colour of the individual or group under scrutiny; with the most light-skinned of 'non-whites' paradoxically often being designated as especially sexually passive, if not asexual. This unstable structure stems from a white racist logic wherein, as Lynne Segal observes, 'black is the colour of the "dirty" secrets of sex – relentlessly represented in the image of the Black "boy" as stud, and Black woman as whore.'[37]

Isaac Julien and Kobena Mercer have underlined the persistence of this mythology within the context of gay male culture:

The gay subculture . . . is dominated by the needs and demands of white males. Black men fit into this territory by being confined to a narrow repertoire of types – the supersexual stud and the sexual savage on the one hand, the delicate and exotic 'Oriental' on the other. The repetition of these stereotypes betrays the circulation of 'colonial fantasy', and traces the way the

contours of this landscape have been shaped by mainstream cultural legacies
of slavery, empire, and imperialism.[38]

Holleran's unnamed New Yorker narrator in *Dancer from the Dance*
exemplifies the largely white-oriented parameters of the mainstream
late 1960s and 1970s American gay scene, which has, in this respect,
changed very little: 'Each year you [read: a white gay man] love someone
new: Orientals in 1967, Italians in 1968; blacks in 1969, and bearded
blonds in 1970; and always the Puerto Ricans, the angels, who take the
form of messenger boys.'[39]

Finally, Petra's song, 'The Miller's Son', can be used to illustrate
another dominant construction of promiscuity, which intersects with
all of the above. Although Petra declares that 'in the meanwhile,/There
are mouths to be kissed/Before mouths to be fed,/And there's many a
tryst/And there's many a bed', she nevertheless assumes that her final
erotic destination will be marriage to 'the miller's son', or 'the Prince of
Wales', or 'the businessman,/Five fat babies and lots of security.'[40] Even
if she is somewhat begrudging of the prospect of monogamy (when
'you're stuck with just one/Or it has to be done on the sly'), she has
already resigned herself to the governing cultural equations between
promiscuity/serial monogamy and youth, and between monogamy/mar-
riage and adulthood. Implicit or explicit in these paired equations is
the assumption that those individuals or groups who are seen to remain
sexually promiscuous beyond the (always vaguely defined) period of
youth have failed to fulfil their socially expected – or 'natural' – life
trajectory, and are consequently infantile (in the deprecating sense),
immature, guilty of evading commitment, and/or refuse to acknowledge
their true, underlying monogamous needs. In Adam Phillips's words,
'as yet, the promiscuous cannot grow old gracefully.'[41] Chapter 2 questions the representation of promiscuous gay men as regressively, and
destructively, 'immature' by analysing Larry Kramer's (and, by implication, many other conservative and liberal gay men's) dogmatically
pro-marital and monogamous gay perspective.

In that chapter, I also stress that the denigrating and punishing
attachment of the notion of 'promiscuity' to gay men – or, for that matter,
to any other category outlined above – is never entirely an act of separation between designator and designatee. For it almost always involves
a degree of fascination, and even desire, on the part of the designator,
that increases in almost direct proportion to the degree of denunciation
or punishment being enacted upon the 'promiscuous' object. In
Foucault's formulation, far from seeking to fully abolish sexual diversity,
'the nineteenth century and our own have been . . . the age of multiplication: a dispersion of sexualities, a strengthening of their disparate
forms, a multiple implantation of "perversions". Our epoch has initiated

sexual heterogeneities.'[42] Thus, whether the scrutinised group or individual (black gay men, working-class heterosexual women, and so on) is
in fact sexually non-monogamous or not, the imposition of a distancing and pathologising notion of 'promiscuity' on to them by dominant
cultural discourse is not only a means of repressing dominant fantasies
and fears concerning sexual diversity; it is also precisely the means
whereby the dominant repeatedly resurrects, publicly airs, and (re)pro-
duces, those otherwise disavowed fantasies and fears.

DEFINING 'PROMISCUITY': MARGINALISED MEANINGS

Promiscuity has, of course, nevertheless also accrued other, contestatory
meanings that run parallel – and also interlace – with those dominant
definitions.

Certainly, in many cases, marginalised people who are actively
promiscuous or pro-promiscuity have resisted defining themselves, or
their sexual practices, as promiscuous because of the prevailing negative
associations that the term holds. Thus, if Kate Millett's *Sexual Politics*
deployed the term in a non-pejorative context in stating that 'society
should cease to punish the promiscuity in women it does not think to
punish in men',[43] other (pro-)promiscuous women have rarely seen the
term as sufficiently impartial, or recuperable, to use to define their
sexual behaviour against dominant anti-promiscuous rhetoric and
material practices. Similarly, as many 'black men [particularly hetero-
sexuals] have adopted and used certain patriarchal values such as
physical strength, *sexual prowess*, and being in control to create a system
of black male gender roles in which macho tactics are used to cope
with the repressive and destructive power of the plantocracy and the
state,'[44] so their sexual self-definition has tended to be through patriarchal notions of the heterosexual male 'stud', rather than through the
quasi-medicalising notion of the 'promiscuous'.

At the same time, black and white gay male discourses alike have
often had a comparable antipathy towards the term, particularly since
the profound backlash against gay sex/uality that much of dominant
culture has desperately latched on to in order to 'rationalise' the
HIV/AIDS crisis. A 1982 article in *The Advocate* on potential links
between sexual practice and the newly discovered virus exemplifies
this well-advised gay suspicion of the term as it declares: 'one word is
like a hand grenade in the whole [health crisis] affair: promiscuity.'[45]
Yet this gay male distrust of the term has also been pronounced since
at least the 1960s, when, as Steven Seidman notes, dominant discourse
(as earlier in the century) 'often assumed . . . the inherently promiscuous,
carnal nature of homosexual desire, a sign of its pathological or deviant

status,' or else responded to the actual growth of opportunities for
publicly avowed gay male promiscuous sex during the 1970s and early
1980s in the same demonising manner.[46]

Difference of opinion amongst gay men about the connotations and
usefulness of the term also increased during 'the Age of Promiscuity',
and has continued to do so in the process of rethinking sexual practice
since the arrival of AIDS. Samuel R. Delany's ironised use of the term
in 1988 to describe his New York cruising adventures during the early
1960s is symptomatic of the frequently provisional and cautious gay
male deployment of the word, remaining self-conscious about its
dominant meanings: 'Parks and Forty-second Street movies were what
my "promiscuous sex" more or less consisted of at eighteen.'[47] Alternatively, though, while Dennis Altman points out that 'the dictionary
meaning of promiscuity implies a lack of discrimination that is not
necessarily the case',[48] in his discussion of sex in urban American gay
bathhouses before AIDS he also exemplifies another gay male use of the
term that suggests its potential for positive – or at least non-judgemental
– connotations:

The willingness to have sex immediately, promiscuously, with people about
whom one knows nothing and from whom one demands only physical contact, can be seen as a sort of Whitmanesque democracy, a desire to know and
trust other men in a type of brotherhood far removed from the male bonding
of rank, hierarchy, and competition that characterizes much of the outside
world. It is equally true, however, that age and physical beauty set up their
own hierarchies and barriers.[49]

In Chapter 1, we will even find 'promiscuity' used to signify revolution
and liberation, in John Rechy's classic narrative of 1970s macho urban gay
cruising and tricking, *The Sexual Outlaw*. And more recently, Douglas
Crimp has famously crystallized a certain gay male reclamation of the
term in the context of safe/r sex, as he argued – contrary to those gay
men who 'insist that our promiscuity will destroy us' – that 'gay promiscuity should be seen instead as a positive model of how sexual pleasures
might be pursued by and granted to everyone if those pleasures were
not confined within the narrow limits of institutionalized sexuality.'[50] In
a more explicitly anti-monogamous spirit, novelist Dale Peck comments:
'I wish that there could be a more profound sense of a gay community
based on promiscuity, but it never seems to go very far. I wish we could
really dismantle the family, sexual monogamy and sexual jealousy.'[51]

As Holleran summarises in his late 1980s 'Notes on promiscuity':
'some gay men think promiscuity is a revolutionary ideal that can
transform the world, release human energy, and make the planet a better place to live. . . . Others think promiscuity is the freeway to hell.'[52]

In the following chapters, I am interested in the unresolved – and in many ways unresolvable – tensions between these two extremes, and in the range of more ambivalent meanings and experiences of promiscuity that complicate any unrelenting adherence to either of these two poles.

True to such ambivalence, my use of the term 'promiscuity' in this study has links with most of the differing gay male uses I have just cited. Like Seidman, I acknowledge and resist the punitive deployment of the word as part of a spectrum of normative cultural practices that seek to marginalise, pathologise or destroy gay male sexual diversity, and gay men in general. Like Delany, I partly use the term for want of a better one that is equally wide-ranging. Somewhat like Holleran, I use it in a non-pejoratively descriptive sense, to mean multiple sexual acts – but also desires and fantasies – with multiple (known or unknown) partners. And while I do not share Rechy's predominant celebration of promiscuity as necessarily liberatory and transgressive in *The Sexual Outlaw*, I do, like Crimp, use the term to foreground the erotically and socially beneficial aspects of non-monogamous sexuality. Unlike Peck in the above interview statement, however, I do not believe that we could or should presume promiscuity as the basis for all of gay (or any other) culture, over and above monogamous sexuality.

As will become clear, I move between using the term specifically in relation to gay male cultural understandings and experiences of promiscuous sexuality, and applying it in a wider sense that broadly relates to all sexual groups. Moreover, as I have already suggested (and as I explain in greater detail later), I understand promiscuity to be psychical as much as it is physical. By this I mean that I include as promiscuous activity the widely condoned and encouraged range of public and private sexual fantasising in relation to star figures and popular cultural narratives; and I also include the less encouraged, but nevertheless widely condoned, range of public and private sexual fantasising in relation to known or unknown individuals seen in everyday circumstances: the yearnings of a married woman for a different stranger each day at the bus stop; an anti-promiscuous middle-aged man's momentary desires as he passes a number of women on the street; a celibate gay man's repertoire of solitary masturbatory fantasies, with or without the aid of porn; and so on. While these erotic events are obviously not all of the same intensity or consequence, and are not all promiscuous in the same way, I am suggesting that they can still all be linked to the always unbounded category of 'promiscuity'.

In so doing, I reject the reductively literal dominant cultural myth that the 'reality' or 'evidence' of sexuality is located primarily in the act of intercourse, and in other forms of interpersonal erotic physical contact (that are commonly marginalised as foreplay to 'the real thing').

The dominant deployment of this myth strives to sustain a compart-mentalisation of desire and sexuality within conventional social arrangements – the couple, the family, monogamy, marriage – that depends on an uneven disavowal of the far broader eroticism of every-day life. (Uneven – like all disavowal – because of, for example, the capital-motivated circulation of promiscuous public sexual fantasies in the media.) As Lauren Berlant and Michael Warner similarly observe:

These border intimacies give people tremendous pleasure. But when that pleasure is called sexuality, the spillage of eroticism into everyday social life seems transgressive in a way that provokes normal aversion, a hygienic recoil even as contemporary consumer and media cultures increasingly trope toiletward, splattering the matter of intimate life at the highest levels of national culture.[53]

Using a wide definition of promiscuity, then, that embraces both psy-chical and material forms of reality *without collapsing them together*, a central part of my argument will be that even though fantasmatic and physical manifestations of promiscuity are clearly separable, the relatively universal occurrence of promiscuous fantasies and desires – and the promiscuousness of desire itself – complicates any simplistic discursive attempt to rigidly separate, and hierarchise, 'properly familiar' monogamous sexual arrangements and 'improperly alien' promiscuous sexual arrangements.

In this, I follow the psychoanalytic (and widely popularised) notion of fantasy as – amongst other things – an integral supplement and resistance to cultural and practical constraints, as outlined in Freud's famous metaphorical comparison between fantasy and the nature reserve.

The human ego is . . . slowly educated by the pressure of external necessity to appreciate reality and obey the reality principle; in the course of the process it is obliged to renounce, temporarily or permanently, a variety of the objects and aims at which its striving for pleasure . . . is directed. But . . . [humans] have always found it hard to renounce pleasure; they can-not bring themselves to do it without some form of compensation. They have therefore retained a mental activity in which all these abandoned sources of pleasure and methods of achieving pleasure are granted a further exis-tence – a form of existence in which they are left free from the claims of real-ity and of what we call 'reality-testing.' . . . Thus in the activity of phantasy human beings continue to enjoy the freedom from external compulsion which they have long since renounced in reality. . . . Indeed, they cannot subsist on the scanty satisfaction which they can extort from reality. . . . The creation of the mental realm of phantasy finds a perfect parallel in the establishment of 'reservations' or 'nature reserves' in places where the requirements of agriculture, communications and industry threaten to bring about changes in the original face of the earth which will quickly make it unrecognizable. A nature reserve preserves its original state which every-where else has to our regret been sacrificed to necessity. Everything, including what is useless and even what is noxious, can grow and proliferate there as it pleases. The mental realm of phantasy is just such a reservation with-drawn from the reality principle.[54]

Freud's parallel between fantasy and the nature reserve is arguably less than 'perfect' in its neat separation of material and psychical realities.[55] On the one hand, it seems true that consciousness is persistently framed by the core primal (or original) fantasies,[56] so that even the most con-scious 'day-dream will . . . involve an unconscious wish underlying its manifest content and the structure of that unconscious wish will be related to the primal fantasies.'[57] But on the other hand, the many gra-dations between fully unconscious and conscious modes of fantasising can also be seen to indicate a persistent *cross*-flow beween material and psychical realities. Like an actual nature reserve, visits from the outside world are frequent, altering the landscape of the defended fantasy realm in subtle but significant ways. Chapter 3, for example, partly considers the overlap between specific cultural factors and more gen-eral desires for a paternal substitute within David Wojnarowicz's sexual fantasies.

For the most part, however, the nature reserve analogy is apt, and is useful here for its emphasis on the psychical persistence – alternately avowed and disavowed throughout society – of the polymorphous perversity of infancy and early childhood throughout later life. In the context of promiscuity, this means that whether one is culturally pres-sured into or happily embraces monogamy (or both occur together), sexual desire – mediated through fantasy – necessarily exceeds its immediate material satisfaction through one regular partner.

But as I have already stated, unlike a number of pro-promiscuous gay male discourses from 'the Age of Promiscuity' and beyond, I am not attempting to naturalise promiscuous sexual practice as an 'under-lying need' that all monogamous arrangements 'wrongly constrain'. After all, the psychical nature reserve often also contains compensatory fantasies of an idealised monogamous partner, as well as abiding, 'monogamous' traces of our first incestuous manifestations of desire. In Chapter 3, for instance, we will find romantic fantasies of eternal union with a paternal figure. So while this study is centrally arguing for the immense social gains to be had from the material and psychical acceptance and proliferation of diverse sexual practices, it does so with the knowledge that the intrinsic promiscuousness of sexual desire produces complex, contradictory and often unpredictable social effects, wherein monogamy and promiscuity are always interdependent.

Neither do I view promiscuity as inherently positive and beneficial. Like Leo Bersani in his widely influential – if also highly problematic[58] – essay on gay male sexual practice, 'Is the rectum a grave?', I dispute the notion upheld by some gay men (both during the Gay Liberation era and since) that supposedly 'radical sex means or leads to radical politics.'[59] There are of course important political reasons for defending and celebrating promiscuous sexual practices, particularly in the context of marginalised social individuals and groups who are condemned out of hand by normatively monogamous aspects of dominant culture, and of their own cultures. The following chapters are partly just such a political intervention against the shrill anti-pluralism of so many prevalent sexual discourses, which, well over a decade into safe/r sex awareness, still seek to equate all forms of non-monogamous sex with danger and disease. Consequently, returning to Holleran's and Crimp's comments, I am also concerned with the possible ways in which supporting consensual forms of promiscuity – alongside denaturalised forms of (permanent and serial) monogamy – might indeed 'transform the world' for the better (or rather, portions of the world at different times) by realising domestic and wider cultural arrangements that are 'not confined within the narrow limits of institutionalized sexuality.' But at the same time, as Bersani emphasises, 'the ways in which *having sex* politicizes are highly problematical',[60] and a loosening and reordering of dominant structures of sex and intimacy – however widely adopted – would clearly only ever constitute one move in the right direction, rather than a guarantee of a 'progressive' society.

For just as with monogamy, the relationship between promiscuous sexual practice and sociopolitical subjectivity is characterised by conscious and unconscious ambivalences and contradictions. On the one hand, as Bersani notes, sexual experimentation or diversity and political conservatism frequently co-exist in the same gay male subject: 'Many gay men could, in the late '60s and early '70s, begin to feel comfortable about having "unusual" or radical ideas about what's OK in sex without modifying one bit their proud middle-class consciousness or even their racism.'[61] – a combination that is, of course, reflected in any other cultural group. On the other hand, as all of the following chapters demonstrate in different ways, promiscuous sex will have a range of conflicting connotations and effects within any single gay man. These continuing contradictions remind us that the *comparative* lack of structure in multiple unattached sexual encounters can at times involve significant psychical risks (such as a regularly renewed sense of loss and alienation), or even destructive patterns – as well as providing intense, varied pleasures and productively destabilising insights (such as a regularly renewed recognition, acceptance, and even enjoyment, of the permanent fact of loss and contingency).[62]

In summary, then, the term 'promiscuity' might be seen to have a similarly ambiguous and flexible connotative capacity as 'queer' in the 1990s. Like that now widely embraced word, it retains the traces of its dominant derogatory usage, and hence enables resistant people to confront that policing usage, rather than simply censoring or avoiding or giving the term over to the dominant by adopting other words and phrases (although the motivation behind these latter responses to the term are, in some cases, understandable). Like 'queer' counter-discourses, therefore, it is sometimes used to defend or celebrate the exciting and complicating erotic and cultural heterogeneity also implicit in the term throughout its history. Like those uses of 'queer' that implicate all cultures broadly in non-normative sexuality at the level of fantasy, it can also be used to address an all-inclusive psychical promiscuity. And like those uses of 'queer' as a shorthand for lesbians, gays and bisexuals (or all non-heterosexuals), it can be used to refer to multiple sexual encounters with multiple partners, or to refer to the people who have those multiple sexual encounters, without any assumption of radical or progressive intention or outcome from that sexual activity.

Thus, I thread my discussions of gay male sexual diversity in this study through the term 'promiscuity' not only because it is relatively inescapable within prevailing sexual discourse – which remains narrowly structured around the binarism of monogamy and promiscuity (with occasional recognition of celibacy) – but also because it is able to evoke multiple, conflicting and ambiguous meanings that are as diverse as the range of non-monogamous sexual practices, fantasies, desires and subjectivities to which it can be applied.

FRAMING CONCEPTS

Before placing those differing gay male notions of promiscuity within an historical context, I should briefly explain my use of other central terms.

I have sought to use historically accurate terminology to reflect broad shifts in cultural descriptions and perceptions of same-sexual desire and homosexual identity. For the sake of brevity, however, I occasionally use 'queer' transhistorically to mean either gay men, or lesbians and gay men, or all non-heterosexuals (in each case, the surrounding context should imply which meaning I intend). Unless specifically stated, then, I do not use 'queer' to signify a progressive or 'cutting edge' political stance, but more as a form of abbreviation.

Like many others, I believe that the familiar use of 'gay community' tends to have misleadingly 'cosy, togetherness connotations. We don't, we now realise, have to be clones – though we can if we want.'[63] However, the general preference for 'subculture' is also, I think increasingly, unhelpful. In the process of trying to describe prevalent ways of categorising culture, and marginalised spaces of resistance, it still ends up invoking overly vague, inaccurate cultural hierarchies. The question always remains: a subdivision of which 'whole' culture? Or put another way, binary thinking takes hold here in such a way as to imply levels of dominant cultural consolidation and across-the-board agreement that are at odds with the multiple, fractured realities of actual 'non-subcultural' discourses and lives. After all, different interweaving dominant cultures will be identified and prioritised by different aspects of different oppositional groups. (While I do persistently refer to 'dominant culture' as a shorthand for prevailing discourses and perspectives, I do not equate that 'dominant' with all heterosexuals – or all of any other group – and sometimes also use it in relation to prominent aspects of gay male, or another marginalised, culture.) I therefore prefer to simply use the term 'culture' (or 'marginalised culture'), to foreground the equal cultural *complexity* and *significance* – if not power and influence – of gay, lesbian, bisexual and heterosexual lives, discourses and practices.

My final keywords are 'masculine' and 'feminine'. Like many other critics and theorists whose work is centrally informed by feminism, I use these gender terms to describe dominant, patriarchal, culturally constructed and regulatory notions of what men and women are respectively expected to be. Men are, of course, generally supposed to be masculine (active, rough, tough, physically sturdy, virile, resistant to emotional expression . . .), and women feminine (passive, soft, gentle, vulnerable, physically weaker and/or smaller, less sexual or sexually naïve, emotional/less intellectual . . .), and those who exhibit characteristics from the opposite category – most determinedly, queers – are conventionally seen either to have got it wrong, or in more resolutely discordant cases, to have something intrinsically wrong with them. Yet as Alan Sinfield argues, 'the supposition that masculinity and femininity are the essential, normative properties of men and women respectively . . . is scarcely valid in respect of heterosexuals – they don't in fact fall tidily into masculine and feminine attributes, all the time or in every respect; so it is perverse that lesbians and gay men should be interpreted as some kind of contorted variation upon it.'[64] Moreover, there is no teleological reason whatsoever why any of the individual attributes I have sketched out above should have been designated as 'masculine' or 'feminine' in the first place.

So although we can – and desperately need to – disturb normative notions of gender through cross-gender identification, through validating and complicating a denaturalised notion of the 'feminine', and so on, the masculine/feminine binary will, regardless of context, still always remain far too narrow to adequately (or even approximately) articulate the immeasurable diversity of female and/or male forms of behaviour, attitudes, identifications or desires. For this reason, my use of 'masculine' and 'feminine' to signify the prevalent gendering of male and female behaviour, appearance and attitudes is highly critical and provisional, and hence ironised throughout to counter the insidious naturalisation of both terms even in much progressive critical work, as well as more widely.

At the same time, though, as Biddy Martin notes, 'the separation of anatomical sex and social gender implied by the sex/gender split has had the consequence of leaving the assumption of biological sexual difference intact and of introducing a damaging body/mind split.'[65] Contrary to a clear-cut distinction between purely physical 'sex' and externally imposed 'gender', Martin (in a very similar way to Judith Butler) underlines that 'sex . . . is always already gender.'[66] In other words, our shared conceptualisations of 'sex' are never purely anatomically grounded, but are instead resolutely bound up in (subtly or overtly) gendered understandings of 'sexual difference'. Throughout the following chapters, then, when I use 'sex' to designate anatomical differences between men and women,[67] I do so with the proviso that any notion of 'maleness' and 'femaleness' is also culturally contingent.

HISTORICISING AMERICAN GAY
MALE PROMISCUITY

I have so far tracked dominant and marginalised modern American understandings of promiscuity largely through etymology and ideology, rather than through the existing documentation of material sexual practices. While the ensuing chapters will explore particular gay male concepts and practices of promiscuity in more detail, I include here a necessarily brief outline of twentieth-century gay promiscuity in America, to contextualise those later specific examples.[68]

In the context of American history, incidences – and fantasies – of male same-sexual promiscuity have been invoked ever since the seventeenth-century Anglo-European colonisation of the New World. Jonathan Goldberg has notably dissected 'the colonialist's [narratives of] promiscuous natives and degenerate underclasses', who were recurrently – if by no means primarily – demonised for alleged same-sexual activities strenuously disavowed within the colonisers themselves.[69]

For our purposes here, however, the earliest documented period of significance lies at the turn of the twentieth century. George Chauncey's groundbreaking *Gay New York* has provided copious insights into the extensive homosexual/gay sociosexual arrangements in the nation's cultural capital from 1890–1940. This historical evidence is clearly not representative of the country as a whole: John D'Emilio points out that 'as late as 1920, 50 per cent of the US population lived in communities of fewer than 2500 people', making financial and social independence from the traditional cross-sex family structure – aside from the mass dispersals of the war years – impossible and/or unthinkable.[70] On the other hand, Chauncey notes that 'while little research has been conducted yet on other American cities, scattered evidence nonetheless indicates that Chicago, Los Angeles, and at least a handful of other cities hosted gay subcultures of considerable size and complexity before the war, and that many small towns also sustained gay social networks of some scope.'[71] Chauncey's focus on metropolitan erotic spaces therefore underlines the far greater opportunities for promiscuous sex within the comparative anonymity, diversity and human plenitude of the city.

Gay New York documents a wide range of contexts and environments, both public and private, in which New York men were able to have sex together, whether as 'fairies', 'queers', 'gays' or 'normal' ('masculine' and heterosexually-identified) men.[72] Interestingly, in many respects, the diversity of sexual spaces that he describes approximates the range of options available (if not the specific historical circumstances) for urban American gay men during the 1970s and more recently: 'Some gay men were involved in long-term monogamous relationships they called marriages; others participated in an extensive sexual underground that by the beginning of the century included well-known cruising areas in the city's parks and streets, gay bathhouses, and saloons with back rooms where men met for sex.'[73]

More precisely, Chauncey illustrates that 'the most visible gay world of the early twentieth century . . . was a working-class world, centred in African–American and Irish and Italian immigrant neighborhoods.'[74] If gay men 'sometimes had to fight to claim their place', they were still 'remarkably integrated into the life'[75] of these communities, providing many opportunities for congregating and having casual sex with one another, as well as with so-called 'normal' men. Most famous of these districts in the pre-Depression years was Harlem, where, as Eric Garber documents, the prolific black cultural activity of the Harlem Renaissance, combined with 'costume balls, parties, speakeasies and buffet flats . . . provided an arena for homosexual interaction.'[76] '"Buffet flats were after-hours spots that were usually in someone's apartment,"'[77] which became progressively notorious for drinking, gambling and prostitution, but also enabled 'a variety of sexual pleasures [offered] cafeteria-style' without payment, catering to 'all variety of sexual tastes'.[78] Contrary to the conventional image of the sexually furtive 'twilight' homosexual before Stonewall, Garber also cites writer, painter and dancer Richard Bruce Nugent, 'the most bohemian' figure of the Harlem Renaissance, 'who delighted in shocking the prudish with his erotic drawings and his openly homosexual promiscuity.'[79]

One more feature of this era should be dwelt upon briefly here. If 'indifference or curiosity – rather than hostility or fear – characterised many New Yorkers' response to the gay world for much of the half-century before the [Second World] war',[80] nevertheless, a wide network of legal and more general social prohibitions and punishments against homosexual activity – imprisonment, fines followed by scandal, blackmail, violence – made cruising and having sex in most (ostensibly) public spaces extremely risky. Hence, from the turn of the century – as in the 1970s and 1980s – gay-tolerant and gay-only bathhouses provided a widely used antidote to hostile scrutiny, and often also enabled a greater degree of sexual experimentation: 'In sharp contrast to most social situations, which negated the body and homosexual desire, the baths affirmed them by facilitating public interactions, group encounters (or "mass sex," as it was usually called), and, at the least, overt expressions of homosexual interest.'[81] Also like their post-Stonewall counterparts, these baths-goers commonly developed friendships (and sometimes long-term sexual relationships) with one another, as did many of the countless men who met while cruising on the streets, in parks and elsewhere in the city.

However, as so often in the history of marginalised groups, with an increasingly integrated gay public presence came increasing dominant cultural surveillance and intolerance. Chauncey remarks that:

The very growth and visibility of the gay subculture during the Prohibition years of the 1920s and early 1930s precipitated a powerful cultural reaction in the 1930s. A new anxiety about homosexuals and hostility toward them began to develop, which soon became part of the more general reaction to the cultural experimentation of the Prohibition era that developed in the anxious early years of the Depression.[82]

The postwar years continued this trend. For as 'the gay world continued to thrive and became even more extensive in the 1940s and 1950s than it had been before the war', it also 'became less visible in the streets and newspapers of New York, gay meeting places did become more segregated and carefully hidden, and the risks of visiting them increased.'[83]

Yet at a national level, the war provided unprecedented opportunities for many men – whether already gay, repressed, or mainly straight but bisexually curious – to have sex with other men.[84] In many cases, these encounters (and often, the homophobic responses to them) also encouraged men to develop some tentative, or even forthright, sense of homosexual identity in relation to their sexual activity. Allan Bérubé notes that:

The tension of living in the all-male world of the military, the comradeship that came with fighting a common enemy, and the loneliness of being away from home in strange cities looking for companionship all helped to create a kind of 'gay ambience,' as one veteran put it. Servicemen openly cruised each other in the anonymity of crowded bus and train stations, city parks, restrooms, YMCAs, beaches, and streets. They doubled up in hotel beds, slept on the floor in movie theatres, and went home with strangers when there was no other place to sleep.[85]

In part, the unattached nature of many of these wartime sexual encounters was due to the great risk of attacks, psychiatric interrogation and experimentation, imprisonment and/or being discharged (and hence facing social ostracism) if same-sexual activity or romance was discovered. If the war brought a great number of men together for periods of intense bonding, then equally, 'lovers were transferred to other bases; couples and circles of friends split up as troops . . . were sent overseas. Sometimes lovers never came back.'[86]

   Yet clearly, the many brief sexual encounters military men had together, and with male civilians in the cities they passed through, were pleasurable in isolation as well as for their indication of a potential new life once the war was over. As in previous decades, the gendering of these sexual practices was strenuously masculinist, particularly in the defensive all-male work environment and military living quarters. Hence, even as 'feminine' men were frequently propositioned by masculine-identified men as 'female substitutes', Douglas Sadownick notes that these so-called 'sissy men found it hardest of all to fit in, unless they turned their effeminacy into seductiveness; but that some-times went against their own moral code.'[87]

   For thousands of butch, femme and butch/femme men alike, however, the end of the war ushered in less circumspect opportunities for gay sex and friendship.[88] As Bérubé, amongst others, records:

Many returning veterans based their decisions for civilian life on their newly discovered homosexuality . . . [and therefore] left their parents, abandoned their small towns, and migrated to large cities they had seen for the first time during the war. There they created [more extensive] lesbian and gay neighborhoods, risked going to the growing number of lesbian and gay bars, and looked for work that would allow them to lead relatively open lives.[89]

More specifically, though, we need to distinguish here between the greater mobility of white homosexual men in the late 1940s–1950s and the continuing crucial significance of the extended family and neighbourhood for a considerable number of black homosexual men in the face of white racism: 'If white gay men had to leave their native cities [and towns] to become gay, many black gays did the opposite and stayed close to home.'[90]

Generally speaking, then, the quantity and spectrum of promiscuous and monogamous gay male sexual arrangements grew considerably in the postwar years – and was met by increasing dominant cultural antipathy and policing initiatives: 'Hundreds of gay men were arrested in New York City every year in the 1920s and 1930s for cruising or visiting gay locales; thousands were arrested every year in the postwar decade.'[91] Nevertheless, the normative designation of urban public spaces primarily as male property provided gay men with considerably more communal erotic environments than those available for lesbians – a factor that has remained consistent for the rest of the century.

Equally, postwar American gay culture 'benefited from . . . more open public discourse about sexuality which at times, as in the case of [Allen Ginsberg's notorious poem] *Howl* [1955–56], presented affirming images of homosexual love' and recreational sex.[92] (The availability and explicitness of gay sexual material increased dramatically from the late 1950s onwards, following a series of trials that 'progressively contracted the domain of obscenity', enabling, for example, Rechy's *City of Night* to become a bestseller.[93]) In 1948 – the same year that Gore Vidal's novel of gay promiscuity and frustrated fidelity, *The City and the Pillar*, first appeared – Alfred Kinsey's avidly read report on *Sexual Behavior in the Human Male* suggested that half of all adult American men had been attracted to another man; more than a third had had homosex to orgasm; 4 per cent were exclusively homosexual; and one out of eight was predominantly homosexual for at least three years.[94]

But the gradual loosening of representational and other social restrictions on sexual diversity really only gathered speed at the tail-end of the frequently normative 1950s. As has been widely documented, during that decade, Cold War paranoia about national security and vigilant attempts to resuscitate the nuclear family after the war produced immense governmental, military and wider social scapegoating and punishment of gay men and lesbians, spearheaded in the early 1950s by the McCarthy witchhunt trials against supposed queers and Communists. Increased gay visibility was therefore met with extreme institutional suppression, encouraging low self-esteem, sexual guilt and furtiveness in a great many gay men – but also the emergence of complex (if often apologetic) lesbian and gay political organisation in the form of the homophile movement, focused around the Mattachine Society and the Daughters of Bilitis.

In opposition to homophobia, then, the combination of liberal and conservative homosexual mobilisation in these nationwide organisations illustrates how, in Steven Seidman's words, the 1950s concurrently 'laid the groundwork for many of the changes in American sexual mores and behavior in the 1960s', particularly for the black Civil Rights, women's, student/youth, and later the lesbian and gay, movements. 'Not only were the social conditions that spawned sexual liberation movements created in the 1950s, but the ideology of sexual purity and restraint was already under attack by liberal reformers, sex radicals, and segments of the youth culture.'[95]

Thus, 'by the 1960s, . . . there appeared discourses and representations providing rationales for eroticism solely on the grounds of its pleasurable, individualising or communicative qualities,' in contrast with the preceding decades' greater emphasis on 'framing sex as a medium of love', predominantly within the context of marriage.[96] Like a number of other historians, Eric Hobsbawm has summarised that 'the Western sexual revolution of the 1960s and 1970s was made possible by antibiotics – unknown before the Second World War – which appeared to remove the major risks from sexual promiscuity by making venereal diseases easily curable, and by the birth-control pill which became widely available in the 1960s.'[97] Yet the considerable sexual liberalism of this era also derived from the postwar economic boom, which enabled 'entrepreneurs . . . [to extend] the logic of consumer capitalism to the realm of sex.'[98]

The initial benefits of the 'permissive' 1960s were, on the whole, ambiguous for gay male sexuality. While gay culture continued to expand, the so-called sexual revolution[99] was inevitably most slanted towards dominant (middle-class) cultural concerns, privileging the heterosexual white male promiscuity symbolised by the vast success of Hugh Hefner's *Playboy* empire.[100] But if the rise of the 1960s middle-class urbanite singles set often reproduced conventional sex/gender dynamics, the increasing dependence of the economy upon working women prompted an ambiguously sexualised address of the female consumer, and a generally more sexually adventurous climate wherein women could experience considerable sexual diversity and reciprocity (within and beyond marriage), as well as facing continuing sexism.[101]

Most importantly, however, the explosion of second-wave feminism, and particularly the emergence of a radical feminist call for non-marital sexual freedom, produced a blueprint for the subsequent growth of the lesbian and gay liberation movement – and all of these mobilisations on behalf of self-declared marginalised groups were in turn centrally influenced by the great success of the black Civil Rights movement. The frequent (though also internally disputed) radical feminist emphasis on the interdependence of sexual freedom and other forms of social change was succinctly summarised in Kate Millett's *Sexual Politics*:

A sexual revolution would require, perhaps first of all, an end of traditional sexual inhibitions and taboos, particularly those that most threaten patriarchal monogamous marriage: homosexuality, 'illegitimacy', adolescent, pre- and extra-marital sexuality. . . . The goal of revolution would be a permissive single standard of sexual freedom, and one uncorrupted by the crass and exploitative economic bases of traditional sexual alliances.[102]

While lesbian and gay political and cultural organisation was already well-established across the country during the 1960s, the Stonewall riots of June 1969 provided the material and symbolic catalyst for a more consistently radicalised – and hence more unapologetically visible – gay and lesbian movement to amass in urban areas, with national attention focused on New York. As Michael Bronski puts it: 'the promise of Stonewall was (among other things) the promise of sex: free sex, better sex, lots of sex, sex without guilt, sex without repression, sex without harassment, sex at home and sex in the streets.'[103] As the Gay Liberation Front (GLF) quickly emerged with its emphasis on revolutionary sociosexual emancipation for all minorities, the outpouring of groups, marches and more informal gatherings reconfigured the largely heterocentric promiscuous 'sexual revolution' trumpeted in the preceding decade within homosexual terms:

For the first time ever, a community standard developed that transformed anonymous sex into a good thing – another choice on the broadening sexual palatte. Casual sexual encounters no longer took place simply because men needed to conceal their identities, but because it was considered hot to separate sex from intimacy. . . . The more tricks one had, the more one helped to push the revolution along, according to editors at the Canadian gay magazine *The Body Politic*.[104]

Of course, as I have tried to suggest, gay promiscuity in earlier decades had numerous motivations aside from furtiveness. Anonymous and casual sex was 'a good thing' for countless men before the 'Age of Promiscuity', but now it became a positive choice; a release from the frequent secrecy of the past; and in many men's eyes, a beneficial, or even radical, act for gay culture as a whole. Correspondingly, the range of sex venues already available in the early decades of the century – bathhouses, backrooms, parks and so on – grew greatly in number, and in many instances, were far more openly used than in the pre-Stonewall years.

At the same time, though, the prevalent couple structure retained its

advantages for a great many men, even as they reshaped it to accommodate multiple sexual needs. In Seidman's words, 'observers of gay
men's intimacy patterns in the 1960s and 1970s have frequently commented on the way they combined the emotional exclusiveness typical
of heterosexual romantic love patterns with sexual nonmonogamy.'[105]
So the common simultaneous desire for intimate monogamy and lustful
promiscuity (or, indeed, for intimate promiscuity and lustful monogamy)
did persist in many ways in the post-Stonewall era, even as most gay
male discourses and practices denaturalised the dominant equation of
sex with romance, monogamy and intimacy to a far greater degree than
in lesbian and heterosexual cultures.

However, early attempts to agitate against sexual norms, and to combine sexual 'radicalism' with activism against other forms of social
injustice, soon lost their promising momentum, becoming replaced by
a general preoccupation with liberal reform within the existing dominant social framework – seen in the campaigning of the Gay Activists
Alliance (GAA) – or *laissez-faire*ism:

As with feminism, the revolutionary expectations of the early gay liberation
movement never materialized. For one, the rebellious milieu that spawned
it had lost its vigor by the mid-1970s, and the nation entered a more conservative political era. Then, too, the gay movement adapted to the times, for
the most part pulling back from its radical critique of the effects of sexual
repression and instead recasting itself as a movement in the long tradition of
American reform. Proponents . . . campaigned for civil rights legislation
rather than a restructuring of family life and sexual socialization. And the
commercialism that came to characterize the gay male subculture of the 1970s
was not different in kind from the consumerist values that had already made
sex a marketable economy.[106]

In summary, then, the 1970s made possible a considerable range of
openly promiscuous gay male sexual experimentation – criticised by
some as an empty avoidance of culturally ingrained fears of same-sex
intimacy; and valued by others as a vital means of constructing a new
form of society, where sexual diversity could be publicly accommodated,
rather than spectacularised and pathologised from a distance. (As will
become clear later, even though my emphasis is clearly on the latter
reading, the former interpretation of promiscuity also has a great deal
of relevance in some contexts as well). At the same time, the growing
demand for gay venues for socialising, cruising and sex enabled the
development of an unprecedentedly strong commercial gay scene. On
the one hand, this commercial scene/culture strengthened a sense of
collectivity and promoted wider recognition of gay identity. But on the
other hand, it also encouraged a general depoliticisation of sex, and a
dissociation of sexual freedom from other social issues. This separation

of sexual pleasure from its various political meanings and effects is epitomised in the prevailing reauthentication of 'masculine' ideals by gay men.[107] In one sense this has been a strategy against heteropatriarchal culture's presumption of all gay men's 'effeminacy' – a strategy already used by a number of gay men long before Stonewall. But in another sense, this normalisation of the macho/masculine gay man was greatly accelerated by the homogenising trajectory of gay male consumer culture from the late 1970s onwards.

For African–American gay men, the promiscuous sexual possibilities promised by the post-Stonewall mainstream gay scene(s) have generally been far more compromised. In negotiating dominant forms of gay culture, gay black men have frequently found themselves caught between the implicit or explicit white exclusivity of many sexual venues (including some outdoor cruising grounds), and the white fetishisation of black male sexual 'virility' mentioned earlier. (This is in stark contrast to the pre-1960s focus of a considerable part of the urban American gay scene in and around black communities. 'Let me tell you,' describes [sic] Ira L. Jeffries, who came out in Harlem in the 1940s, 'Harlem's lesbian and gay community was *thriving* until certain white business men realised the money we generated and wanted to tap into it. Starting in the 1960s, our clubs were either systematically closed or mysteriously burned down. Finally, there was nothing left, so we were all forced to go downtown.'[108]) If, at a superficial level, white fascination with the black male body provided a range of promiscuous opportunities for black gay men, many – promiscuous or otherwise – have rejected the unspoken white bias of mainstream gay culture's frequent celebration of sexual liberty as tantamount to liberty in general. Looking back on the 1980s from the early 1990s, Essex Hemphill reflected that:

At the baths, certain bars, in bookstores and cruising zones, black men were welcome because these constructions of pleasure allowed the races to mutually explore sexual fantasies and, after all, the black man engaging in such a construction only needed to whip out a penis of almost any size to obtain the rapt attention withheld from him in other social and political structures of the gay community. These sites of pleasure were more tolerant of black men because they enhanced the sexual ambience, but that same tolerance did not always continue once the sun began to rise.[109]

This absolute disparity between sexual and other social interactions amongst white and black gay men (another example of the common conjunction of sexual 'pluralism' and political conservatism pinpointed by Bersani) led Hemphill to hyperbolise provocatively that 'white gay men may only be able to understand and respond to oppression as it relates to their ability to obtain orgasm without intrusion from the church or state.'[110] What Hemphill saw as missing in white gay culture is a sustained and widespread acknowledgement of the multifaceted nature of subjectivity, which includes, but is not reducible to, sexuality and sexual practice (nor, for that matter, consumerism).

This resistance to white sex-centred gay discourses may be seen to partly account for the focus in much African–American gay fiction to date on sustaining monogamous relationships (whether interracial or between two black men) and negotiating with the nuclear family, to find a 'safe harbour'[111] against the double bind of racism and homophobia, rather than on the ramifications of cruising and promiscuous sex with strangers.[112] On the other hand, the lesser concern with promiscuity in African–American gay writing may also be partly accounted for by the lesser publication of black gay authors thus far, narrowing the range of available representations. As Andrew Gillings puts it in a 1997 *Village Voice* article, 'not only are black gay men writing more literary fiction, they are writing about a variety of black gay experiences. Yet publishers remain willfully ignorant about these stories and their market.'[113] By contrast, Samuel R. Delany's autobiographical accounts of cruising in *The Motion of Light in Water* (1988); the pre-Dennis Cooper sexual extremism of his novel, *Hogg* (1969–73, published 1995); his 1994 novel *The Mad Man*; and Gary Fisher's short stories and often harrowing journal entries, collected posthumously in *Gary in Your Pocket* (1996), suggest the gradual emergence of a body of literature exploring the potentials and risks of promiscuous sex for African–American gay men. Non-African–American gay male fiction and autobiography writers of colour are currently even less visible.

To be more precise, then, this study focuses on a selection from the more widely circulated white American gay male discourses of promiscuity. My central concern is to foreground the general implications of these narratives for gay and other cultures alike. However, equally, my particular emphasis is clearly on the prevailing gender patterns within gay promiscuity, involving a predominantly deracialised reading of gay sexual practice. My decision to leave aside racial and ethnic dynamics in subsequent chapters is therefore partly symptomatic of my own identificatory and critical preoccupations to date, but also partly due to the scarcity of publicly disseminated promiscuity-centred black gay literature.

To conclude my historical overview, I turn now to gay sexual practice since the emergence of the AIDS epidemic. A concerted anti-gay backlash from the right had already begun in the mid-1970s in response to growing mass gay visibility (rather like the backlash during the Depression, and the scapegoating of the 1950s). But of course, with the appearance of HIV and AIDS (initially identified as GRID and then ARC) in the early 1980s, the backlash against gay culture and sexuality in general, and against gay male promiscuity in particular, rose to unimagined heights. The complex initial and subsequent effects of AIDS upon gay men and gay male sexual practice (aside from a crushing cultural backlash) have been widely documented,[114] and are addressed later.

In broad terms, though, we can summarise thus. First, a period of absolute uncertainty over the causative agent of AIDS in the early 1980s, leading to advice against promiscuity and anal sex. Then the discovery of HIV enabled safer sex guidelines on condom use to be widely disseminated from the mid-1980s onwards, together with an (unevenly acknowledged) distinction between safe, safer and unsafe promiscuous practice. These crucial developments enabled gay men to begin to make clearer distinctions between the necessary warnings against risky fluid exchange, and the unhelpful warnings they had initially received, and continued to receive from misinformed cultural discourses, about having multiple sexual partners.

In the States – primarily in New York and San Francisco – 'a high proportion of sexually active gay men had already become infected with HIV even before the first cases of AIDS were diagnosed.'[115] Nevertheless, the development of safer sexual practice amongst gay men during the 1980s, both through peer support and 'reinforced by educational interventions by groups recognised as a part of that community and by the gay press, played a key role in helping gay men put factual information about safer sex into practice.'[116] Far from being blithely or destructively irresponsible (the popular homophobic/anti-gay image throughout the epidemic), many gay men rapidly initiated dramatic changes in their sexual practice, and produced educational advice that was usually frank, clear and encouragingly eroticised.

Any hopes that condom awareness would create sustained safer sex practice across gay male culture, and a corresponding consistent fall in HIV seroconversions, have, however, been quelled in the 1990s with the 'so-called second wave of HIV infection, meaning that people who were in grammar school and high school in the mid-80s are now testing positive for HIV in numbers not much lower than ten years ago.'[117] The 'so-called' here is well advised, as Eric Ciasullo – a San Franciscan AIDS activist interviewed by John Weir – underlines: 'The rate of infection among teens and guys in their early twenties isn't new, it's just newly acknowledged.'[118]

There are, of course, numerous intersecting reasons for the continuing rise of HIV and AIDS amongst gay men. Edward King, amongst other critics, has pointed to the 'degaying' of AIDS in the late 1980s and early 1990s: 'a vast overreaction' to the possibility of HIV spreading amongst non-drug-using heterosexuals, 'in which the present realities of the epidemic were deliberately played down.' (This reframing of the crisis was uneasily supported by many gay men, who had 'genuine fears that the epidemic would not be taken seriously for as long as it was thought to only affect gay men.'[119]) The outcome of this heterocentric tactic is that 'in the 1990s, most of the spontaneous, self-organised HIV education at a gay community grassroots level has undoubtedly been lost,'[120] restricting the range of advice and support available for newly sexually active gay men. The sense of immortality, and of being separated from 'old' AIDS-torn gay culture, felt by many of these younger gay men is therefore not being met by sufficient culture-specific counter-information.

Another central factor behind the continuing rise in HIV seroconversions in gay male culture is, obviously, the difficulty of sustaining safe/r sex practices, for a number of extremely complex reasons. Most general of these is the difficulty of having to continuously rationalise the danger of certain basic forms of sexual pleasure, within the often irrational and chaotic context of sex. In her 1992 short story/essay 'Slipping', Pat Califia writes with great eloquence of this struggle, which is all too quickly trivialised or ignored in much didactic AIDS discourse.

Most of us are doing the best we can, trying to scrape through this epidemic with as much of our libidos and our sanity as we can rescue. . . . Some of us know what we should do, do it most of the time, and sometimes we slip.

We slip because the condition of being aroused creates moisture. Hazardous footing. Melts boundaries. Makes the edges fuzzy. Creates immediate needs that overwhelm our ability to plan for the future. . . . When the sexual flesh is hard, engorged, it has no conscience.[121]

Moreover, as I will be arguing in relation to dominant understandings of promiscuity, the sense of 'forbiddenness' attached to unsafe sexual acts can make them all the more alluring. Eric Rofes writes:

As a man who has never enjoyed getting fucked and who has experienced varying levels of discomfort and pain during my few ventures in this area, I have noticed an escalating interest in getting fucked appearing in my masturbatory fantasies since the early years of the epidemic. How common is it for humans to eroticize the exact activities which they are told not to actualize?[122]

The task of maintaining safer sex practices, whether in a promiscuous context or otherwise, is further complicated by the fact that the right to openly enjoy these now 'forbidden' unsafe activities was only gained in the very recent past (and even then only partially), through great cultural and psychical upheaval – as Rofes underscores:

Masses of men emerging from the closet over the past twenty-five years have clamored for sexual freedom and the urban cultures they created elevated

the value of communal sexual options. AIDS educators who have underestimated the powerful meanings of anal sex, oral sex, and semen exchange to
significant numbers of gay men may have imperiled the effectiveness of their
efforts.[123]

For gay men who grew up during those upheavals, as for many of the
younger generation, the relentless loss, grief and anxiety attending
AIDS have also produced a range of self-endangering sexual responses,
including sexual compulsiveness (as well as sexual aversion) and – in
particularly devastated cities like San Francisco – guilt amongst many
HIV-negative men, or resignation to the likelihood of eventually sero-
converting.

Recent years have seen a resurgence of backrooms and both private
and public sex clubs in major American cities, reflecting a broader gay
cultural attempt to re-eroticise sex within the ongoing crisis. On the
one hand, while a large number of gay men are learning to accept that
'our relationship to pleasure and sexuality cannot return to what it was
before the intervention of HIV',[124] this communal return to public and
private cruising spaces indicates the possibility of enjoying a promiscuous gay male sexuality in the face of AIDS. On the other hand, however, sexual activity is understandably not always monitored in these
clubs,[125] underlining the greater possibility of unsafe temptations for
many promiscuous gay men – as well as raising the fraught question of
how far a community should proscribe its individual members' sexual
behaviour.

This possibly greater risk for gay men who have multiple sexual
partners needs to be put into context: although abandonment to pleasure
at the expense of safety may happen unexpectedly in any encounter,
regardless of who the individuals involved are, factors such as safer
sex awareness, peer group support and individual character are not
insignificant. Yet that notion of promiscuous gay men's exposure to a
wider range of potentially risky encounters than the (truly) monogamous
couple experiences cannot be simply dismissed as anti-promiscuous
scaremongering. While this study will be arguing against normative
representations of promiscuity as, a priori, impractical or dangerous (and
pointing out the comparable risks of unsafe sex within a monogamous
relationship), I will also be partly addressing the practical and psychical difficulties of promiscuous sex for gay men since the appearance of
AIDS.

To reiterate, then, Chapter 1 examines the gendering of promiscuous
gay male sex through John Rechy's gay-themed novels of the 1960s and
1970s, taking issue with the prevailing normative masculinisation of
male promiscuity (and sexual potency in general) by drawing attention
to the critically neglected ambivalence of Rechy's representations of

butch gay sex. Rechy's strong investment in 'masculinity' is shown to be qualified by his repeated dissection of the anxieties and inconsistencies of the butch stud, and sometimes, by the inclusion of the rarely heard promiscuous femme gay male voice as well.

Chapter 2 begins by unpicking the self-contradiction of Larry Kramer's fictional and non-fictional representation of gay male promiscuity as innately destructive, regressive and deceitful, both before and since HIV/AIDS awareness. Kramer's contortions are used to illustrate the ways in which dominant (straight and gay) culture's detachment from, and demonisation of, promiscuity are always dependent upon a self-troubling disavowal of the promiscuousness of desire itself, regardless of one's conscious monogamy or promiscuity. However, as with Rechy, I am also concerned to replace the conventional dismissive reception of Kramer's fictional texts amongst progressive critics with a more careful analysis of their self-reflexivity. From this angle, *The Normal Heart*, and *Faggots* in particular, appear considerably more self-conscious about the promiscuousness of desire, and the fascination of promiscuous sex, than is often acknowledged (even by Kramer himself).

Chapter 3 addresses the writings of the late visual artist and AIDS activist David Wojnarowicz. His semi-poetic sexual narratives usually take place along the highways of America, and hence raise and imply questions about the various relationships between promiscuity, travel and public space. At the same time, the sexual explicitness of these travelogues serves to throw into relief the heavy homoerotics of Jack Kerouac's Beat classic, *On the Road* (1957), and of the American pioneer archetype by which both writers are influenced. Within the general context of this study, however, Wojnarowicz's writings are seen to be most important for their acute awareness of the key role that fantasy, in all its unpredictability, plays in the production and perception of sexual pleasure (promiscuous or otherwise) – an awareness that has significantly disruptive implications for normative cultural assumptions of a stabilised, fully knowable monogamous sexual identity. Conversely, though, like Rechy's texts, Wojnarowicz's narratives are also shown to express monogamous yearnings that complicate any notion of an unproblematically promiscuous sexuality as well.

Notes

1. Sondheim and Wheeler, *A Little Night Music*, pp. 101–3.
2. Holleran, *Dancer*, p. 196.

3. Ibid., p. 204.
4. Holleran, 'Steam, soap, and sex', p. 99. Holleran dates this 'age' as 1975–85, but as will become clear, any attempt to periodise gay promiscuity is, at best, tentative.
5. However, Holleran's novel is often more ambivalent about foregrounding normative heterosexual culture's implication in the very sexual desires and practices that it derides gay culture for openly expressing.
6. Holleran, *Dancer*, p. 210.
7. Hence, too, Sondheim's discomfort with the decision – allegedly made by the show's producer, Harold Prince – to replace his cynical finalé number for *Company*, 'Happily Ever After', with the more commercially viable 'Being Alive', wherein Bobby finally declares his wish for a monogamous long-term partner. (On the other hand, Mary Rodgers is convinced that Sondheim wrote some of the lines in 'Being Alive' about himself: '"Someone to sit in my chair", she says, "that's the way he really feels."' Gottfried, *Sondheim*, p. 88.)
8. The continuing relevance of Crowley's play was underlined by its critically acclaimed and popular off-Broadway revival in 1996.
9. In the case of *Rent*, however, this mainstream success is as much due to Larson's prioritisation of a heterosexual love story over any gay and lesbian sexual expression, as to the actual lesbian and gay content of the piece. Nevertheless, one show-stopping number, 'Take Me or Leave Me', compellingly repeats the monogamy/promiscuity couple debate seen in *Boys in the Band*, within the context of a relationship between a lesbian and a bisexual woman (who are, on the other hand, predictably typed as a strictly monogamous lesbian who 'love[s] margins and discipline' and an unreliably flirtatious bisexual).
10. This includes stand-up comedy and (usually drag) cabaret writing, performed in bars and clubs as well as theatres, together with the generally more 'high' cultural play and one-person show.
11. A study of promiscuous representation in American gay male poetry would most obviously include the works of Dennis Cooper, Allen Ginsberg, Thom Gunn, Frank O'Hara and Walt Whitman.
12. Schulman, *My American History*, p. 166.
13. John Rechy fits into both of these loose categories: his first novel, *City of Night* (1963), was an unprecedented commercial success, yet his later – and more confidently sexual – gay-themed works of the late 1960s and 1970s were principally read by smaller gay audiences. Andrew Holleran and Larry Kramer also straddle both categories.
14. In his 1993 Harvard lecture, John Preston quipped that 'Ed White might have the crowd from *The New York Review of Books*, but I was the star of [the leatherman's magazine] *Drummer*. The prestige might not be the same, but the numbers worked out pretty well.' Preston, *My Life*, p. 7.
15. *Advocate Men*, p. 7.
16. Preston, *My Life*, p. 344; emphasis added.
17. Ibid., p. 13.
18. *Straight to Hell*, p. 1.
19. 'Promiscuous' entry in the Oxford English Dictionary.
20. Ibid.
21. Ibid.
22. Schofield, *Promiscuity*, p. 17.

23. Rubin, 'Thinking sex', p. 280.
24. Ibid., pp. 280–1. The imprecision of the term 'public sex' to describe sex encounters in parks, public toilets and similar spaces is well illustrated by a fascinating news item reported in a 1994 issue of London's *Pink Paper*: 'A New York judge has ruled that bushes in a public park do not constitute a public place. The decision, by Brooklyn Federal Judge Raymond Dearie [sic!], may mean that New York police have to desist from arresting gay men having sex in public parks. The case centres on a businessman who appealed against a fine of $6 he received after being found guilty of sex in a Brooklyn park in April. The businessman appealed, arguing that the arresting officer had to wade through bushes to witness the arrest.' 'When park sex is not public.'
25. Rubin, 'Thinking sex', p. 282.
26. Although Rubin's diagram is now fifteen years old, and despite some progressive dominant cultural shifts in the recognition and representation of queers, the normative stratification of sexual practices that she outlines remains relatively the same.
27. Rubin, 'Thinking sex', p. 283.
28. Ehrenreich et al., *Re-Making Love*, p. 167.
29. Ibid., pp. 162–3.
30. Wilton, *Finger-Licking Good*, p. 24.
31. D'Emilio and Freedman, *Intimate Matters*, p. 167.
32. Ibid., p. xvi.
33. Sondheim and Wheeler, *A Little Night Music*, p. 96.
34. While based on Ingmar Bergman's *Smiles of a Summer Night* (1956), the narrative also echoes the rampant upper-class promiscuity implied in *A Midsummer Night's Dream*.
35. Douglas, *Where the Girls Are*, pp. 65–6.
36. Sondheim and Wheeler, *A Little Night Music*, p. 95.
37. Segal, *Slow Motion*, p. 176.
38. Julien and Mercer, 'True confessions', p. 169.
39. Holleran, *Dancer*, p. 131.
40. Sondheim and Wheeler, *A Little Night Music*, pp. 101–2.
41. Phillips, *Monogamy*, p. 29.
42. Foucault, *The History of Sexuality*, p. 37.
43. Millett, *Sexual Politics*, p. 122n. See also Wolf, *Promiscuities*.
44. Julien and Mercer, 'True confessions', p. 171; emphasis added.
45. Fain, 'Is our "lifestyle" hazardous to our health? Part II,' p. 19; cited in Weeks, *Sexuality and its Discontents*, p. 47.
46. Seidman, *Romantic Longings*, p. 169.
47. Delany, *The Motion of Light in Water*, p. 354. On the same page, Delany also equates promiscuity with anonymity: he writes that a semi-coerced sexual experience in his youth 'had as much to do with my turning toward "promiscuous sex" and away from social sex as any single happening.' Here the distinction appears to be between 'promiscuous sex' with strangers (usually in public spaces) and 'social sex' with known partners, such as his wife and their live-in male lover. Earlier, however, Delany argues that his sexual encounters in the riverside trucks 'with thirty-five, fifty, a hundred all-but-strangers . . . [were] hugely ordered, *highly social*, attentive, silent, and grounded in a certain care, if not community' (p. 202; emphasis added).
48. Altman, *Homosexualization*, p. 175.

49. Ibid., pp. 79–80.
50. Crimp, 'How to have promiscuity', p. 253.
51. Quoted in Parkes, 'Silences and secrets', p. 56.
52. Holleran, *Ground Zero*, p. 114.
53. Berlant and Warner, 'Sex in public', p. 560.
54. Freud, 'General theory of the neuroses', pp. 419–20.
55. Of course, Freud is well aware of the constant overlap between these two realms throughout much of his writing.
56. 'Typical phantasy structures (intra-uterine existence, primal scene, castration, seduction) which psycho-analysis reveals to be responsible for the organisation of phantasy life, regardless of the personal experiences of different subjects,' and which 'have one trait in common: they are all related to the origins. Like collective myths, they claim to provide a representation of and a "solution" to whatever constitutes a major enigma for the child. Whatever appears to the subject as a reality of a type as to require an explanation or a "theory", these phantasies dramatise into the primal moment or original point of departure of a history.' Laplanche and Pontalis, 'Primal phantasies' entry in *The Language of Psychoanalysis*, pp. 331–2.
57. Cowie, 'Fantasia', p. 75.
58. I particularly oppose Bersani's misguided interpretation of certain other gay and lesbian critics' hope for the increasing cultural acceptance and proliferation of sexual diversity as 'unnecessarily and even dangerously tame.' (Bersani, 'Is the rectum a grave?,' p. 219.) To my mind, Bersani's alternative notion of gay male sexual practice as resolutely unassimilable and anti-social is butch essentialism dressed as radical truth. For a more detailed critique of this essay along similar lines, see Merck, 'Savage nights'.
59. Bersani, 'Is the rectum a grave?' p. 205.
60. Ibid., p. 206.
61. Ibid., p. 205.
62. I do not mean to imply here that numerous unattached sexual encounters define all forms of gay male promiscuity. For instance, many would consider a gay man who has more than one regular partner, even in a shared domestic setting, to be 'promiscuous'. 'Multiple unattached sexual encounters' is therefore intended more as a key example.
63. Sinfield, *The Wilde Century*, p. 206.
64. Ibid., pp. vii–viii.
65. Martin, 'Sexualities without genders', p. 104.
66. Ibid., p. 119.
67. As opposed to my more frequent use of 'sex' to mean sexual activity.
68. This section borrows from a number of historical and critical studies, but is also informed by a broad range of newspaper and magazine articles in the gay and lesbian press too numerous to list here, and more cumulatively than individually influential upon my understanding of modern American gay sexual history.
69. Goldberg, *Sodometries*, p. 26. In stressing the incoherences and projections that characterise these colonial narratives, Goldberg also points to the construction of 'the figure of the promiscuous Indian woman' (p. 234), the earliest American regulatory equation between women, 'non-whiteness' and monstrous non-monogamy.
70. D'Emilio, 'Capitalism and gay identity', p. 103.

71. Chauncey, *Gay New York*, p. 12.
72. The distinctions between these terms are highly significant. '*[F]airy* (as a noun) and *queer* (as an adjective) were the terms most commonly used by "queer" and "normal" people alike to refer to "homosexuals" before World War II' (Ibid., p. 14). 'Essentially synonymous with "homosexual," *queer* presupposed the statistical normalcy – and normative character – of men's sexual interest in women; tellingly, queers referred to their counterparts as "normal men" (or "straight men") rather than as "heterosexuals." But *queer* did not presume that the men it denoted were effeminate, for many queers were repelled by the style of the fairy and his loss of manly status, and almost all were careful to distinguish themselves from such men.... [T]hey usually applied terms such as *fairy*, *faggot*, and *queen* only to those men who dressed or behaved in what they considered to be a flamboyantly effeminate manner' (p. 16). 'The term *gay* began to catch on in the 1930s, and its primacy was consolidated during the war. By the late 1940s, younger gay men were chastisting older men who still used *queer*, which the younger men now regarded as demeaning' (p. 19). (Ironically, this shift has been reversed in the 1990s, with some older gay-identified men chastising younger gay men for adopting the previously demeaning 'queer', while conversely, some younger queer-identified men are presumptuously asserting that 'gay' is restrictive and outmoded.) 'In calling themselves *gay*, a new generation of men insisted on the right to name themselves, to claim their status as men, and to reject the "effeminate" styles of the older generation' (p. 19). Chauncey also cites evidence that by 1940, 'gay' was an adjective used mainly by homosexuals not only 'to denote homosexuality', but also to signify 'sexual attractiveness, *promiscuity*, . . . or lack of restraint, in a person, place or party.' Legman, 'The language of homosexuality', p. 1167; quoted in Chauncey, p. 379, n. 36; emphasis added.
73. Chauncey, *Gay New York*, p.1.
74. Ibid., p. 10.
75. Ibid., pp. 44–5.
76. Garber, 'A spectacle in color', p. 325.
77. 'Celebrated entertainer Bricktop,' quoted in ibid., p. 322.
78. Ibid., pp. 322–3. Garber's description of patrons being openly promiscuous, to the extent of watching one another have sex, suggests an even more polymorphous variation of the gay male bathhouse (alongside the more formalised prostitution that took place in the buffet flats).
79. Ibid, p. 327. Of course, Nugent's prominent position in artistic/literary society made such erotic ostentation far easier, and even expected, particularly of a 'Negro' male. Yet Nugent's openness is echoed – albeit in different circumstances – in a number of Chauncey's accounts of non-secretive working-class gay male promiscuity in districts such as Harlem.
80. Chauncey, *Gay New York*, p. 2.
81. Ibid., pp. 219–20.
82. Ibid., p. 8.
83. Ibid., p. 9.
84. Little is as yet known about the effects of the First World War on gay life. Chauncey argues that 'it is likely that the first war had a less dramatic effect than the second, in part because it led to the mobilization of a far smaller number of people for a shorter period of time' (p. 144). Yet most

of the developments I gesture towards here in relation to the Second
World War clearly applied, on a smaller scale, to the previous war's disruption of familial life and the postwar burgeoning of urban gay cultures.
Moreover, as in the Second World War, many Americans overseas discovered 'a cultural and political climate for homosexuals that was almost
unimaginable at home', in the sexually precocious metropolitan milieux
of Europe (ibid.).

85. Bérubé, 'Marching', pp. 386–7.
86. Ibid., p. 390.
87. Sadownick, *Sex Between Men*, p. 34.
88. My use of 'feminine', 'masculine', 'butch' and 'femme' here does not
    only refer to how men identified themselves, but also to how they were
    categorised by those around them, often in antagonism with their self-
    perception.
89. Bérubé, 'Marching', p. 393.
90. Sadownick, *Sex Betweeen Men*, p. 61.
91. Chauncey, *Gay New York*, p. 9.
92. D'Emilio and Freedman, *Intimate Matters*, p. 291. Interestingly, *Howl*
    polymorphously blurs together images of straight, gay and implicitly
    bisexual male 'public' promiscuity, thereby disturbing the normative
    distinction between gay male sexual 'depravity' and young straight
    men's celebrated sexual exploits: Ginsberg celebrates 'angelheaded hip-
    sters . . . who blew and were blown by those human seraphim, the
    sailors, caresses of Atlantic and Caribbean love,/who balled in the
    morning in the evenings in rosegardens and the grass of public parks and
    cemeteries scattering their semen freely to whomever come who
    may, . . . who sweetened the snatches of a million girls trembling in the
    sunset, . . . joy to the memory of his [Neal Cassady's] innumerable lays
    of girls in empty lots & diner backyards, moviehouses' rickety rows, on
    mountaintops in caves or with gaunt waitresses in familiar roadside
    lonely petticoat upliftings & especially secret gas-station solipsisms of
    johns, & hometown alleys too.' Ginsberg, *Collected Poems*, p. 128.
93. D'Emilio and Freedman, *Intimate Matters*, p. 287.
94. Ibid., pp. 291–2.
95. Seidman, *Embattled Eros*, pp. 18–19.
96. Seidman, *Romantic Longings*, p. 169. This unsettling of the marital
    norm is part of a much longer (and extremely varied) American history
    of increasingly separating sexual pleasure from a reproductive impera-
    tive, which reaches back at least to the Victorians. (See, for example, Part
    One of *Romantic Longings*.) However, despite the dramatic changes of
    the 1960s and 1970s, the twentieth-century conflation of sex and monog-
    amous love remains dominant.
97. Hobsbawm, *Age of Extremes*, p. 270.
98. D'Emilio and Freedman, *Intimate Matters*, p. 302.
99. While a great many people did envisage an actual transformative revo-
    lution, some progessive historians have underlined that the notion of a
    'sexual revolution' was 'more rhetoric than reality' for others. (Seidman,
    Romantic Longings, p. 122.) Seidman suggests that 'the claim of a com-
    ing sexual revolution, like the idea of black or women's liberation, func-
    tioned as a powerful, emotionally charged symbol. The rhetorical intent
    [for many, at least] may have been to imbue sex and sexual conflicts with

a moral and political seriousness hitherto lacking' (ibid.).

100. See, for example, D'Emilio and Freedman, *Intimate Matters*, pp. 302–3; and Weeks, *Sexuality and its Discontents*, pp. 23–5.
101. Weeks, *Sexuality and its Discontents*, pp. 25–6.
102. Millett, *Sexual Politics*, p. 62.
103. Bronski, 'How sweet', cited in Sadownick, *Sex Between Men*, pp. 80–1.
104. Sadownick, *Between Men*, p. 83.
105. Seidman, *Romantic Longings*, p. 173.
106. D'Emilio and Freedman, *Intimate Matters*, p. 323.
107. I want to stress here that I am not opposed to the embodiment of traditionally 'masculine'-identified physical and behavioural codes by gay men *per se*. Nor am I simplistically suggesting that we should reject gay men's complexly motivated erotic investments in these codes. Instead, I am taking issue with the *normalisation* of a masculine ideal, such that male embodiments of so-called 'femininity' are presumed to be 'playing' with gender roles more than 'masculine' men do, and are therefore less authentically sexual, and ultimately in thrall to 'real' men. Yet at the same time, given the close proximity – or often, virtual equivalence – between dominant heterosexual, bisexual and gay male forms of masculinity, even the most self-consciously denaturalised gay manifestations of 'masculinity' are never exempt from their overarching patriarchal cultural context. These extremely fraught issues are pursued later.
108. Cited in Sadownick, *Sex Between Men*, p. 62.
109. Hemphill, Introduction to *Brother to Brother*, p. xix.
110. Ibid., p. xx.
111. The phrase comes from David Frechette's poem, 'Safe harbour', in Hemphill, *Brother to Brother*, p. 61.
112. See, for example, Steven Corbin's *Fragments that Remain* (1993); James Earl Hardy's *B-Boy Blues* (1994) and *2nd Time Around* (1996); and Darieck Scott's *Traitor to the Race* (1995). Of course, much white gay fiction shares these themes, though often without an emphasis on racial and ethnic considerations within the couple or family.
113. Gillings, 'B-boy blues,' p. 42.
114. See, for example, Dangerous Bedfellows, *Policing Public Sex*; King, *Safety in Numbers*; Odets, *In the Shadow of the Epidemic*; Patton, *Sex and Germs* and *Inventing AIDS*; Rofes, *Reviving the Tribe*; Sadownick, *Sex Between Men*; Watney, *Policing Desire* and *Practices of Freedom*.
115. King, *Safety in Numbers*, pp. 30–1.
116. Ibid., p. 75.
117. Weir, 'Is there life after sex?,' p. 13.
118. Ibid., p. 18. On the problematics of 'second wave' discourses, see Redick, 'Dangerous practices'.
119. King, *Safety in Numbers*, p. 223.
120. Ibid., p. 75.
121. Califia, 'Slipping', pp. 94–5.
122. Rofes, *Reviving the Tribe*, p. 170.
123. Ibid., pp. 166–7.
124. Ibid., p. 297.
125. Walt Odets notes that of the current sex clubs, 'the most liberal prohibit – though not always diligently – only unprotected anal sex.' Odets, *In the Shadow of the Epidemic*, p. 129.

'Crushed Intimacy':
John Rechy and the
Masculinisation of Gay Male
Promiscuity

Since the publication of his bestselling debut novel *City of Night* in 1963, John Rechy's gay-oriented writings have remained the most famous literary emblems of the myths and realities of pre-AIDS-awareness American 'masculine'-identified gay promiscuity.[1] While porn author Sam Steward (a.k.a. Phil Andros) and erotic artist Tom of Finland tapped into many men's fantasies of endless butch sex during the pre-liberation years, and gay-authored novels like Gore Vidal's *The City and the Pillar* (1948) and James Baldwin's *Another Country* (1962) had presented largely dismissive literary images of promiscuous urban gay sex, *City of Night* was a more diverse first-hand account of homosexual and bisexual promiscuity, which gained a degree of national attention preceded only by the failed 1957 obscenity case surrounding Allen Ginsberg's queerly promiscuous poem, *Howl*. The now-classic *City of Night* was read by gay and straight audiences alike (functioning as a key entry point into gay culture for the latter);[2] it 'became a landmark of gay literature and has been translated into some twenty languages.'[3] And if Rechy's later, more confrontationally sexual gay-themed novels of the late 1960s and 1970s were less widely read, their influence upon gay culture's sexual self-perception up until the mid-1980s was potent enough in 1982 for Dennis Altman to cite 'above all the novels of John Rechy' in his list of a gay male-related 'literature of cruising'.[4]

Rechy's fame, and infamy, within gay culture after *City of Night* was reinforced by his visual self-promotion in the press and on book covers as an embodiment of the 'masculine' bodybuilding gay stud ideal, muscles always flexed flirtatiously for the reader. Candidly admitting his 'enormous vanity, not to say egomania,'[5] in prefaces and interviews he underlined the thoroughly autobiographical nature of his narratives of restlessly promiscuous macho hustlers and bodybuilders,[6] who are torn between defying and succumbing to Catholic sexual guilt: 'All of my books are, in a sense, confessions.'[7]

But while Rechy's other gay-related, pre-AIDS works – principally, *Numbers* (1967), *The Sexual Outlaw: A Documentary* (1977) and *Rushes* (1979) – are no longer in fashion (probably mainly due to their relentlessly portentous tone), they remain important not only as semi-fictionalised historical documents, but also as unusually nuanced depictions of the effects of normalised masculine sexual codes within promiscuous gay culture. Throughout these narratives, Rechy's strong investment in macho forms of promiscuity is iconically on display, from his early hustling days to his uneasy alliance with gay liberation. Yet in both deliberate and unintended ways, his writings can also be seen to persistently question, and in *Rushes* to partly reject, their own allegiance to the seductive myth of the forever impervious and dominating hustling or cruising 'masculine' stud.

In life as in his writings, Rechy's early status as a homophobically defensive hustler 'outlaw' from gay culture (who nevertheless depended upon gay men for much of his clientele) developed into the ambiguous stance of a post-Stonewall butch gay 'sexual outlaw' who admonished the increasingly extreme machismo of his own sexual culture, crystallized to his mind in the rise of SM. (Rechy's mixed ethnicity also made him an 'outlaw': 'My father was Scottish, my mother Mexican. . . . I ended up rejected by both *Chicanos* and *Anglos*.'[8] However, while he has written about Mexican characters [*The Miraculous Day of Amalia Gomez* (1991)], and complained in the above interview that he is 'a Chicano writer omitted from anthologies of Chicano writers,'[9] his gay-oriented texts never draw attention to their narrators' ethnicity in any detail.) Tracing Rechy's differing allegiances to, and representations of, promiscuity from the early 1960s to late 1970s will enable us to examine the deeply ambiguous effects of the overwhelmingly 'masculine'-biased gendering of male same-sexual practice, and promiscuity, across straight, gay and implicitly bisexual cultures during those decades. Yet at the same time, I want to clarify the relevance of Rechy's pre-1980s promiscuous narratives for the continuing normalisation of masculinity in much of contemporary American gay sexual culture (and by extension, for other, American-influenced and/or similarly masculinist gay cultures as well).

GAY MALE PROMISCUITY AND
NORMALISED 'MASCULINITY'

Early on in *City of Night*, its unnamed young hustling narrator explores the gay bars and areas of New York City in the late 1950s for the first time,[10] and discovers the sexual 'jungle of Central Park':

Unexpectedly at night you may come upon scenes of crushed intimacy along the dark twisting lanes. In the eery mottled light of a distant lamp, a shadow lies on his stomach on the grass-patched ground, another straddles him: ignoring the danger of detection in the last moments of exiled excitement.[11]

The hustler's reference to the 'crushed intimacy' of these coupling 'shadows' suggests the possibility of an intimate connection within the brief, compressed span of an 'anonymous' sexual encounter (a possibility that we will be returning to later). Equally, though, 'crushed intimacy' unintentionally describes the recurrent effect of the narrator's brittle sexual machismo, and that of Rechy's subsequent hustling and cruising fictional stand-ins: namely, their disavowing rejection of intimacy or reciprocity – whether in monogamous or promiscuous sex – even as they sometimes yearn for that interconnection.

Leaving aside the complicating question of the macho hustler/cruiser's divided desires for a moment, we can sometimes see Rechy's texts (re)producing[12] the conventional gay cultural image of the potently promiscuous gay stud (or in the case of the 1960s hustlers, the bisexually active but straight-identified 'trade') who aspires to 'masculine' sexual dominance by shunning the supposedly 'effeminate' vulnerability of (momentary or long-term) closeness with another man. For all their complexity, Rechy's narratives prior to *Rushes* do tend to uphold the normative gay cultural equation between promiscuous sexual potency and male 'masculinity', and correspondingly, tend to downplay willingly promiscuous male 'femininity'.[13]

Thus, even as *City of Night*'s narrator is frequently self-conscious about the performative basis of his butch pose for adoring johns and queens, his first-person accounts of interacting with gay men sometimes serve the purpose of covertly naturalising his own macho sexual persona in contrast to the other men's flagrantly contradictory behaviour. For example, while visiting a fascistic SM queen's house in San Francisco, he meets 'Carl, a large, masculine, somewhat goodlooking man in his 30s', who 'strutted in arrogantly in motorcycle clothes. His breath reeked of liquor'. Before long:

Carl's transformation has become complete: All the masculinity has been drained out of him as if by the liquor. His legs are curling one over the other.

The once rigidly held shoulders have softened. . . . His look liddedly mellowed, and he began to thrust flirtatious glances in my direction. 'Im [sic] Unhappy,' he drooled in wine-tones. . . . 'you wanna know why Im Unhappy? . . . [B]ecause – I – wanna – wanna – lover. Yes! A Lover! And all this – this motorcycle drag – it doesnt mean shit to me. I'd wear a woman's silk night-ie if it got me a Lover. . . . If he wants me to be a woman, I'll be the greatest lady since Du Barry. I'll be all things to One Man! . . . I – am – lonely.' . . .

The glass smashed on the floor.

He was still passed out on the couch when I left.[14]

Here, another proudly masculine-identified man, who has initially been portrayed as a promiscuous SM 'top', is disapprovingly shown to confess a yearning for monogamy that is conventionally feminised both by the defiant Carl himself and by the pitying narrator. While Rechy has repeatedly emphasised the factual basis of all of his characters ('I can't write make-believe'),[15] at the same time, this coolly detached depiction of Carl serves to heighten momentarily the narrator's misogynist and homophobic sense of distance from the 'shaming effeminacy' of queerness and/as monogamous romantic love. As Stephen Adams notes in his insightful discussion of Rechy, this hustler's 'sympathies are more easily aroused by those who offer no threat to his masculinity and heterosexual pose.'[16]

Rechy has since acknowledged the frequent defensiveness of *City of Night*, which, as Adams points out, attempts 'to make homosexuality symbolic of some more universal condition with which . . . [Rechy's] narrator may safely identify'.[17] The author similarly commented in 1977 that:

City of Night is a book about a male hustler who does not ever really admit that he's gay. . . . It represented quite honestly where I was at the time. I didn't bullshit. I was honest. So I am fond of confessing that *City of Night* is a very honest book about a dishonest person.[18]

This narrational 'dishonesty', and the author/narrator's frequently normative gendering of gay sexual practice, need however to be placed in the broader cultural context of the late 1950s and 1960s. As we saw in the introductory chapter, despite the gradual loosening of social restrictions on sexual diversity from the mid-1950s onwards, and despite the gay boom of the migratory war years, the postwar trend towards aggressively renormalising the heterosexual family unit (especially in emerging suburbia) meant that the expanding gay world 'became more segregated and carefully hidden, and the risks of visiting . . . [it] increased.'[19] Seymour Kleinberg reminisces that:

As students in the mid-fifties, most of the gay men I knew thought about marrying. . . . If very few gay men actually married, it was not for want of spending thousands of dollars and years in therapy trying to be straight.[20]

For those unable to afford therapy, the psychological effects of this contradictory combination of gay cultural expansion and increased dominant demonisation were often the same, as with Carl and his queeny host's attempts to appear more conventionally masculine than each other for the amused narrator: 'Carl's not quite as butch as hes [sic] pretending to be. Hes really the end!'[21]

In this last example, as well as mirroring wider homophobia, the two queens' battle for butchness, and the narrator's similarly defensive machismo, are also symptomatic of the closely related rigid gender norms of the period. George Chauncey notes that 'only in the 1930s, 1940s, and 1950s did the now-conventional division of men into "homosexuals" and "heterosexuals", based on the sex of their sexual partners, replace the division of men into "fairies" and "normal men" on the basis of their imaginary gender status as the hegemonic way of understanding sexuality.'[22] Indeed, 'the homosexual displaced the "fairy" in middle-class culture several generations earlier than in working-class culture; but in each class culture each category persisted, standing in uneasy, contested, and disruptive relation to the other.'[23] Thus, the archetypes of the feminine 'fairy' and the masculine 'normal man' persisted within postwar, pre-liberation homosexual male culture in ways that often replicated straight gender conventions, including the idealised figure of the promiscuous 'real man' versus the less sexually potent femme – not that all gay men identified with one of these gender-specific roles.[24]

Nor did those homosexually active men who identified as 'real men' always consider themselves to be gay. Take, as a key example, the hustler (and his straight-identified johns). Adams observes that the narrator's 'vocation as a hustler has no economic basis, it merely allows him to practice homosexuality without incurring any of its opprobrium, particularly the presumption of effeminacy. . . . The exchange of money is a symbolic, though necessary, token, by which his masculinity [and heterosexuality] is "absolved."'[25] As we will see in more detail later, the pre-liberation hustler commonly took on a drag queen, or a succession of drag queens, as his 'girlfriend' or 'wife' in order to maintain some semblance of traditional heterosexual gender roles, even within a publicly homosexual relationship.[26] The reproduction of 'masculine' codes is therefore equated not only with promiscuous sexuality, but also with being a 'normal' straight-identified man, echoing the primary division of sexuality along gender lines in earlier decades.

At the same time, though, the hustlers documented in *City of Night* 'periodically prove their masculinity'/'heterosexuality' by having sex with women.[27] In this sense, they are central examples of 'the trade man, or the heterosexually identified, homoerotically inclined man,'[28] who, in straddling both heterosexual and homosexual affiliations, can be read more precisely as 'bisexual', albeit without identifying themselves as such.[29] Yet in a number of cases, as with *City of Night*'s narrator, heterosex appears to function almost entirely as a status symbol, rather than a sustained desire: 'we kept on studiedly digging a cute young girl nearby – because youre [sic] supposed to want real girls only . . . for "love" [as opposed to hustling johns and being non-committal with drag queen "girlfriends"].'[30]

Like *City of Night*, *Numbers* – a 1967 sequel of sorts – occasionally normalises promiscuous, non-gay-identified 'masculinity'. Its ex-hustler protagonist, Johnny Rio, is described early on as having an occasional – and 'self-defeating' – 'tough' persona, yet beneath that persona lies 'an easy masculinity – not stiff, not rigid, not blundering nor posed'[31] – in other words, a properly masculine normal man underpins the macho façade. (Incoherently and anxiously, we are also told here that 'there is something very, very subtly female about him' – and yet, confusingly enough, 'there is nothing feminine, there is nothing effeminate' about Johnny.)

But in the post-1960s gay liberation years as well, in *The Sexual Outlaw* – the 1977 so-called documentary text[32] that is most commonly associated with Rechy's promiscuous gay public persona – he famously epitomises the dominant normative masculine gendering of promiscuity (and active sexuality in general) in gay male and straight culture alike. The text juxtaposes an account of the prodigious sexual exploits of ex-hustler Jim over a weekend in Los Angeles[33] with media reports on anti-gay activity, and Rechy's own observations on gay promiscuity and politics. Rechy, who is now gay-identified, reverently praises the 'queens, who are true hero-heroines of our time, exhibiting more courage for walking one single block in drag than a straight-looking [read: masculine-identified] gay to [sic] "come out" on a comfy campus.'[34] Yet this excessive reverence is decidedly desexualising. For the text's central thesis, that 'the promiscuous homosexual is a sexual revolutionary', who in 'each moment of his outlaw existence . . . confronts repressive laws, repressive "morality" [in the] battlefields [of] parks, alleys, subway tunnels, garages, streets,'[35] consistently masculinises promiscuous public sex to the virtual exclusion of femme gay men. In his list of the range of promiscuous outlaws, Rechy does self-referentially include the less-than-butch professions of writers, teachers,[36] dancers, actors and painters alongside the construction workers, cowboys, truck drivers, motorcyclists and weightlifters.[37] Nevertheless, his focus is on their butch cruising personas, rather than their – and his own – more ambiguously coded professional personas.

This equation between male masculinity and active promiscuous sexuality is underlined by recurring military metaphors (the 'battle-fields'; 'the shock troops of the revolution'[38]), by heroic rhetoric ('No stricture – legal, medical, religious – will ever stop him. It will only harden his defiance'[39]) and by references to a seemingly primal male/masculine tough promiscuous sexual drive ('Male and male and male, hard limbs, hard cocks, hard muscles, hard stomachs, strong bodies, male and male'[40]; after sex, two butch men 'hesitate . . . , resist-ing the ancestral pull to become strangers again after the intimacy.'[41]). This latter notion of a shared primal promiscuous maleness is contra-dicted by references to *conflicting* gay male attitudes to promiscuity elsewhere in the text.[42]

Nevertheless, the macho sexual outlaw is mythically envisaged as the privileged bearer of a transhistorical 'ancestral rage. Death by sword or other torture decreed for homosexuals by ecclesiastical courts. Burnings at the stake into the nineteenth century'.[43] Moulded by Rechy's Catholicism-imbued worldview, the 1970s sexual outlaw becomes a modern-day martyr crossed with an action hero, living a perversely 'monastic life [of] total commitment and dangers, risks, sacrifices [as he] confronts cops and [anti-gay] maniacs [with his] fully awakened, living, *defiant* body.'[44] Unconsciously reproducing the dominant American patriarchal ennoblement of masculine-coded practices and ideology largely on the basis of their allegiance to an abstract masculine ideal, Rechy contends that merely avoiding or escaping anti-gay entrapment and violence is enough to heroicise the macho cruiser: 'each night after the [sex]hunt, the outlaw knows he's won an ancestral battle – just because he's still alive and free.'[45]

However, this notion that the butch sexual outlaw is necessarily more alive and free than dominant culture, or than non- or anti-promiscuous gay men, is obviously insubstantial on two fronts. As Rechy himself highlights at other points in the text, normative gender codes prevail on the supposedly culture-free outlaw's turf: as another man's finger 'tries to penetrate Jim's ass, . . . Jim jerks away immediately, pulls his cock out of the other's mouth, pushing him away, rejecting even the hint of penetration.'[46] (Not that the desire to be penetrated would, by itself, make Jim more progressive in relation to gender norms. Rather, his violent over-reaction illustrates how aggressively he seeks to embody the ideal of the implacably butch stud.) Later that same night, Jim lies in bed with 'a very handsome dark youngman' he met leaving a park:

Used to being pursued, each waits for the other to advance first. Both are severely turned on, cocks rigid. Now they glance at each other, each wanting the other even more now. But they look away. Their cocks strain in isolation.

Nothing. . . . Looking away from each other, both dress hurriedly, each cut deeply by regret that they did not connect.[47]

Against his own assertion of heroic freedom, Rechy draws attention here to another instance of 'crushed intimacy', in the sense of a potentially intimate promiscuous connection being 'crushed' by machismo (as opposed to a monogamy-centred reading of this scene as a potentially monogamous connection being 'crushed' by promiscuity). In effect, these purportedly revolutionary macho 'sexual outlaws' are, themselves, 'cocks strain[ing] in isolation.'[48]

Which brings us to the second way in which *The Sexual Outlaw*'s championing of promiscuous outlaw freedom rings hollow – in its portrayal of public gay sex as a revolutionary transgression of normalised heterosexual monogamy: 'a radical statement is made each time a man has sex with another on a street.'[49] For at other moments in the text, Rechy incoherently undermines his own manifesto by admitting that for the most part, *gay promiscuity is visible only to homosexuals and to the cops*'[50]; sex between men 'on a street' sounds less disruptive when Rechy specifies that it usually occurs in a dark alley or park chosen for its likely seclusion from hostile onlookers. Moreover, in Foucauldian mode, Rechy acknowledges that dominant anti-gay and anti-promiscuous norms help to produce the defiant shadowland cruiser when he rhetorically asks: 'Does police harassment stop sexual outlawry? No. It increases it – *creates it* – by resultant defiance. The police count on that.'[51] (This is not to say that all gay 'public', or semi-public, promiscuity is mainly motivated by its antagonism with repressive forces, nor that it would disappear if it was no longer outlawed. It might well increase – although the fear of potential entrapment heightens the attraction for some.) Adams wittily responds that:

The separation of sex from the individual's everyday world and its relegation to the safety-valve of 'outlaw country' is a dubious model of revolutionary freedom. . . . Rechy is committed to the maintenance of an underground, demanding only 'better conditions for the workers,' not the overthrow of the system.[52]

However, as with the hustlers' normative gender allegiances in the earlier novels, the masculinisation of promiscuity and normalisation of masculinity in *The Sexual Outlaw* are partly symptomatic of mainstream mid- to late-1970s gay culture in general. We saw in the introduction that while the gay liberation movement (following the women's movement) began by denaturalising dominant norms of gender, sexuality and sexual practice, a broader cultural shift towards political conservatism from the mid-1970s onwards was reflected in the decreasing directness of gay male challenges to heteropatriarchy (and capitalism). Central to this retreat from socialist and revolutionary forms of sexual-political analysis was the increasing normalisation of the macho 'clone' or leather or SM figure, who, as Jamie Gough notes, 'reflects a *combination* of sexual freedom [i.e., a confounding of dominant cultural assumptions that all gay men were 'effeminate'] with the *un*freedom of the institution of masculinity (i.e., of the gender system).'[53]

Yet Jack Fritscher, editor of the leatherman's magazine *Drummer* during this period, provides a prominent example of how the post-liberation normalisation of 'masculine' sexuality – particularly in SM forms – was often perceived by butch gay men as transgressively powerful in comparison with 'vanilla' femme gay sexuality: 'He believed the essence of gay style owed too large a debt to the "great ladies of the silver screen," and he postulated the idea of the "homomasculine man" as someone for whom S&M was a celebration of masculinity and a second "coming out".'[54] While Rechy was vocally (if ambivalently) opposed to SM sex and style, his paeans to heroic butch promiscuous sex clearly espouse a comparable 'celebration of masculinity' that implicitly desexualises the supposedly outdated gay male femme.

It is important to remember, however, that the rise of gay macho styles in the 1970s had many precedents, both in the masculine-identified, homosexually active 'normal men' of late nineteenth to mid-twentieth-century America, and in the earlier and concurrent social acceptance within diverse cultures of the 'active' – inserting/dominating – masculine-identified man who engages in homosex (though usually not exclusively). Alan Sinfield similarly emphasises that:

The idea of gay manliness does not derive only from post-1960s liberalization. In diverse social arrangements, from the ancient Greeks through the seventeenth-century rake . . . [and so on], same-sex passion has been legitimated through the claim that it is manly. Usually that has meant justifying the 'active' role and despising the 'passive' as inferior, i.e. womanly. In fact, matters may not be so clear-cut.[55]

Usually attendant upon this normative equation between masculinity and active sexuality is the implication of promiscuity as part of that activeness.

Equally, the normalisation of masculine sexual (and other behavioural) codes within gay culture, and the linking of promiscuous gay sex primarily to 'masculinity', has persisted into the late 1990s. If the categorisation of sexuality according to gender identification has been supplanted by the hetero/homo/bisexual distinction since mid-century, the influence of gender difference upon gay male (and all other) subjectivities remains as profound as ever. Witness, for instance, the dearth of gay cultural acknowledgement – let alone encouragement – of promiscuous or otherwise sexually active femme and drag queens[56] (with rare exceptions; for example, cinematic representations like the promiscuous young drag queen in *The Adventures of Priscilla, Queen of the Desert* [1995, dir. Stephan Elliott], or the eroticised late 1960s coupling of drag queen and 'masculine' gay man in *Stonewall* [1995, dir. Nigel Finch].[57]) Even rarer is any cultural validation specifically of femme-on-femme gay male desire or sex, which represents a considerable challenge to the masculine sexual norm (and can be seen in the budding relationship between two queens living with AIDS in Terrence McNally's *Love! Valour! Compassion!* [1994; film version 1997]).[58]

Viewed within this surrounding cultural context, Rechy's intermittent normalisation, and even naturalisation, of masculine-identified forms of gay male promiscuity can be seen as symptomatic both of the long-ingrained dominant cultural privileging of gender-conformist male sexuality (and male experience in general), and of the specifically gay male reproduction of this heteropatriarchal ideology.

THE TROUBLE WITH STUDS: DENORMALISING 'MASCULINE' GAY MALE PROMISCUITY

It might seem from the examples given so far that Rechy's works are, by and large, uncritically invested in 'masculine' forms of promiscuity. However, readers would be hard-pressed to find many other outright endorsements of the normatively masculine gay stud in any of his texts – despite the fact that Rechy is commonly associated with this unproblematically masculinist image. On the contrary, these texts can be seen to ruthlessly expose the contradictions, anxieties and self-doubts of their butch hustling and cruising protagonists far more frequently than they reinscribe myths of masculine sexual virility.

This self-reflexivity begins in the first pages of *City of Night*, which provide a brief account of the narrator's (and Rechy's) deeply disturbing early family life in El Paso, where, he tells us:

When I was about eight years old, my father taught me this: He would say to me: 'Give me a thousand,' and I knew this meant I should hop on his lap and then he would fondle me – intimately – and he'd give me a penny, sometimes a nickel. At times when his friends – old gray men – came to our house, they would ask for 'a thousand.' And I would jump on their laps too. And I would get nickel after nickel, going around the table.

And later, a gift from my father [of a prized ruby ring passed down from his grandfather] would become a token of a truce from the soon-to-blaze hatred between us.[59]

The young narrator's hatred is further provoked by the persistent mood swings of his embittered father, a failed musician trapped in unrewarding jobs, whose 'violence erupted unpredictably over anything':

In an instant he overturns the table. . . . He would smash bottles, menacing us with the sharp-fanged edges. He had an old sword which he kept hidden threateningly about the house.[60]

The narrator eventually leaves home for the army without speaking to his tearful father. He is soon brought home by news of his father's illness, but when he arrives, his father has already died, initiating a grief-stricken (and Catholic patriarchy-influenced) sense of guilt and alienation, at 'failing' to take responsibility for the break in communication effected by his father's violence:

I know now that Forever I will have no father . . ., that as long as he had been alive there was a chance, and that we would be, Always now, strangers . . . *my Father* was gone, *for me*. . . . And throughout the days that followed – and will follow forever – I will discover him in my memories, and hopelessly – through the infinite miles that separate life from death – try to understand his torture: in searching out the shape of my own.[61]

There is, of course, a more precise way in which the dead father continues to influence his son. The adult narrator's eroticised 'craving for attention'[62] from paying men, who are often 'near-middle-aged or older . . ., mostly uneffeminate,'[63] can be traced fairly obviously to his ostensibly 'straight' macho father's prostitution of his eight-year-old son for himself and a number of other men.[64] Yet at the same time, the masculine/straight-identified men's disavowal of their same-sex desires through the ritual exchange of money (and by abstracting the child's body itself into economic currency: 'Give me a thousand') clearly influences the narrator's later disavowal of his own desire for multiple male sexual partners[65] through the excuse of 'doing it for the money',[66] and through a 'masculine' identification that is culturally equated with heterosexuality. The narrator's father therefore instils in his son a confusing contradiction: a desire for sex with (preferably) straight/masculine-identified men,[67] and a repudiation of those desires through a defensive identification with the straight (or in some cases only straight-identified) male object of desire.[68]

The novel ironically foregrounds the narrator's resistance to drawing

such direct connections between his childhood sexual abuse and com-
pulsive yet emotionally withdrawn adult hustling. Towards the end of
the novel, his macho sexual reserve is challenged by Jeremy Adams, a
pick-up he goes home with during the New Orleans Mardi Gras:

'Wouldn't your masculinity be compromised much less if you tested your
being "wanted" with women instead of men?'
   'It's easier to hustle men,' I defended myself quickly. . . .
   'I think it's something else,' he went on relentlessly. 'Even a wayward
revenge on your own sex – your father's sex. . . .'
   I winced. He had aimed too cruelly.[69]

The narrator then recalls his father 'reassuring me, in that strange way
– so briefly! – that he did . . . want me,' yet is shown to over-emphati-
cally reject the implications of that memory: '"I can't blame my
father – for anything," I said sharply, sitting up.'[70] Similarly, the initial
psychoanalytic positioning of this memory of childhood sexual abuse
at the start of the novel implies its significance as the source for the
hustler's money-mediated promiscuity.

These brief yet pointed references to the narrator's childhood sexual
abuse/prostitution roughly frame the novel's central hustling narratives,
complicating the narrator's macho adult self-representation by gestur-
ing towards the traumatic patriarchal family life on which his disavowing, 'childhood-tampered ego'[71] is founded. The inclusion of this
childhood material also indirectly complicates the 'masculine heterosexual' dominant cultural male ideal that the adult hustler strives to
embody, by providing an example of homoeroticism at work within
the stringently heteropatriarchal homestead (and *promiscuous* homoeroticism between the father and his male friends, which is deflected
on to the 'feminised' male child). What might also be seen to be implicitly
called into question here, then, is the crude normative cultural distinction between the idealised, safely monogamous heterosexual nuclear
family and the disturbingly/enticingly unruly and often promiscuous
sexual realm outside the family. As it has become almost commonplace
to note from the more recent publicisation of domestic child and youth
molestation largely carried out by straight(-identified) men within
the family, it is precisely through the still widespread belief in this
simplistic cultural distinction that child/youth sexual abuse (or, put
another way, non-consensual adult male domestic promiscuity) can
remain so prevalent.

But while *City of Night* links its protagonist's macho hustling/
promiscuity back to his sexual abuse, it also implicitly links his macho
sexual stance to the dominant cultural imperative that men should
strive to embody impervious, dominating masculine sexual codes (an

imperative of which his father's controlling sexual abuse is the darkest underside). While the narrator – like so many other fearful homosexually active men of the late 1950s and early 1960s – steers away from criticising dominant culture itself, his frequent emphasis on the performative basis of 'masculine' sexual power within the marginalised world of hustlers, queens and johns can be seen to reflect on the prevailing straight male sexual ideal as well: 'I would discover that to many of the street people a hustler became more attractive in direct relation to his seeming insensibility – his "toughness." I would wear that mask'[72]; 'as the queens began to dish each other [about which hustler belongs to which queen], myself and the two other [hustler] "husbands" felt ourselves so Goddamned absurdly Masculine.'[73]

This last scene – where the marriage-minded queens fight over their frequently unfaithful butch 'husbands' – also exemplifies Rechy's awareness that the hustler depends upon the monogamous feminine-identified queen's presence in order to prop up his own embodiment of masculine promiscuous sexual potency. Miss Destiny, a fearless LA drag queen, underlines this point while railing against the hustlers for sneaking off from their drag wives to have sex with women: 'You know whats [sic] the crazy matter with you, all of you? youre so dam [sic] gone on your own damselves you have to hang around queens to prove youre such fine dam studs. . . .!'[74]

Furthermore, in both the pre- and post-liberation texts, the butch hustler or promiscuous gay man is shown to have uncomfortably close encounters with the misogynistically feminised, 'weaker' spheres of emotional intimacy, mutuality and vulnerability that exist *within himself*, during his purportedly unconnected and dominating participation in promiscuous sex. In *The Sexual Outlaw*, for example, Rechy recalls an interviewer from a literary magazine asking him:

'Is your entire sexual scene one of not responding to other people?'
I answer: 'My primary scene, yes.'
But I should say: Not totally. When I hustle, yes; when I'm into 'numbers,' mostly.
But there are other times of mutual exchange, yes. Yes; and I do cherish those times.[75]

While the different types of sexual experiences Rechy mentions here are all promiscuous,[76] the combination of unconnected and mutual encounters he mentions nevertheless serves to remind us that, whether they were 'masculine' *or* 'feminine'-identified (or otherwise), gay men in the 1970s often 'combined the emotional exclusiveness of heterosexual romantic love patterns with sexual non-monogamy.'[77] Rechy's quintessential embodiment of the mainstream gay cultural ideal of the

emotionally untouchable butch gay male stud is thus shown to be subject to more complex 'ambivalences and contradictions'.[78] On the other
hand, though, Rechy's confession to the reader that he kept his 'times
of mutual exchange' secret during the above interview self-consciously
illustrates the masculine promiscuous gay man's common resistance to
admitting his sexual and emotional 'ambivalences and contradictions'
to himself or others.

At other moments in these texts, such emotional resistance on the
part of the macho protagonist is challenged by an unsettling encounter
with potentially monogamous desires that are similarly feared for their
'feminising' effect upon the butch cruiser (and arguably also for their
reminder of the father's enforced sexual intimacy). In *City of Night*, the
shrewd pick-up Jeremy Adams tells the narrator, 'bluntly: "You want,
very much, to be loved – but you dont [sic] want to love back, even if
you have to force yourself not to."'[79] The narrator unusually opens up
enough to tell Jeremy his whole name (which is still withheld from the
reader), and although he rejects Jeremy's offer to come away with him
'before the [promiscuous] Carnival is over,'[80] he only reaches his hesitant
decision after a protracted confessional conversation:

Were we strangers? Or had we, rather, known each other too intimately? . . . .
    I leaned over him and kissed him on the lips.
    And I was thinking: Yes, maybe youre right. Maybe I could love you. But
I wont.
    The grinding streets awaited me.[81]

By the time of the sequel, *Numbers*, the ex-hustler bodybuilder
Johnny Rio takes the further step of interrupting his stream of non-
reciprocal sexual encounters with 'numbers' to make a fumbling
attempt at a mutual encounter with an actor he meets at a friend's
dinner party. After they kiss goodbye, Johnny drives away, thinking:

That other – that further country ['of sharing mutually, . . . [a]nd – perhaps – . . . finding *one* . . . number'[82]] . . . I just . . . explored it. And . . . it
isn't mine.
    Nauseated, he stops the car; and he vomits convulsively out the window.
    That country – . . . he thinks. It wasn't mine.[83]

The butch stud is shown here attempting to physically abject the sex-
ual/emotional mutuality and possible monogamy that threatens to
trouble his overdeterminedly promiscuous 'masculine' identity, which
is defined over and against its supposed opposite of (monogamous or
even promiscuous) sexual intimacy. As Julia Kristeva has influentially
outlined, the subject – in this case, the promiscuous macho gay

man – defines himself or herself most clearly in opposition to that which he or she considers abject; yet that distinction produces an ongoing interdependence between subject and abject which renders the abject thing – in this case, 'feminised' sexual intimacy and/or monogamy – 'above all [an] ambiguity' that remains 'inseparable' from the subject, constantly threatening any notion of a stable self-identification.[84] Here, Johnny Rio's overinvestment in reaching an ever-growing target figure of sexual numbers makes this encounter with a tempting mutuality all the more threatening to his nervously upheld butch stud self-image.

Finally, in *Rushes*, Rechy produces his most pointed, and most intricate, representation of the butch gay stud's unwilling confrontation with his own sexual and emotional vulnerability and partially monogamous desires. The novel is set during one night in and around a late 1970s exclusively 'masculine' leather and Western urban bar called Rushes, situated next door to the Rack, 'one of the city's most popular [SM] orgy rooms.'[85] Rechy's fictional representative, Endore, an ambivalently masculine-identified regular at the Rushes, and his hyperbutch SM friend, Chas, both align themselves with the post-liberation gay male embrace of promiscuity as a chosen and freeing pleasure, in contrast to some other liberationists' denunciation of promiscuity as 'alienating':

Both feel that abundant sex – what others but not they call 'promiscuity' – is – Endore says 'can be' and 'should be' – an enriching, unique experience not to be denied or surrendered to conventionality posing as liberation; and both agree that sex need not occur with love – Chas says 'does not.'[86]

While Endore has been drawn to SM in the past, and momentarily agrees with Chas that 'there's no difference between us,'[87] he has, for the most part, rejected the macho extremes of mainstream gay male sexuality that he sees embodied most forcefully by Chas (who 'despises women . . ., weak heterosexual men . . . and weak homosexuals. All weakness!'[88]) and by the increasingly butch SM scene in general (more on this later). With more self-implicating insight than Rechy's 1960s protagonists, Endore – a journalist – 'has written against the hostility burgeoning in the macho ghettos against women'[89] and 'transvestites', and observes that precisely because of its studiedly tough stance,

The new masculinity [in gay culture] is damned to bouts with . . . [a] tenacious vulnerability. At recurrent moments, especially when liquor slackens control, the forced rigidity snaps. . . . Poised tenuously, the hard pose tilts, falls, shatters. Astonished, the mean look softens.[90]

Yet alongside Endore's deep ambivalence, and even resentment, towards the macho ethos and environment he continues to inhabit, the bar narrative is punctuated by his memories of rejecting his potential lover Michael's growing affection: 'Endore remembers Michael's lips brushing the words ["I love you"] against his cheek. The gentle opening of the secret wound, with a mere breath.'[91] Near the end of the night at the bar, Endore's first talk with Michael since rejecting him reveals that even though Endore withdrew to prevent their monogamous 'surrender . . . to any imprisoning concept of "fidelity" as ownership,' he had also become jealous of Michael's other sexual partners: 'After all your bullshit about selfish "fidelity," *you* couldn't cope with it,' Michael reminds him.[92] Later, Endore similarly rejects Robert, an inexperienced newcomer to the Rushes who oversteps the bar clientele's predominant resistance to public or private emotional intimacy:

'I love you,' Robert says.

    'Don't say that!' The terrified words bolt out of Endore's lips. 'There's no such- . . .'. . . . Robert frowns. 'We are gonna make it, aren't we?'

    'No!' Endore says, and now he knows and can answer why he told him to leave: 'Because you threaten the cynicism by which I survive,' he says angrily. 'And it was threatened once before.' And now by memories, of Michael. And he is here in the jungle I prepared him for without wanting to, and you'd inherit it too. . . .

    Robert erupts, 'Then fuck you – you're as fucked as Chas in your own way. . . . Fuck you!' he shouts.[93]

Robert's linking of Endore to the aggressively promiscuous Chas highlights the masculinist basis of Endore's aversion to sexual/emotional interconnection and to monogamy – or at least to having a primary partner. However, on the one hand, Endore's argument against the 'imprisoning concept of "fidelity" as ownership' is important in its own right, and not a mere smokescreen to repel intimacy. He argues elsewhere that his sexual jealousy was culturally pressured: 'the hated attitudes like venom injected too deeply, too early, in him.'[94] On the other hand, his patronising attempt to patriarchally protect the younger man from 'inheriting' the tough sexual 'jungle' *does* serve to prevent further emotional involvement. Similarly, Endore's remark that Robert 'threaten[s] the cynicism by which I survive' can be seen to refer to his disbelief in monogamy, but also (and unintentionally) to the threat Robert's passionate openness represents to his cynically detached masculine pose.

    Moreover, earlier in the evening, Endore has acknowledged to himself that the unprecedented appearance of two heterosexual women and a drag queen in the bar has unsettled his 'previously uncluttered attitudes toward women' by provoking previously unnoticed 'emergent feelings toward the Rushes as impenetrable territory except by the masculine men. Like him.'[95] His conscious ambivalence towards the rigid butch stud ideal is thus counteracted by his insidious allegiance to 'masculinised' promiscuity within a butch sexual space that guards against any reminders of the 'feminine', including the 'secret wound' of intimate or monogamous desires.[96] Yet as Endore's awkward deflection of potential lovers within this masculine environment indicates, the perceived threat of that abject wound is produced by the rigidity of the Rushes itself, where 'terror of rejection wars with the desire to connect.'[97]

I should perhaps clarify here that my intention in spotlighting these various examples of potentially mutual or monogamous desires within butch promiscuity is not to suggest that Rechy's (or any other) butch gay studs really want or need monogamy more than promiscuity, or that all their promiscuous encounters ought to be more intimate and emotionally open. Instead, these uncomfortably close encounters with previously unconscious or subconscious desires to bond more closely with other men through sex illustrate the instrinsic promiscuousness (or in Endore's words, the 'blurring boundaries'[98]) of all sexual desire, wherein contradictory needs and wishes perpetually clash and intertwine. The 'masculine' gay stud's desire for unattached and/or emotionally unreciprocal sex is therefore no less valid or real than someone else's yearning for romantically intimate monogamous sex. However, the more insistently the gay stud invests in his non-reciprocal sexual identity, the more disturbingly unexpected any contact with his own 'tenacious vulnerability' becomes.

Another significant way in which Rechy's texts denormalise and interrogate the masculine promiscuous archetype is by repeatedly drawing attention to their macho protagonists' depressive, and even suicidal, sense of alienation and self-doubt amidst their public display of sexual bravado. At one level, this sociosexual alienation is represented as a response to the ever-present threat of anti-gay violence and social hostility – a threat which is muted by the momentary comforts of unattached sex, where emotional distance can numb the fear of further rejection:

We cruise and fuck away the knowledge of the stalking hatred. Whipped by strobe lights, young warriors desert the battle for sequined disco graves. In bars we numb it away.[99]

At another level, though, in *The Sexual Outlaw*, Rechy admits that he also sometimes feels isolated and self-destructive *during* his cruising and promiscuous sex: he tells an interviewer from a gay magazine that 'sometimes . . . after a night of hustling and dark cruising alleys, I think of suicide.'[100] In one sense, this extreme depression could perhaps be traced to what Rechy calls 'the psychic danger of constant loneliness' in anonymous sex.[101] However, the less overwhelming 'sad joy'[102] that Jim feels after sex in a public restroom in *The Sexual Outlaw* is a far more common example of the cruising gay man's ambivalent response to the 'fast-forward relationship' structure of one-time-only promiscuous sexual encounters, wherein the thrill of the first intimate contact is swiftly followed by the final parting.[103] By contrast, the more extreme despair and nihilism that Rechy/Jim experiences at other moments can be seen to stem more specifically from the self-isolating passivity of the supposedly supremely active butch cruiser, as he exhibits himself for the desiring gaze of other cruising men but frequently refuses to initiate contact or reciprocate emotionally.[104] Stephen Adams ironically notes that 'Rechy's hero takes himself so seriously that there is neither joy nor honest lust in his promiscuity; . . . for all his readiness to display his wares he is the helpless victim of physical inhibition.'[105] We saw this passive inhibition earlier in the image of the two butch men together in bed, 'each wait[ing] for the other to advance first,' their 'cocks strain[ing] in isolation.'

In one respect, Rechy's (anti-)heroes *are*, to some extent, 'helpless victim[s] of physical inhibition,' if we view their masculine reticence to interact physically or emotionally with their sexual partners as an unconscious re-enactment of the sexual passivity forced upon them in childhood by a father with whose machismo they also identify.[106] More broadly, however, their physical inhibition is symptomatic of the way in which the macho stud's gay cultural status as pre-eminently desirable also requires that he is the most sexually objectified figure, and he therefore paradoxically makes himself somewhat passive – a state conventionally associated with femininity – in the very act of straining to exhibit masculine virility by posing for other men and resisting initiating sexual contact.[107] And with this sexual self-objectification also comes the traditionally feminised fear of rejection, which is all the more disturbing when so much proclaimed potency is at stake: 'One rejection – real or imaginary – can slaughter Johnny Rio, even among 100 successes.'[108]

In *Rushes*, Endore recognises this contradiction between masculine potency/dominance and feminine objectification/vulnerability (or *apparent* contradiction, if we take for granted the fact of human complexity that the gender binarism attempts to annul). As the bar finally closes, he watches the other butch patrons lingering outside, hoping to be picked up: 'In their uniforms of defiant masculinity – slightly tarnished now – they exude a collective desperate beauty, a desperate sexuality, dozens and dozens of men waiting, just waiting.'[109] Here, rather like the child narrator in *City of Night*, these masculine gay studs may be seen to simultaneously reproduce the emotional unresponsiveness and distance of the masculine patriarch, and passively display themselves in the hope of receiving attention and affection from another butch stud.

Following on from this last image observed by Endore, I want to turn finally to two key examples of Rechy's fictional representatives in *The Sexual Outlaw* and *Rushes* casting a critical (if also partly cruising) eye over other promiscuous butch gay men, as opposed to the protagonists' self-analysis I have predominantly focused on so far. Unlike the narrator's self-normalising depiction of 'feminised,' monogamy-yearning Carl in *City of Night*, in these examples the 'masculine' protagonist's disgust and dismay at the behaviour of other butch studs throws into sharp relief the repressive and restrictive – but also ambiguous – effects of macho gay sexuality. In turn, though, the observing protagonist is shown to remain enmeshed in 'masculinity' himself, despite his partial sense of distance from the men he observes.

In *The Sexual Outlaw*, Jim is cruised in an LA park by Tony, a 'wiry, sexy, dark, moodily Italian' young man 'with a boxer's tight body', who takes Jim home to spend 'one or two or even three blurred days of drugs and sex and hatred' together with Tony's 'roommate . . . Steve, a wild-looking muscular blond man – very handsome.'[110] Led by Steve, Jim joins him in 'topping' the slightly less butch-defined Tony: 'Barking, Steve commanded Tony to do whatever he was ordered: to Jim first, then to Steve, often to both.'[111] Proudly butch Jim both identifies with and desires Steve, and waits to sexually 'conquer' – read: penetrate – him: 'that – and the dope (he has to rationalize at least partly for his aroused excitement [sic]) kept him there.'[112] After Steve gives a visiting 'sex client' or two the same treatment as Tony, 'laughing contemptuously', he finally orders Tony to watch as he has sex with Jim alone. At first Steve is resistant to Jim's attempts to 'top' him, but finally he lets him fuck him, apparently in order to upset Tony by showing his butch 'top' being 'humiliated' (through 'feminising' penetration) by another butch: 'Tony turned away. "Watch, you goddam queer!" Steve demanded.'[113] Jim, who has been ambivalent about taking part in the 'ugly orgies'[114] all along, pulls away from Steve in disgust at his treatment of Tony and leaves.

In one sense, this scenario stages the masculine gay man's momentary rejection of those normatively sanctioned masculine qualities of implacability and aggressive domination he usually upholds himself. Viewed more broadly, though, this scenario also reflects a central dilemma that many self-reflexive gay men experience, regardless of their conscious or unconscious gender identification: namely, the conflict between their (often primary) desire for the butch/masculine stud, and their resistance to identifying with, or their active self-identification against, the politically and emotionally repressive ideology

and behavioural codes attending 'masculinity'. Unusually in this particular case, the macho stud who is used to both desiring and identifying
with the masculine ideal (muscularity, emotional/physical impenetra-
bility, competitiveness and control) finds himself in the position of
those less butch-invested men who pursue him with a combination of
desire and disdain: 'Because physically – *and only physically, he
emphasizes* – Steve turned him on, and he obviously turned Steve on
equally – they kissed, licked each other's body, sucked each other
before Tony's hurt eyes.'[115]

Jim's belief that his desire for Steve's muscular body can be fully
separated from masculine ideology is rather unlikely. For while it
might be possible to desire male muscularity without associating it
with coventional masculine values, the relentless dominant cultural
valorisation of muscular body types as 'natural' expressions of a 'natural'
promiscuous potency[116] and patriarchal worldview makes this separation of aesthetics from ideology extremely difficult and rare. Even the
most self-consciously anti-masculine gay man (which butch Jim clearly
isn't) who desires butch men will be responding to those men's affect
as well as to their aesthetic appeal. To take one case, the desire for the
distant, dominant and/or aggressive man can frequently be traced to
the emotionally and physically withholding masculine father (and
other patriarchs) of childhood and youth, whose distance and control
is subsequently eroticised in often insidious ways, and with widely
varying effects. (In *City of Night*, and in David Wojnarowicz's writings,
the child's desire is actively brought into play by the father at the same
time that he withholds affection.)

Yet if desiring masculine-defined men isn't 'natural', but rather
normatively encouraged in patriarchal culture, it also isn't simply a
politically reactionary act, to be avoided at all costs. This chapter, and
this study as a whole, is certainly concerned with denormalising and
criticising the many repressive aspects of 'masculine' forms of promiscuous male sexuality that are privileged in much of gay culture and
beyond. But I do so with the important qualification that the oppressive
effects of normalising masculine male sexuality can be counteracted to
some extent by (an always unevenly sustained) self-consciousness
about the performative constructedness of those sexually potent masculine signifiers, and about the absence of any intrinsic link between
male physical strength and masculine ideology, despite the pervasive
cultural equation between the two.

The ambiguous relationship between masculine-coded erotic signifiers
and masculine ideology is all the more apparent in the context of gay
male SM practices and iconography. In the LA threesome scenario in
The Sexual Outlaw, Jim is provoked into questioning his erotic and
identificatory relationship to machismo during what can be seen as a

type of SM scene, albeit one where consensuality is not maintained. Although Steve's taunting of an upset Tony suggests an overstepping of mutually agreed boundaries, Tony ultimately rises to Steve's defence when Jim calls him a 'sick motherfucker': 'Don't you say anything about him!...I love him.'[117] (However, Steve then responds dismissively with 'Bullshit', reinforcing the sense of a lack of consensus.) Jim's questioning of masculinity through a rejection of the butch extremes of gay male SM is echoed in all of Rechy's gay-oriented novels of the 1960s and 1970s. However, the central protagonist is also repeatedly shown to retain a disavowed erotic investment in the SM practices he denounces, raising the fraught issue of the relationship between fantasy and material/political culture.

These contradictions are most interestingly addressed in *Rushes*. Endore remarks in the club that 'I have a deeper knowledge of our [gay men's] contempt than Chas. I long ago faced what the "top-man" sees when he looks down at the groveling masochist. He sees himself.'[118] Rather than making a general statement here about the co-existence of sadistic and masochistic desires in everyone, Endore is referring to his belief that the rise of SM sex and macho iconography within the sexual promiscuousness of post-liberation gay male culture – 'something kept in hibernation throughout the more overly repressive years ... [now] awakened'[119] – is at root a self-destructive 'slavish' reproduction of dominant culture's masculinism, and its macho suppression of gay male sexuality. Endore sees this most vividly in the SM rooms of the Rack, which stands directly next door to the Rushes' less 'total ... commitment'[120] to machismo:

The Rack is the inevitable extension of the Rushes – and ... what ... [Endore] loves and has vaunted in the sexhunt is not [to be found] in the nightly deaths of mean bars nor in the charade of filth and pain. No, the Rack is permeated by the punishment for sex. He sees this clearly and with anger: This is what they have done to us! ... And this is what we do to ourselves in ritual re-enactment of *their* hatred, and we masquerade it all as masculine strength.[121]

(Incoherently enough, while Endore is separating the broader masculine-identified sexhunt from the more overt machismo of SM, he is also linking these two realms of masculine promiscuous sexuality together by seeing the latter as 'the inevitable extension' of the former.)

At one level, then, Rechy is underlining the notion that, whether top or bottom, the muscularly masculine-coded leather/uniform role play of the gay male SM scene is always indicative of an ideological adherence to 'masculinity' – an adherence that is variously echoed throughout other strands of masculine gay sexual culture.[122] This perspective has been theorised from a slightly different angle by Leo Bersani, who stresses 'the question not of the reflection or expression of politics in sex, but rather of the extremely obscure process by which sexual pleasure *generates* [or rather, *can* generate] politics.'[123] In other words, the butch gay male SM top or bottom (or any combination of the two)[124] is not necessarily expressing his conscious political support for patriarchy through his sexual appearance and behaviour. Indeed, in one sense, being a butch bottom in SM might be seen as an erotic undermining of supposedly non-masochistic traditional 'masculinity' (although the butch bottom frequently interacts with a butcher top).[125] But the butch gay male SM devotee does necessarily have an erotic investment in dominant 'masculine' norms (even in the act of complicating their conventional meanings, as with the butch bottom), that will inevitably bear some relationship to his conscious political identity. Even though he may be politically opposed to heteropatriarchy, his erotic pleasure in a combination of masculine behavioural and visual signifiers can never be entirely explained as a non-invested form of semiotic playing with, or subversion of, dominant gender norms, which 'just so happens' to reprioritise the sexual potency and cultural significance of masculinity over femininity[126] (particularly when, as so often in the SM scene, that masculine-coded sexuality is a central element of one's social identity).

Rushes ultimately seeks to distinguish between 'healthy' forms of promiscuity and the destructive 'decay – the death – of fantasy'[127] in SM, in gay machismo generally, and in the Rack's fantasy reconstructions of unprotected and supposedly unsavoury sex environments from the outside world within the relative privacy of a gay sex club:

Why, after the bursts of 'liberation' – why, now, the courtship of filth, even when sterilized filth? Within the safe, enclosed bars and orgy rooms, why the imitation of the dank tenebrous places into which others had been shoved by oppression – toilets, crumbling buildings, prison cells?[128]

There is, however, an unintentional irony in Rechy's decision to criticise SM's machismo by constructing Endore (and hence, implictly, himself) as a Moses-like patriarchal prophet in the Rushes, vainly seeking to lead his unenlightened people out of one patriarchy and into his own 'Israel'. The novel closes with Endore standing despondently outside the Rack and the Rushes as 'distant bells, announcing Sunday, resonate across the blighted streets',[129] raising his hand 'as if in a benediction impossible to complete. Then it falls to his side in a fist.'[130]

Yet at another, self-reflexive level, as with Jim's simultaneous identification with/desire for/repudiation of the macho stud Steve in *The Sexual Outlaw*, Endore's disgust at what he calls the 'psychic bleeding' of the Rack is consciously unsettled by his own continuing erotic fascination with SM, from which he unevenly tries to distance himself. When he stands in the street looking despairingly at the gay world around him at the end of the novel, he has just finished visiting the Rack, where the image of a man being whipped on an elevated platform had reactivated his longstanding desires for the sexual submissiveness, domination and self-debasement he denounces in other gay men:

Endore saw the head of the strapped man twisting to one side, then the other, and to one side it was Chas's, and to the other it became his own, then Chas's, then his own . . . and then it was a stranger's! . . . Endore told himself – and felt the lash of the belt on his own raw flesh and saw himself lashing the same belt across the twisting naked body.[131]

Here, the novel's dominant conflation of male SM sex with reactionary gender politics is self-consciously contrasted with Endore/Rechy's own desire for erotic pleasures and positions he assumes can only be socially reprehensible.[132] This momentary acknowledgement of the lure of SM illustrates that even though it is crucial to 'recognize the influence of culture on the construction of desire',[133] the pleasures of SM are informed by individual histories as well as broader cultural imperatives, complicating their meanings and effects. As Chris Straayer notes:

In sadomasochistic sexual practice, *mise-en-scène* is produced to accommodate sexual scripts. SM scenes include characters and situations as well as settings and styles, but they exclude specific motivations and biographies. Precisely because the scene's ingredients are strongly typed, individual participants may invest them with widely varying desires and meanings.[134]

Moreover, our sociopolitical identities exist in an always uneven relationship to the contradictions and multiplicity of our sexual desires, as Endore briefly remembers while watching the SM scene in the Rack. Seen from this angle, the 'sterilized filth' of the reconstructed public bathroom or prison cell in the Rushes is not so much a gay male obeisance to dominant culture's marginalisation of gay sex, but rather an example of gay male culture's frequent acknowledgement and enjoyment of the erotic pleasures of fantasy role play, danger and debasement (however safely 'sterilized') that interweave promiscuously with our other, more socially accommodated, sexual desires. (We will see a remarkably similar example of a patriarchal prophet of sexual doom reluctantly admitting his own erotic fascination with the supposed cause of gay cultural destruction in Larry Kramer's writings in the next chapter.)

In summary, then, Endore – like Rechy's other lead protagonists –
rightly points to the psychically and communally restrictive effects of
normalising masculine gay male sexuality, which he sees as always
retaining ties with dominant culture's masculine norms. However,
Endore (like his predecessors) also oversimplifies the complex relationship between sexual fantasy and sociopolitical identity. While the
machismo, and deference to machismo, in gay male SM is never enacted
completely outside of the dominant cultural masculine imperative, it
is – like the hustler/cruiser protagonists' own masculine-defined
promiscuous desires – also part of a broader psychical web of personal
history and fluctuating desires for submission and control that are not
entirely reducible to conventional gender roles (however deeply
ingrained those gender roles clearly are).

Taken as a whole, though, the examples explored in this section
counteract Rechy's more widely publicised investment in the normative masculinisation of gay promiscuity with numerous dramatisations
of the unconfident and uneven performativity of the butch stud persona. Whether founded in childhood trauma, or in a more general
acceptance of dominant cultural pressure to suppress the 'feminising'
realms of mutuality and intimacy (which subsequently resurface to
disrupt a rigid sense of identity), the masculine or more macho hustler
and gay male cruiser are mainly represented in Rechy's writings as ideals
that invite identification and desire precisely because of their fantastical
impossibility as a sustained reality. The intrinsic flux and ambiguity of
that butch promiscuous fantasy is symbolised most forcefully in the
Tom of Finland-like drawings of hyperbutch gay men in diverse sexual
combinations that cover the walls of the Rushes club. The influence of
time is shown to have rendered the meaning of each panel ambiguous,
just as the persistent complexities of the masculine gay stud's sex life
rarely evade the contradictions and multiplicities of desire for very long:

All unattainably muscular, raunchy fantasies of impossible masculinity, . . .
cocks huge and engorged, balls like ripe fruit – . . . the large cartoon figures
painted without shading or nuance are exalted exaggerations of the real men
who often pose before them. . . . Each panel depicts figures in poses of assault
or submission – but which, is often equivocal because of the melding and
fading of clarity and ambiguity in the lines; a vague surrendering figure in
one panel slides into a bold posture of assault in another.[135]

BAD GIRLS: 'FEMININE' GAY MALE PROMISCUITY

I have so far drawn attention to the critique and deconstruction of this
masculine/macho promiscuous gay male ideal from the perspective of
masculine gay (or bisexually active) men themselves. As we have seen,

shrewd as such self-reflexivity, or analysis of other macho men, can be, it inevitably remains caught up to a significant degree within the terms of masculinity itself. By contrast, though, *City of Night* and *Rushes* sometimes extend their critique of masculine sexuality to include the voices and desires of feminine-identified promiscuous gay men, and in so doing break with Rechy's frequent desexualisation of the queen in comparison to the butch stud. Although some of these promiscuous queens partly subscribe to, and reproduce, normative patriarchal notions of masculine sexual virility and feminine sexual passivity, their confident sexual agency and their verbal assaults on the butch stud's inflated sexual persona also present considerable challenges to the prevailing masculinisation of promiscuity – challenges that are, moreover, almost never foregrounded in gay male literature (or, for that matter, in representation of any kind).

Perhaps unsurprisingly, the drag queens of the pre-liberation late 1950s in *City of Night* are more heavily invested in the dominant gender system than the more consistent femme sexual autonomy we will find in the 1970s in *Rushes*. In the earlier novel, the narrator observes that the 'femmequeens' would frequently 'indicate a kind of contempt for those other men who only desire other males, without posing, as far as the law allows them, as real women the way the queens do.'[136] Here, normative gender roles are shown to be policed by the drag queens as well as by their 'normal' hustler boyfriends, and resisted by those homosexual men who break the dominant cultural taboo of desiring other men without adopting a (culturally denigrated) overt feminine position that would make the relationship intelligible within hetero-centric logic. The feminine-identified queens' complicity here in perpet-uating heteropatriarchal norms within homosexual culture reminds us that cross-gender identification is no guarantee of progressive ideology, and can reinforce gender norms almost as much as male masculine identification when it is unself-consciously naturalised. Chauncey underlines that in pre-1950s gay culture – which inevitably retained traces in the 1950s – 'many . . . men embraced the [fairy] identity because it embodied a way of understanding how they, as men, could have the feelings their culture ascribed exclusively to women,'[137] rather than as a direct resistance to masculinism.

This gender normativity on the part of the overtly feminised fairy/ queen also manifests itself in the 1950s drag queens' self-identification as monogamy-seeking domestic wives who are trying, with little suc-cess, to keep their hustler husbands from straying sexually outside the home (usually with women). In this, the drag queens align themselves with traditional notions of the 'good' (read: 'feminine') woman who aspires to sexually compliant, monogamous – preferably marital – domestic security, despite her 'masculine' husband's inconsistently curbed roving sexual urges, which she alternately denounces and resigns herself to.

This archetype is principally represented through Miss Destiny, the LA queen we encountered earlier admonishing the hustlers for running off from their drag wives to prove their masculinity/heterosexuality by having sex with women. When the narrator first meets her, she has just lost her current 'husband,' Sandy, who has been jailed for selling drugs, and is searching for a replacement to give her the ideal romantic wedding she longs for, 'like every young girl should have at least once':[138]

'Do you know, baby, that I have never been Really Married? I mean in White, coming down a Winding Staircase. . . . And I *will*! I will fall in love again soon – I can feel it – and when I do, I will have my Fabulous Wedding, in a pearlwhite gown –'[139]

The narrator's poignant final meeting with Miss Destiny takes place during a chaotic, drugged get-together at her apartment sometime later, where she 'leans towards me and I can smell the sweet liquor and the sweet . . . lost . . . perfume – and with a franticness that only abysmal loneliness can produce, she whispered: *"Marry me please, dear!"'*[140] (The narrator later hears conflicting accounts of Miss Destiny's eventual marriage to a 'butch studhustler', orchestrated by a voyeuristic 'rich [queer] daddy.'[141])

But there is more to Miss Destiny's (and her femme friends') proclaimed yearning for a monogamous husband than first meets the eye. Certainly, her rapid turnover of husbands ('about every studhustler has [lived with me], at one time or another'[142]) is primarily a result of the difficulty of holding on to the sexual and emotional fidelity of the homophobic hustlers, whose promiscuity is encouraged both by the pre-liberation demand for non-queer-identified 'trade' objects of desire, and by the less historically specific cultural privileging of masculine male sexual agency and power over feminine and female sexuality. Yet beyond all this, Miss Destiny is also fairly quick to seek a replacement for Sandy, rather than remaining conventionally loyal to him ('I tried to be faithful, but the years will be so long – and what can a girl do . . .?'[143]), and appears more preoccupied with the accoutrements of marriage and femininity than the particular husband who would accompany them. Indeed, she defines herself primarily as 'A Very Restless Woman'[144] – a term which becomes her refrain as much as her ode to white weddings: 'havent [sic] I loved every new hustler in town? – but oh this restlessness in me!'[145]; 'a wild restless woman with countless of exhusbands.'[146]

In other words, Miss Destiny's restlessness is provoked by her promiscuously fickle desires for the variety of serial monogamy (or perhaps even multiple sexual partners without the ties of marriage) as well as for a stable loving husband. Despite her publicly proclaimed 'one-man-woman' persona, her delight in pursuing 'every new hustler in town' almost matches that of the hustlers in their macho pursuit of women to prove their 'heterosexuality' (even though her serial monogamy is also necessitated by her repeated abandonment). In this sense, the infidelities of each of Miss Destiny's husbands partly work to her advantage, enabling her to be 'a wild restless woman' through serial monogamy – as monogamous/mutual desires were seen earlier to surface within the staunchly promiscuous butch stud, so promiscuous desires are here seen to intermingle with the queen's proclaimed monogamous yearnings. For Miss Destiny's cruising and flirting with numerous masculine men in the city's parks and bars can be seen to exceed her stated goal of finding a reliable husband to end all her searching, and function as promiscuous pleasures in their own right:

Indeed, indeed! here comes Miss Destiny! fluttering out of the shadows into the dimlights along the ledges [of LA's Pershing Square] like a giant fire-fly – flirting, calling out to everyone: 'Hello, darling, I love you – I love you too, dear – so very much – ummmm!' Kisses flung recklessly into the wind. . . . 'I live on Spring Street and there is a "Welcome!" mat at the door'[147]

In contrast with the dominant cultural trope of feminine monogamous passivity – which the queens themselves sporadically ascribe to – Miss Destiny's search for a stable lover allows her to actively proposition any new hustlers in the area, who are momentarily placed in the position of disarmed seducee by her show of sexual confidence: 'looking alternately coyly and coldly at Chuck [another hustler] then me seductively; all of which you will recognise as the queen's technique to make you feel such an irresistible so masculine so sexual so swinging stud, and queens can do it better than most real girls, queens being Uninhibited.'[148]

This comment on the queen's ability to switch from her deferential wife role into a seasoned seducer (and to combine coy deference and active sexuality within her seduction) 'better than *most* real girls' emphasises that her sexual persona is largely modelled on that of the designated bad girls of society. As Chauncey clarifies in relation to late nineteenth/early to mid-twentieth-century New York homosexual culture:

In crucial respects the fairies' style was comparable not so much to that of some ideal category of womanhood as to that of a particular subgroup of

women or cultural type: prostitutes and other so-called 'tough girls.' The
fairy's sexual aggressiveness in his solicitation of men was certainly inconsistent with the sexual passivity expected of a respectable woman, but it was
entirely in keeping with the sexual character ascribed to tough girls and
prostitutes.[149]

Although the categorisation of the bad/tough promiscuous woman –
usually working class and often non-white – is a convenient way for
dominant middle-class white culture to falsely distance itself from the
unpredictability and multiplicity of its own desires, that categorisation
also enables promiscuous female sexual agency within some circumscribed contexts. With that agency, however, often come allegations of
prostitution (even if one is not a prostitute) and denigrated promiscuousness that serve to punish non-monogamous female sexual agency.
This available model therefore provided highly provisional power gains
for the non-prostitute promiscuous fairy or queen. Chauncey notes
that:

many men seem to have regarded fairies in the same terms they regarded
prostitutes. This conflation may have made it easier for them to distance
themselves from fairies and to use them for sexual purposes in the same way
they used female prostitutes.[150]

In the case of Miss Destiny, both of the polarised normative roles
available to women and feminine queens during that era – respectable
woman and tough girl – can be seen to overlap. Elsewhere in *City of
Night*, however, more unambiguously promiscuous bad girl queens
occasionally punctuate the action, implicitly undermining the prevailing
cultural (and narrational) association between masculine men and
promiscuity, and also counterbalancing the more predictable image of
those other 'fairies . . . [who are] hoping for a Man to settle down
with.'[151] Despite police prohibitions against cross-dressing, Darling
Dolly Dane, a friend of Miss Destiny, and other LA drag queens manage
to cruise the parks if 'they tone down their effeminateness',[152] although
not without ongoing harrassment:

'Well, honeys,' says Darling Dolly, 'your baby sister's gonna be on her way
now. . . . Honestly, if the fuzz don't stop bugging us, there just ain't gonna be
a Decent place where a Respectable Queen can go to in the afternoons. . . .
Why, we'll just have to start cruising the tearooms, and then they'll call us a
menace'[153]

Yet the queens do manage to cruise the cities, from the 'Meat Rack' in
New York's Washington Square – where 'a screamingly effeminate . . .

Negro queen' proclaims herself 'The Queen of This Meat Rack'[154] – to the streets of LA, where another 'girlish Negro youngman' unabashedly passes out sexual invitations to surprised butch men:

'Honey,' she says – just like that and shrilly loudly, enormous gestures punctuating her words, 'you look like you jest got into town. If you aint gotta-place, I got a real nice pad. . . .' I only stare at her. 'Why, baby,' she says, 'don't you look so startled – *this* is LA! – and thank God for that! Even queens like me got certain rights!'. . . . She handed me a card, with her name, telephone number, address: Elaborately Engraved. . . . And the spadequeen breezed away, turned back sharply catching sight of another youngman, with a small suitcase. I heard her say just as loudly and shrilly: 'Dear, you look like you jest got into town, and I – . . . '

I turn the engraved card over, and on it there is written in ink: WELCOME TO LOS ANGELES![155]

These two promiscuous queens on opposite coasts bring a rarely sanctioned element of humour to their cruising, while at the same time contradicting the prevailing cultural pacification of black gay men, who, whether considered 'animalistically' virile in the case of masculine black men, or supremely supine in the case of feminine black gay men, are nevertheless all expected to be sexually deferential from the privileged perspective of the normative white gay male gaze.

Although these confidently promiscuous drag queens are based on actual acquaintances of Rechy, within the context of pre-liberation gay male literature, they might also be seen as indirect descendants of Gore Vidal's promiscuous femme – but not cross-dressing – homosexual men of the 1940s in *The City and the Pillar*. In Vidal's novel, the masculine hero Jim learns about gay promiscuity primarily from a group of femme hotel bellhops:

As Jim got more and more involved in . . . [their] world, he found himself fascinated by the stories they told of their affairs with one another. He could not imagine himself doing the things they said they did. Yet he wanted to know about them, if only out of a morbid desire to discover how what had been so natural and complete for him could be so perfectly corrupted by these strange womanish creatures.[156]

Jim continues to try to anxiously distance his own 'naturally manly' (and ultimately failed) quest to retrieve the butch lover of his youth, Bob, from the 'unnaturally womanly' sexual adventures of the LA queens he befriends:

If he was really like the others, then what sort of future could he have? Endless drifting, promiscuity, defeat? No. It was not possible. He was different,

Bob was different. After all, hadn't he been able to fool everyone [that he was a 'normal' man], even those like himself . . .?[157]

On the one hand, then, Jim, like the hustlers of *City of Night*, anxiously asserts his 'normal masculinity' over the 'queer femininity' of the queens – and at the same time, unlike Rechy's hustlers, asserts that normalcy by naturalising his monogamy over the queens' 'corrupt and drifting' promiscuity. But on the other hand, the novel depicts its convention-ally masculine hero learning about gay promiscuity, and subsequently becoming a serial monogamist (albeit supposedly as a mere diversion from seeking his true love, Bob), through his fascination with the sexual exploits of queens, rather than through the purported masculine virility of hustlers and 'normal' men.

I want to return finally to *Rushes*, where Rechy produces his most significant portrayal of cross-dressing femme promiscuous sexuality, in the sense that it poses a more sustained challenge to the masculine monopoly on gay male promiscuity than the *City of Night* scenarios we have seen so far. Roxy, a white drag queen, and Elaine, a black woman – both prostitutes hanging out on the piers across the street from the club – manage to gain unprecedented access to the strictly anti-femme and misogynist Rushes via Endore (who has persuaded Martin, a famous artist, to use his influence to help the two enter the bar). Rechy underscores the butch clientele's fear of being implicated in the prostitutes' femininity as the femme outlaws enter the bar: 'The two have the power of psychic assault'[158]; 'A path clears before them, as if they are contagious.'[159]

But this ruffling of the macho cruisers' feathers is dramatised most fully in a showdown between Roxy and Chas, the quintessential butch stud. As Roxy and Elaine edge their way further into the bar, we gradually learn that Chas's fury at their appearance is not only grounded in his concern 'to purify his turf',[160] but also in his memory of a con-frontation with Roxy earlier that evening on the piers, where her sexual aggression simultaneously mocked and refused Chas's assumption of masculine sexual dominance:[161]

Chas remembers the transvestite on the piers. Her words to him resound. 'Tonight I'm gonna conquer me a real macho stud for some rough sex, man,' he tries to rub out both the presence and the memory.[162]

Unfortunately for Chas, Roxy recognises him as well when they meet again in the Rushes. Like Johnny Rio's retching after his encounter with feminising sexual intimacy in *Numbers*, Chas 'drinks from his beer, to push back the nausea threatening him at . . . [Roxy's] touch,'[163] reveal-ing the extent to which his purportedly 'truer' masculine identity is predicated upon a never-completed abjection of 'femininity' that calls into question the self-assurance of 'masculinity'.

Indeed, as with Johnny Rio's abjection of intimacy, Chas's attempts to repel Roxy fail to maintain a clear distinction between them both. Instead, their awkward exchanges, and the surrounding narration, ultimately serve to underline the ways in which their differing gender affiliations are equally culturally constructed, and are also similarly flamboyant in their constructedness:

'Hey, well, look who's here!' Roxy recognizes Chas. 'We met on the piers earlier, remember? You ran away.' She slides next to him. The black of her vinyl blends with the black of his leather; the sequins on one shine like the bradded studs on the other. 'See, I was right – we *are* dressed alike! . . . We even wear earrings, both of us.'[164]

Or as Roxy puts it even more explicitly (if also rather heavy handedly) a bit later: 'You know why my drag makes you uncomfortable – why you had to run away from me? . . . Because yours is just as gay is mine.'[165] The equal performativity of hyperbutch and cross-dressing femme gay male identities is also shown to encompass their respective sexual personas; in response to Chas's gruff insistence that 'leather and drag don't mix!,' Elaine (a biological woman, but here aligning herself with her threatened femme friend) remarks that 'we mix when we fuck on the piers!'[166] Elaine's comment points to the promiscuous sexual interplay of butch and femme out of sight of the masculine/macho-oriented mainstream gay scene, and at the same time reasserts the promiscuous sexuality of the femme queen excluded by the masculine gay sexual mainstream.

However, Rechy also understands that the marginalisation of feminine-identified gay men is commonly carried out in the name of naturalised female 'femininity' as well as naturalised male 'masculinity'. In contrast with the supportive alliance between queen and straight woman seen in Roxy and Elaine, Roxy's feistiness towards the butch gay men in the club is shown to be undermined by the claim to real femininity of Lyndy, a famous women's fashion designer who has also gained access to the Rushes for a voyeuristic night amongst the cruising men:

Our eyes are made up the same, Roxy thinks, looking at Lyndy.
'I adore your gowns!' Lyndy exults. 'So "new feminism" – so right for the Rushes!'
. . . Pretending to admire them [Roxy and Elaine], she's trying to thwart whatever power they may have, if any, over her. . . . Roxy's voice becomes very precise. She is choosing her most impressive tones and words. . . . The

defiance and the courage with which she invaded the macho territory have withered before Lyndy's accusative power, Endore understands.[167]

Rather like the drag queens of *City of Night*, then, Roxy embodies an overtly feminine-identified promiscuous gay male sexuality that, to fluctuating degrees, claims its place on the sexual turf of gay culture. Moreover, these drag queens are also shown to interact sexually with the masculine stud norm far more often than their sexual devaluation by the gay mainstream (particularly in the post-liberation years) would suggest. The queens in both novels are certainly not exempt from carrying out their own acts of marginalisation: we found earlier that the 1950s queens demonised non-gender-determined gay men; while Don, a (non-cross-dressing) queen in the Rushes, moves between denouncing the 'mean fake machos,'[168] rejecting an ageing beauty of yore who cruises him, and unwittingly insulting a younger black man he tries to cruise by invoking racial stereotypes. But at the same time, the sexual self-assurance of these promiscuous queens[169] importantly indicates the possibility – and various realities – of resisting the conventional insistence upon 'masculinised' male sexuality within gay culture and beyond.

Such unusual representations of forthright femme gay male sexuality are far removed from the reproduction of masculinist norms that we found in Rechy's texts at the start of this chapter. If Rechy's gay-oriented texts of the 1960s and 1970s are often recalled (and not without cause) as hymns to normalised gay sexual machismo, their occasional acknowledgement of femme gay male promiscuous sexuality, and their predominant butch self-reflexivity, reveal a considerably more intricate and questioning image of promiscuous masculine-identified gay men. In one sense, the gender self-consciousness of these texts underscores the profound (but often culturally trivialised) continuing influence of gender ideology upon gay male sexual practice and self-definition in the postwar period, despite the 'official' replacement of earlier, gender-identification-based definitions of sexuality with the hetero/homo/bi distinction. Yet in another, concurrent sense, Rechy's writings are also significant for the many ways in which they dramatise the perpetual contingency and insufficiency of gay (or any other) male allegiances to 'masculinity'. The painful emotional suppressions of Rechy's central protagonists indicate the great individual and communal costs of normalising masculinity within gay culture, whereby the potential for a wide range of intimacies in both fleeting and lasting sexual encounters is all too often crushed prematurely by an anxious pursuit of butch self-restraint and control.[170]

Notes

1. Although Rechy's earliest fiction depicts straight-identified, bisexually active men, in contrast with his later gay-identifed protagonists, nevertheless, my focus in this chapter (and this study as a whole) is on the gendering of promiscuous gay male sexuality.
2. *City of Night* 'and its sequel, [*Numbers*] . . . have given upwards of a million readers vivid travelogues through the netherworld of homosexual promiscuity.' Isenberg, 'Defiance, despair,' p. 1.
3. Isherwood, 'Beyond the night,' p. 60. Rechy has even claimed that the novel has become 'required reading in the schools.' (Pally, 'A visit with author John Rechy', p. 52.) He offers no details of which, or how many, schools he means; presumably, he is referring to colleges.
4. Altman, *Homosexualization*, p. 175.
5. Quoted in Nagle, 'Sisyphus as "Outlaw"', p. 25.
6. Although there is much overlap between 'masculinity' and 'machismo', I have attempted to distinguish as much as possible between the general category of 'masculinity' and the more strenuous amplification of so-called masculine traits in 'machismo'.
7. Ibid., p. 26.
8. Pally, 'A visit with author John Rechy', p. 53.
9. Ibid.
10. Although it was published in 1963, Rechy writes in a 1984 introduction to the novel that 'four years elapsed between the time I began to write the book . . . and the time it was finished,' as 'I plunged back into my "streetworld."' Rechy, Introduction to *City of Night* (1994), pp. xv–xvi.
11. Rechy, *City of Night*, p. 59.
12. By '(re)producing', I mean that Rechy's butch protagonists both *reproduce* wider ideological beliefs and practices, and, for readers unfamiliar with hustling or gay cruising cultures, also operate as influential literary paradigms that *produce* those readers' initial understandings of the 'masculine' hustler or gay cruiser. Moreover, even for those gay readers of the 1960s and 1970s already familiar with the sexual cultures depicted in these novels, the butch hustler and gay cruiser were still developing and changing as cultural types, and therefore Rechy's own particular representation/embodiment of these types would have often also helped to *produce* gay readers' understandings of them (or, in the case of promiscuous macho readers, understandings of their own identifications).
13. I want to reiterate that I am using 'feminine' and 'masculine' to refer to stereotypical gender categories that are ludicrously at odds with human diversity, even when they are being used in non-normative or oppositional ways, for example, by 'feminine'-identified gay men. By this I do not mean that the femme queens I discuss in this chapter are always simply reproducing the oppressive effects of dominant heteropatriarchal deployments of the gender binarism (although, as we will see, at times they are doing this). Indeed, questioning and overturning gender stereotypes by validating the conventionally marginalised femme queen, or by foregrounding femme gay male embodiments of supposedly 'masculine' characteristics, are politically important strategies within heteropatriarchal culture. However, 'femininity' must also always be

understood to be a reductive cultural construct – whether used in relation to men or women – that would ideally be abandoned (alongside the
notion of 'masculinity') to enable more accurately complex, less sexual-
difference-essentialising, articulations of diverse forms of behaviour,
appearance and attitudes within and across the sexes. My use of both
terms here is therefore a begrudging reflection of prevailing ideology,
rather than an attempt to reconfigure their meanings without criticising
their very existence.

14. Rechy, *City of Night*, p. 264. 'As I wrote [*City of Night*], stirred memories
rushed the "stilled" present, and to convey that fusion I shifted verb tensions within sentences.' (Rechy, Introduction to *City of Night* [1994], p.
xvi.) Perhaps the inconsistent absence of punctuation in the novel is also
a deliberate effect of this 'rushed . . . fusion'; Stephen Adams's observation that Rechy's association with the Beat writers of the 1950s is 'as one
of their imitators' offers another explanation. Adams, *The Homosexual
as Hero*, p. 83.

15. Quoted in Isenberg, 'Defiance, despair,' p. 8. Yet in his 1984 introduction
to *City of Night*, Rechy acknowledges his inevitable partiality when he
notes that 'memory itself, being selective, provides form; each portrait-
chapter found its own "frame."' Rechy, Introduction to *City of Night*
(1994), p. xvi.

16. Adams, *The Homosexual as Hero*, p. 87.

17. Ibid., p. 92.

18. Quoted in Nagle, 'Sisyphus as "Outlaw"', p. 25.

19. Chauncey, *Gay New York*, p. 9.

20. Kleinberg, *Alienated Affections*, p. 78.

21. Rechy, *City of Night*, p. 256.

22. Chauncey, *Gay New York*, p. 13.

23. Ibid., p. 27.

24. For instance, *City of Night*'s narrator observes that, like the sneering
hustlers, the drag 'femmequeens' would frequently 'indicate a kind of
contempt for those other men who only desire other males, without
posing, as far as the law allows them, as real women the way the queens
do.' *City of Night*, p. 154.

25. Adams, *The Homosexual as Hero*, p. 86. On the hustler's ambivalent
involvement in gay culture, see Dyer, *Now You See It*, pp. 140–1; and
Moon, 'Outlaw sex', pp. 27–40.

26. By the time of the post-liberation *Sexual Outlaw*, Rechy notes that alongside the continuing macho 'sexual uneasiness . . . among masculine
hustlers, . . . more and more cross turfs back and forth, from hustling to
mutual cruising of other [masculine-identified] males.' Rechy, *Sexual
Outlaw*, p. 158.

27. Rechy, *City of Night*, p. 113.

28. Cagle, 'Rough trade', p. 235. The term 'trade' refers both to straight-identified hustlers who can be bought for sex, and more broadly, to other
straight-identified men who sometimes have sex with men.

29. Cagle argues convincingly that 'reading the trade man as a bisexual figure
resists the monosexism and identity/behaviour split, which work in tan-
dem. For the trade fails to qualify either as a straight man, on account of
his same-sex behavior, or as a gay man, on account of his straight identity. Any analysis which denies the importance of behavior collapses the
trade man into a straight man, and any which denies the importance of
identity collapses him into a gay or bisexual man.' Ibid., p. 238.

30. Rechy, *City of Night*, p. 321.
31. Rechy, *Numbers*, p. 16.
32. The term 'documentary' is inappropriate, given the extreme authorial mediation of many of the actual events recreated in the book.
33. The book is subtitled 'A non-fiction account, with commentaries, of three days and nights in the sexual underground.'
34. Rechy, *Sexual Outlaw*, p. 243.
35. Ibid., p. 28.
36. Rechy has taught writing classes since the early 1970s.
37. Rechy, *Sexual Outlaw*, p. 28.
38. Ibid., p. 298.
39. Ibid., p. 31.
40. Ibid., p. 27.
41. Ibid., p. 135.
42. 'Only a tiny segment of the vast homosexual world, the outlaw world – secretly admired and envied but publicly put down by the majority of safe homosexuals cozy in heterosexual imitation – is not one easily chosen nor lived in.' (Rechy, *Sexual Outlaw*, p. 299.) The implication here is that monogamy is primarily heterosexual and promiscuity – particularly in 'public' spaces – is primarily homosexual, despite many homosexuals' resistance to it; yet Rechy still draws attention to a significant rift within gay culture on the question of 'public' cruising.
43. Rechy, *Sexual Outlaw*, p. 29
44. Ibid., pp. 299–300.
45. Ibid., p. 299.
46. Ibid., p. 62.
47. Ibid., p. 65.
48. In an interview with the gay press recounted in *The Sexual Outlaw*, Rechy comments more explicitly that 'I would very much like to be completely free. Intellectually, I'm close to that in regard to sex. But I still play roles' (p. 71).
49. Rechy, *Sexual Outlaw*, p. 299.
50. Ibid., p. 99.
51. Ibid., p. 103; emphasis added.
52. Adams, *The Homosexual as Hero*, pp. 97–8.
53. Gough, 'Theories of sexual identity', p. 132.
54. Morrisroe, *Mapplethorpe*, p. 164. See also *Jack Fritscher's American Men*.
55. Sinfield, *The Wilde Century*, p. 192.
56. Of course, 'masculine' stylistic and behavioural codes are forms of drag as well.
57. Another notable exception is the drag queen sex worker, who, like the 'masculine' hustler, is often used by non-gay johns to maintain the illusion of engaging in manly, cross-gender 'heterosex'.
58. Interestingly, though, a survey conducted with a sample of San Franciscan gay men in the late 1970s found that the 'stereotypically "masculine" image ... was sought by only ... about one-quarter of the [686] respondents.' (Bell and Weinberg, *Homosexualities*, p. 86; cited in Chesebro and Klenk, 'Gay masculinity', p. 89.) While this sample is probably unrepresentative of San Franciscan or American gay men on the whole at that time, the general sexual ambivalence towards 'masculinity' voiced by these respondents still jars with conventional notions of that period.

59. Rechy, *City of Night*, p. 16.
60. Ibid., p. 17.
61. Ibid., p. 21.
62. Ibid., p. 20.
63. Ibid., p. 34.
64. Within this eroticised context, the father's gift of the heirloom ruby ring to his son can be seen as a grotesque variation on the ritual of exchanging engagement or wedding rings – which, true to the father's oscillating affections, is given to the young narrator only to be taken back '[a] few days later' (p. 19), and then finally given again much later when the narrator leaves for the army.

    Given that we often eroticise what is withheld (as much as what is enforced upon us), perhaps this parental control is so excessively eroticised because the father has lost control over other areas of his life – principally, his failed career.
65. At seventeen years old, 'I was beginning to feel . . . a remoteness toward people – more and more a craving for attention which I could not reciprocate: one-sided, as if the need in me was so hungry that it couldnt [sic] share or give back in kind' (p. 20). Rechy contextualises this remoteness further, though, by mentioning his 'mother's blind carnivorous love' (ibid.).
66. Unlike many homeless hustlers who are unable to find work in order to survive, this narrator is drawn to his work for other reasons: 'already I had had two jobs, briefly: each time thinking I would put down Times Square. But like a possessive lover [such as his violent father] – or like a powerful drug – it lured me. FASCINATION! I stopped working. . . . And I returned, dazzled, to this street' (p. 32).
67. While the erotic passing of the child between several men provides a model for his subsequent promiscuity, there is also a fairly wide cultural awareness now that children who are sexually abused by one man – whether heterosexually or homosexually – sometimes respond to their abuse by becoming sexually promiscuous. For a literary reflection of this, see, for example, Jane Smiley's novel *A Thousand Acres* (1991), where the middle-aged daughter Rose, who was sexually abused/ 'seduced' by her father throughout her early youth, tells her sister Ginny (who was also abused, but responded by withdrawing from her body) that 'I was promiscuous in college, and maybe a little in high school, too. . . . I always thought one of them would have to supersede Daddy eventually. . . . Later I thought if there were enough of them it would sort of put him in context, or diminish him somehow. . . . Pete [her husband] always said . . . I had what he called frenzied dislike of sex' (pp. 299–300). A connection between male same-sexual abuse and subsequent promiscuity will be seen again in Chapter 3. However, in that chapter I also underline the importance of not simply collapsing these gay male authors' promiscuous sex entirely back into their childhood abuse (and the importance of not designating all adult promiscuity as trauma-induced compensation, without considering the degree of unpleasurable compulsion, or pleasurable choice, involved in their adult sexual lives).
68. Contrary to the classical heterocentric Oedipal injunction, I do not mean that a combination of desire and identification for the same object is, in itself, confusingly contradictory, but that the homosocial repression of

patently homosexual desires through identification with the object of
desire is restrictively convoluted.

In *Numbers*, although the ex-hustler Johnny Rio admits his same-sex
desires more openly, he still partly disavows those desires by embody-
ing the role of the sexually non-reciprocating bodybuilding stud, who,
as Mark Simpson points out, 'makes himself his own love object in lieu
of another man. . . . [T]he more [stereotypically] manly the man's body
the more he can direct his homosexual libido towards himself.'
(Simpson, *Male Impersonators*, pp. 31–3.) The highly narcissistic hustler in *City of Night* can be seen to similarly sublimate his homosexual
desires on to his own 'masculine'/straight-identified body, as well as
sublimating those desires through identification with other macho
straight(-identified) men.

69. Rechy, *City of Night*, p. 352.
70. Ibid.
71. Ibid., p. 56.
72. Ibid., p. 34.
73. Ibid., p. 321.
74. Ibid., p. 114.
75. Rechy, *Sexual Outlaw*, p. 47.
76. Rechy does contrast his 'times of mutual exchange' with his more
     anonymous 'numbers,' but the former category refers to non-monoga-
     mous encounters as well. A 1977 article on the author clarifies that
     'there have been no long-term relationships in his life other than non-
     sexual ones. Asked why, he tries out such answers as his narcissism, his
     fear of losing his identity, his fear of vulnerability. But [unsurprisingly
     enough] none of those answers please him, and he stops: "I'm not sure
     why."' Isenberg, 'Defiance, despair,' p. 9.
77. Seidman, *Romantic Longings*, p. 173.
78. Rechy, *Sexual Outlaw*, p. 285.
79. Rechy, *City of Night*, p. 348.
80. Ibid., p. 367.
81. Ibid., pp. 369–70.
82. These words are spoken earlier by the dinner party host. Rechy, *Rushes*,
     p. 236.
83. Ibid., p. 240. The precariously gay-identifed Johnny's words echo the
     thoughts of Vivaldo, a heterosexually identified character in James
     Baldwin's *Another Country*: 'Love was a country he knew nothing about'
     (p. 296). Unlike Johnny, Vivaldo ultimately experiences vulnerability
     and intimacy through an unexpected homosexual encounter.
84. Kristeva, *Powers of Horror*, p. 9.
85. Rechy, *Rushes*, p. 15.
86. Ibid., p. 33.
87. Ibid., p. 193.
88. Ibid., p. 66.
89. Ibid., p. 48.
90. Ibid., p. 19.
91. Ibid., p. 85.
92. Ibid., p. 163.
93. Ibid., pp. 183–4.
94. Ibid., pp. 163–4.
95. Ibid., p. 95.

96. Endore's inability to consistently distance himself from the 'masculine' values he consciously derides is in turn reflected in the stilted laboriousness of much of Rechy's dialogue and narration, which might be partly read as an unself-conscious authorial display of 'masculine' self-importance within a novel that, on the whole, consciously criticises gay machismo.

97. Rechy, *Rushes*, p. 171.

98. Ibid., p. 94.

99. Ibid., pp. 170–1.

100. Rechy, *Sexual Outlaw*, p. 71.

101. Ibid., p. 156.

102. Ibid., p. 34.

103. Alternatively, this 'sad joy' could be seen as the more general post-coital melancholy 'come-down' commonly experienced after monogamous or promiscuous sex. Or even more generally, it might be taken as an example of the mundane low that usually follows any dramatic high, sexual or otherwise.

104. In an influential essay on the 'masculine' male pin-up image, Richard Dyer complicates the notion of total passivity: 'Even when not actually caught in an act [of doing something], the male image still promises activity by the way the body is posed. Even in an apparently relaxed, supine pose, the model tightens and tautens his body so that the muscles are emphasized, hence drawing attention to the body's potential for action.' (Dyer, 'Don't look now', p. 110.) This observation applies equally to Rechy's hustlers and cruisers, and to the flexed author photographs on his books.

105. Adams, *The Homosexual as Hero*, p. 94.

106. Although the details of childhood abuse are mentioned only in *City of Night*, the heavily autobiographical status of each successive central protagonist implies a chronological continuity from the first young hustler.

107. While the supposedly 'feminine' vulnerability of sexual objectification was more often projected outwards by butch gay men on to femme gay men in the earlier decades of this century (just as it is still mainly projected on to women in straight culture), this evasion has become less tenable with the widespread visibility of masculine-identified gay men desiring one another.

108. Rechy, *Numbers*, p. 83.

109. Rechy, *Rushes*, p. 201.

110. Rechy, *Sexual Outlaw*, p. 239.

111. Ibid.

112. Ibid., p. 240.

113. Ibid., pp. 240–1.

114. Ibid., p. 239.

115. Ibid., p. 240; emphasis added.

116. As we will see in the sexually monogamous fantasies of David Wojnarowicz in Chapter 3, the dominant (gay and straight) cultural paradigm of the promiscuous butch stud co-exists with another dominant ideal of the romantically monogamous and protective 'masculine' domestic husband/partner. A prominent gay cultural example of this domestic ideal appears during a club scene in Holleran's *Dancer from the Dance*, where two boys 'in black with tired, beautiful eyes' sit down and discuss a plaid-shirted 'clone': '"I call him the Pancake Man," said one. "*He* doesn't use make-up!" said the other. "Oh, no," the first replied.

"The opposite! Because he's the kind of man you imagine waking up with on a Saturday morning, and he makes pancakes for you, and then you take the dog for a walk in the park. And he always has a moustache, and he always wears plaid shirts!"' (p. 45).

117. Rechy, *Sexual Outlaw*, p. 241.
118. Rechy, *Rushes*, p. 195–6.
119. Ibid., p. 93.
120. Ibid., p. 18.
121. Ibid., p. 218.
122. This notion of reproducing patriarchal norms through fantasy and role play obviously becomes less closely bound up with sex/gender norms within the context of lesbian and bisexual women's use of butch/'masculine' signifiers in SM.
123. Bersani, 'Is the rectum a grave?' p. 208.
124. While it is possible to dissociate gay male SM from butchness, this is extremely rare within the prevailing leather, uniform and muscles iconography of the scene.
125. Hypermasculine top Chas declares that '"in S & M there's a top-man and there's a bottom-man. It's all clear and honest." "Is it?" Endore asks him' (p. 39).
126. Ironically, in the process of criticising the normative social effects of gay macho styles, Bersani also unknowingly replicates this conventional presumption of 'masculine' sexual potency over 'feminine' asexuality. He rightly points out that rather than being inherently socially disruptive of heteropatriarchy, 'the gay-macho style . . . is [primarily] intended to excite others sexually'; yet in his preoccupation with the erotics of machismo, he also ignores the possibility that some gay men – butch, femme or otherwise – might, and do, desire feminine-coded men. Instead, he discusses femme gay men only in terms of their parodic embodiment of 'femininity': 'Much campy talk is parodistic, and while that may be fun at a dinner party, if you're out to make someone you turn off the camp.' (Bersani, 'Is the rectum a grave?' p. 208.) Overtly femme gay men are here equated with 'camp', in a move that dismisses the existence – however culturally marginalised – of the sexualised queen, or drag queen.
127. Rechy, *Rushes*, p. 218.
128. Ibid., p. 93.
129. Ibid., p. 221.
130. Ibid., p. 222.
131. Ibid., p. 221.
132. Jonathan Dollimore has remarked that in *Rushes*, 'S & M is incorporated by being bestowed with . . . [a] redemptive potential' at odds with Rechy's more consistent rejection of SM. (Dollimore, *Sexual Dissidence*, p. 216.) While my reading of the novel similarly underlines the ambivalence in Rechy/Endore's relationship to SM, I cannot find any suggestion in the novel of the 'redemptive potential' of SM, apart from in Chas's heavily criticised dialogue.
133. Straayer, *Deviant Eyes, Deviant Bodies*, p. 199.
134. Ibid., p. 191. Where I disagree somewhat with Straayer is in her assertion that 'the external image of a fantasy or sexual act is meaningless; only the act's meaning to its participant(s) is significant' (ibid.). While it is true that only the SM participants can understand the specific personal significances of their actions, an onlooker can observe the encoding of

wider gender (or racial, or other) paradigms within the SM scene, which
are never entirely supplanted by an individual's recoding of those cultural paradigms in personal terms.
135. Rechy, *Rushes*, p. 22.
136. Rechy, *City of Night*, p. 154.
137. Chauncey, *Gay New York*, p. 50.
138. Rechy, *City of Night*, p. 101.
139. Ibid., p. 112.
140. Ibid., p. 120.
141. Ibid., p. 121.
142. Ibid., p. 99.
143. Ibid., p. 101.
144. Ibid., p. 98.
145. Ibid., p. 97.
146. Ibid., p. 112.
147. Ibid., p. 97.
148. Ibid., p. 98.
149. Chauncey, *Gay New York*, p. 61.
150. Ibid.
151. Rechy, *City of Night*, p. 180.
152. Ibid., p. 134.
153. Ibid., p. 135.
154. Ibid., pp. 50–1.
155. Ibid., p. 92.
156. Vidal, *The City and the Pillar*, pp. 64–5.
157. Ibid., p. 80.
158. Rechy, *Rushes*, p. 110.
159. Ibid., p. 120.
160. Ibid. p. 81.
161. Although Roxy is more overtly sexualised than most queens as a prostitute, she is of course still perceived as less actively and potently sexual
than the butch cruiser within dominant gender terms.
162. Rechy, *Rushes*, p. 52.
163. Ibid., p. 151.
164. Ibid.
165. Ibid., p. 153.
166. Ibid., p. 151.
167. Ibid., pp. 148–9. Lyndy's dismissal of Elaine and Roxy is also predicated
upon her class privileges (she exposes Roxy's crude attempts to appear
'high cultured' by speaking French) and, with Elaine, her racism ('She
designs her clothes on naked black models. She calls them her savages,'
Elaine is told; p. 150).
168. Ibid., p. 117.
169. With the exception of introverted Don, whose middle-aged 'femininity'
makes him doubly redundant amidst the young muscled machismo of
the Rushes.
170. Again, this does not mean that control and toughness need be banished
to the margins of gay male sexual practice. My concern is for the continuing – perhaps increasing – assumption of those qualities as sexual
and social norms amongst gay men.

====== **2** ======

Loving the 'Alien':
Larry Kramer and the Politics
of Gay Male Promiscuity[1]

Looking back at his writing career in an interview with the *New York Native* in 1986, Rechy noted regretfully that 'the whole idea of the things I supposedly stood for, like The Life – sex, promiscuity, coupling – has been attached to me all these years. People never realize that you have to *revise* things.'[2] The firmly ex-sexual outlaw attempted to distance himself even further from his previous notoriety in a sidebar printed alongside the main interview, entitled 'Rechy on AIDS: Stop, Live, Change'. Resentful that at times 'many of the last decades' attitudes about open sex have been "blamed" on his writings', he stressed his decision since the advent of AIDS awareness that 'sex, even safe sex in most instances, should really be something of the past.'[3] Moreover, in response to accusations that he had '"taken back" all he stood for', Rechy defiantly expanded his own embrace of sexual abstinence to apply to society at large:

I miss . . . [the whole life] just as much as anyone else. But we can't fall into the fucking trap of revisionist thinking, man. A new factor has come into being, an enormous one – death. I haven't revised ideas. They've changed.
   [His fists pound the table.]
   Sex was once a daily part of my life. It took me and many other intelligent people a while to believe that this was really happening. Believe it. There are so many dangers present. The spectrum of no sex is healthy.[4]

Elsewhere, Rechy has acknowledged the contradictions and evasions that sometimes inform his interviews.[5] Here, however, his retreat from promiscuity and even sexual practice in general, and his suggestion that others do the same, spring from a less self-conscious confusion

about the possible methods of HIV infection: namely, from a false
assumption that even the absence of risky body fluid exchange (blood,
semen and vaginal fluids) in safe, or safer, sex is insufficient, and that
only complete sexual abstinence will protect us.

Furthermore, his words are not spoken from the very earliest years
of the AIDS crisis, when, in Edward King's words, 'gay men struggled
to understand and adapt to the epidemic',[6] as conflicting reports and
insubstantial evidence meant that 'the earliest safer sex advice
warned . . . [against] a high number of sexual partners, and practising
anal sex.'[7] Rather, Rechy's statements come from a slightly later moment
in the 1980s when many gay- and lesbian-led AIDS organisations (if
not their heterosexual counterparts) had discovered that risky body
fluid exchange, rather than sex in and of itself, enables HIV infection.
Consequently, these organisations, along with gay discourse in general,
had begun to promote the more concretely informed message that
protected sexual practice and safe intravenous drug use – not
monogamy, or low quantities of sexual partners – is of key importance.
Or, put simply, 'it ain't how much you do, it's the way that you do it.'

However, despite the growing dissemination of this knowledge, conflicts of opinion over safe and safer sexual practice (do condoms provide
adequate protection? is oral sex safe?) continued into the late 1980s
and beyond, and at times understandably sustained the tendency in
the earliest safe/r sex advice 'to err on the side of caution'.[8] These tendencies have also always been most pronounced in North American
AIDS discourse, largely due to the extremity of devastation caused by
AIDS throughout the US. As King has summarised:

In the USA, where safe sex is the order of the day, guidelines emphasize the
presence of risk, albeit a low one, in acts such as oral sex; consequently,
American safer sex materials often read as though they are aiming at the total
elimination of any possibility of HIV infection. However, the model of safer
sex advice used elsewhere focuses more pragmatically on the *relative* risk of
transmission, and offers advice that is intended drastically to reduce the risk
of HIV transmission, but not necessarily to remove that risk altogether.[9]

So it was within this increasingly – but also still unevenly and warily
– informed cultural context that the iconically promiscuous Rechy's
warning against sexual activity in 1986 signalled his abandonment of
the optimistically erotic practices and politics of the years of Gay
Liberation: 'I miss . . . [the whole life] just as much as anyone else. But
we can't fall into the fucking trap of revisionist thinking, man.'[10]

The confusion in Rechy's words also extends beyond the logistics
of HIV infection, though. On the one hand, he insists that he 'hasn't
revised ideas. They've changed' purely in response to HIV/AIDS. But

on the other hand, he implies a necessary reappraisal of sexual experimentation over time, regardless of AIDS: 'The Life . . . has been
attached to me all these years. People never realize that you have to
revise things.' And in fact, his thinly fictionalised attempts to abandon
promiscuity, in *City of Night* and *Numbers* especially, and his long-
standing ambivalence towards a promiscuous sexual life that contained
both 'ecstatic freedom' and 'loneliness [and] desolation,'[11] provide
multiple evidence of his continuing assessment of sexual practice
throughout the decades of sexual liberation. Yet equally, Rechy's contention that 'the spectrum of no sex is healthy' isn't purely a misinformed reaction to HIV/AIDS either: in a sense, it also reaches back
beyond the known emergence of AIDS to his comment in a mid-1970s
interview that 'sometimes . . . after a night of hustling and dark cruising
alleys, I think of suicide.'[12] Indeed, it also reaches even further back to
the guilt-ridden and doom-laden *City of Night*, profoundly influenced
as it is by the 'iron-binding echoes of [a Catholic] childhood you cant
[sic] shed no matter how you try.'[13]

    With these earlier texts in mind, then, Rechy's retreat from sex in the
wake of AIDS can be seen to have a longer, more complex history within his own ambivalently promiscuous past. Far from being 'a new factor',
death has been linked to sex both implicitly and explicitly throughout
his writings, whether as an articulation of religious guilt or, more generally, of the psychical dislocations and vulnerabilities (not to mention
the host of physical diseases) that have always accompanied – and
even to a great extent defined – sexual activity. So although Rechy's
pronouncements on the need for sexual abstinence since AIDS are in
one sense clearly the result of misinformation, they are also symptomatic
of the ways in which older incoherent doubts and defences surrounding
sexuality at the personal and wider cultural levels must always con-
tribute in some way to debates – gay or otherwise – about sex in the
age of HIV and AIDS.

    My intention here, therefore, is not simply to 'catch Rechy out' for
being confused in his response to AIDS. He may well have shifted
his opinions on safe/r sex since the mid-1980s. Instead, I invoke this
example of a cultural figure who has, at various times, straddled heterosexual, gay and bisexual affiliations, in order to underline the circulation of contradictory and confused AIDS rhetoric in diverse discourses,
not necessarily dependent on the speaker's sexuality. The most wilful
and obvious example of such confused rhetoric lies in normative heterosexual anxiety about gay men's intrinsically 'infectious' bodies and
'deadly hypersexuality'; an anxiety that works both unconsciously and
deliberately to externalise fears of infection, along with more general
fears connected with sex, on to a reassuringly distanced target group.
Nevertheless, blame, dogma and basic uncertainty – including the

fears about gay 'hypersexual' behaviour I have just mentioned – also operate, inescapably, within lesbian and gay culture in relation to sexual practice since AIDS.

Nor is it my contention that such anxieties over gay male sexual desires and practices always enter gay culture entirely from an 'outside world' of homophobic and heterocentric discourse. This chapter is certainly concerned with the unceasing shaping influence of normative and more adamantly hostile heterocentric discourses upon gay male sexual culture. Yet it will also be directing its attention to the (re)production of such sex-phobic and normalising ideology from within gay culture.

In either case (and at the risk of reiterating the painfully obvious), the question of promiscuity has, of course, been all the more acutely contentious within debates and antagonisms in gay and lesbian culture since the first appearance of AIDS. For although the diverse dissemination of safe/r sex information within gay and lesbian culture seeks, as far as possible, to clarify the actual, and dispel the fantasised, methods of HIV transmission, nevertheless, even with the far wider circulation of clear facts and guidelines now through the lesbian and gay media and social spaces, contemporary queer sexual discourses cannot help but also draw upon a conflicting range of ingrained and emergent cultural notions of promiscuous sexuality. Whether in public discourse, private thought or the unconscious, punitive and hostile beliefs continuously interweave with open and affirmative conceptions of non-normative sexual practice. And as we were reminded in the introduction, this un/conscious ambivalence is astronomically multiplied by living long-term with AIDS fears and deaths.

Thus, while the history of postwar gay male culture is, to a great degree, a history of dramatic growth in visible sexual variety and autonomy, the level of ongoing contestation and dissent within that culture around the question of sexual behaviour, particularly in response to the confusion and destruction wrought by AIDS, should never be conveniently underestimated. On the contrary, internal disagreement and debate regarding sexual practice have continuously contributed in crucial ways to the productive diversity, as well as the bitter fragmentation, of gay cultural self-perception.

In her survey of lesbian and gay activist work and dialogue since the 1970s, for instance, Sarah Schulman observes that, as with the 'sex wars' within the women's movement during the 1980s (over acknowledging lesbians, over SM, over whether to censor or appropriate porn, and over developments in female/feminist sexual discourse in general), so AIDS quickly provoked widespread and long-running arguments within gay male culture, as 'one faction of the gay male community invited the state in to regulate or close bathhouses and the others insisted on the community's right to sexual territory.' Schulman remarks that while 'the coming together [in AIDS activism] of feminist political perspectives and organizing experience with gay men's high sense of entitlement and huge resources proved to be a historically transforming event,' on other crucial and related 'internal affairs' concerning erotic expression, 'we divided, once again, along the lines of sexual practice.'[14]

As a way of illustrating and elaborating on some of that immense gay history of competing sexual beliefs, this chapter focuses primarily on Larry Kramer as a highly prominent nexus for a range of debates and lived differences concerning promiscuity within post-liberation gay male culture, both before and since HIV/AIDS awareness. Seen by many as one of 'the heroes of AIDS'[15] or even 'the father of AIDS activism',[16] Kramer confronted government and grassroots apathy early on in the epidemic in 1982 by co-founding New York City's Gay Men's Health Crisis (GMHC), the world's largest non-government-supported AIDS service organisation.[17] In 1987, he incited the founding of the AIDS Coalition to Unleash Power (ACT UP) in New York, a direct action coalition group that has agitated for institutional and cultural support in response to AIDS, with subsequent chapters begun around the world. As just one representative indication of Kramer's influence, the late singer and AIDS activist Michael Callen – himself a great influence on public awareness – commented in 1992: 'I cannot tell you the number of people who have told me that something Larry said or wrote is what startled them into activism.'[18]

In literary and theatrical terms, too, Kramer is a significant figure, both for the wide, cross-cultural popularity of his own writings before and since AIDS, and for the mounting volume of cultural response generated by his determinedly provocative work and opinions. Kramer's discussions and representations of urban American gay male sexuality from the 1970s onwards have given him an iconic status, placing him at the centre of gay, and often straight, debates over the cultural gains and losses effected by post-1960s gay promiscuity, and by gay reappraisals of conventional relationship structures. As with Rechy before and alongside him, Kramer's literature, journalism and many speeches and interviews have functioned as primary or key entry points into gay male culture, and into gay debates on HIV/AIDS, for a broad range of audiences. So for instance, like his predecessor, he enjoys the irony of *Reports from the Holocaust*, his collection of non-fictional writing on AIDS, reportedly being 'used as a text in many schools, as are my plays,'[19] and indicates that 'I have received letters from all over the world thanking me for [my novel, *Faggots*].'[20] In 1997, America's leading gay and lesbian weekly magazine, *The Advocate*, reported that it had 'never . . . received more mail than we received regarding Larry Kramer's "Sex and sensibility" [essay]. Equally impressive: the fact that 75% of respondents agree with Kramer and that so many women were motivated to respond.'[21] His most acclaimed play, *The Normal Heart*, is also finally being filmed.

Also like Rechy, Kramer often positions himself on the periphery of what he defines as gay culture, and has in turn been positioned and rejected as an 'outsider' by numerous gay critics, both radical and mainstream. For example, following the publication of *Faggots*, 'New York's Gay Activists Alliance . . . put . . . Kramer . . . on its "dishonour roll"'[22]; and in 1994, Britain's *Attitude* magazine included Kramer in a list of names under the heading 'Sorry they're gay'.[23]

But there are more significant differences than similarities between these two gay literary outsiders. Where Rechy has generally kept his distance from an organised gay culture that he has perceived as overly homogenising, particularly in relation to sexual practice,[24] Kramer's spoken and written words pivot on a recurrent, if inconsistent, call for a gay community strengthened mainly by unity rather than diversity, and in need of strong leadership. In other words, and broadly speaking, ideological homogeneity alienates Rechy, and ideological heterogeneity alienates Kramer.

Equally, Rechy's ambivalently pitched pre-AIDS hustling and tricking texts are in many ways at odds with Kramer's comparably autobiographical representations and statements, which criticise the supposedly categorically 'dehumanising' effects of much of gay male sexuality: 'I get very angry when I see [*Hustler*] on the newsstands, or the backpage ads of [*The Advocate*] – how we treat each other as objects.'[25] In a literary career that spans a bestselling novel, *Faggots* (1978), four plays, including the hugely influential *The Normal Heart* (1985),[26] and a collection of essays, journalism and speeches, *Reports from the Holocaust: The Story of an AIDS Activist* (1989, revised 1994), promiscuity remains for Kramer the central cause of communal disruption, estrangement, and now even extinction, within gay male culture. (He has had little to say about lesbians or lesbian sexuality.)

However, his argument is not always entirely this clear-cut. In 'Report from the holocaust', for example, the central essay in his 1988 non-fiction collection, he aimed 'to say a few words about "gay promiscuity," and let it go.'[27] Unusually for a writer who deliberately deals in, and is widely associated with, 'hyperbole . . . [and] broad strokes',[28] he sought on this occasion to problematise the term: 'Promiscuity is a loaded word . . . and what exactly constitutes promiscuity – how many more than one encounter with how many more than one person? – seems to differ depending on whom you ask.'[29] Quoting John Boswell on the absence of any findings that 'gay people are more or less sexual than others',[30] Kramer argues that 'promiscuity is liberating for some people while for others it's dehumanizing, and thus it's hard to come down on one side or the other without taking into account who's being promiscuous.'[31] Then, turning his attention to exoticising heterosexual assumptions of gay men's promiscuity, and to punitive notions of gays 'spreading AIDS', he emphasises that 'the gay community, both before and after the arrival of AIDS, has taken a bad rap for [promiscuity in general].'[32] This displacement by normative heterosexual culture of promiscuous desire on to gay men, he notes later on, teeters precariously beside copious evidence that 'being promiscuous is a characteristic that straight men congratulate each other on achieving'[33] – albeit with more macho terminology.[34] (Or as Andrew Holleran has quipped: 'If a young [straight] man is promiscuous, we say he is *sowing his oats*; if a young woman is promiscuous, we say she is a *slut*; if a homosexual [man] of any age is promiscuous, we say he is a *neurotic example of low self-esteem*.'[35])

In those moments in 'Report from the holocaust', Kramer can be seen to propose a non-pathologising definition of promiscuous sexual behaviour, which rightly acknowledges that instead of collapsing together and condemning all non-monogamous sexuality from a distancing perspective, the notion of promiscuity can be expanded to articulate and address – and hence critically examine or even celebrate – diverse forms of sexual activity in all cultures. Within this framework, then, the generalising term promiscuity can be used non-pejoratively to bring into discourse and explore further a panoply of contextually specific sexual interactions and ideologies that otherwise remain conventionally marginalised as untenable or unthinkable. Yet as another gay essayist and journalist, Scott Tucker, has observed, Kramer generally 'uses [the word promiscuity] as vaguely as most everyone else.'[36] And through this unreflexive incoherence, Kramer creates a slippage between his more intricate definition of promiscuity, seen above, and a normative, repressive understanding of promiscuity, that represents the principal strain in his discussions of gay male sexual practice and desire, ever since his initial notoriety with *Faggots*.

Thus, in a 1992 two-issue cover story interview with *The Advocate*, he reiterates his 'pre-plague morality', which he has continued to adhere to since the AIDS crisis:

I think that what has destroyed us [as gay men] has been our determination to celebrate our promiscuity. And I will never change the way I feel about that, I am sorry. It's childish. It has turned out to be unhealthy, and I think that we are capable of much, much more.[37]

Here, in arguing that gay promiscuity 'has turned out to be unhealthy', Kramer partly makes characteristic use of the same confused absolute equation between promiscuity and HIV transmission advocated by Rechy in 1986, and throughout mainstream (and sometimes gay) discourse generally. But Kramer is also speaking from a considerably later date in AIDS awareness, and from the position of a relative expert in gay culture on the logistics and politics of AIDS. Nevertheless, he continues to reiterate the kind of wholesale warning against promiscuity that characterised gay (and other) discussions of AIDS prior to safe/r sex, as in his own vanguard journalism of the early 1980s. While it is true that unknowingly unprotected promiscuous sex exacerbated the dramatic rates of gay male HIV infection during the late 1970s and early 1980s, promiscuity is obviously neither a sufficient nor a necessary condition for transmission of the virus.

In the 1990s Kramer still continues to incoherently conflate all forms of sexual promiscuity with the actual cause of HIV transmission – the exchange of infected body fluids – most dramatically in 'Sex and sensibility', the largely well-received 1997 *Advocate* article where he warns that:

You cannot fuck indiscriminately with multiple partners, who are also doing the same, without spreading disease, a disease that has for many years also carried death. Nature always extracts a price for sexual promiscuity.[38]

Certainly, links between sex and disease are well-noted within gay culture: the perennial trip to the clap clinic is a standard trope in fictional and factual accounts of 1970s and 1980s urban gay life. Indeed, these links stretch throughout history, as Pat Califia points out:

Sex has always been a life-threatening experience. Sex has always been a high-risk activity. Because of the pill and penicillin, we forgot that for a little while. But for most of human history, people have had to close their eyes and hope they are lucky before they put it in or let somebody else stick it in.[39]

However, the problem with Kramer's argument lies in its anthropomorphisation of these biological occurrences into agents of moral retribution, deliberately punishing humans for their 'sinful' promiscuous pleasures. Equally, the crucial importance of countering disease by continuing diversely to propagate safe/r sex practice in gay male culture is conveniently left out of the equation, making monogamy appear to be the only logical way forward against the health crisis. (A similar manoeuvre is used in Gabriel Rotello's influential study, *Sexual Ecology: AIDS and the Destiny of Gay Men* [1997].[40])

Moreover, unlike Rechy's (admittedly often maudlin) understanding of the diverse spectrum of promiscuous sexualities throughout his work, Kramer loses sight here of his brief observation in 1988 in 'Report from the holocaust' that 'promiscuity is a loaded word . . . and what exactly constitutes promiscuity... seems to differ depending on whom you ask.' And it is precisely his decontextualised use of the term in the above examples, and elsewhere, that enables him to demonise gay sexual promiscuity without having to address the vastly wide-ranging, and frequently conflicting, forms of sexual behaviour that are crowded within this category. The generalising effect of the term is now deployed to cloak complexity, rather than to foreground, and distinguish between, the multiple realities of promiscuous practice and desire. If Kramer were consistently to pursue his occasional acknowledgement that 'it's hard to come down on one side or the other without taking into account who's being promiscuous', then his dominant view of an amorphous promiscuity destroying gay culture would fall apart. For as Kramer's contemporary, novelist and journalist Andrew Holleran, writes in his wilfully contradictory 'Notes on Promiscuity':

Sex is a pleasurable experience repeated many, many times during our lives that, if experienced with the same person each time, is considered responsible, adult, mature; if experienced with a different person each time, is considered promiscuous.[41]

Standing as only one of Holleran's series of ninety-two aphorisms, this comment is somewhat oversimplified: many monogamous couples are marginalised as 'irresponsible' in direct proportion to their disturbance of normative notions of sexuality, racial and ethnic differences, disability and so on. And you don't have to have sex 'with a different person each time' to be considered promiscuous either: as Kramer himself asks, 'how many more than one encounter with how many more than one person' constitutes promiscuity? But after taking these qualifications into account, Holleran's words do serve to underline the virtual ubiquity of sexual acts and relationships that, in one way or another, fall within the realm of the promiscuous. So if Kramer were correct that promiscuity, rather than unsafe sex, is destroying gay men, then by rights a vast proportion of humanity ought to have degenerated or disintegrated as a necessary consequence of promiscuous sexuality long before AIDS.[42]

Also unlike Rechy, Kramer is explicit about the deliberate continuity between his 'pre-plague' and AIDS era perspectives on gay promiscuity. His reproduction of anti-promiscuity rhetoric since the development of safer sex knowledge in the *Advocate* articles above is consistent with his earlier and other current public pronouncements, despite the momentary gesture towards problematising promiscuity in 'Report from the holocaust'. For instance, in a 1979 interview with *The Advocate* following the scandal surrounding the publication of

Faggots, he criticised the prevalence of gay men making 'fucking around . . . [their] be-all and end-all'[43]; while in a 1992 BBC *Arena* documentary on his life, he denounced the 1970s upsurge in open gay promiscuity by complaining that 'there are ways of coming to terms with your sexuality without sharing it with the entire world.'[44]

What all these quotations also clarify, though, apart from Kramer's basic ideological consistency, is his objection to gay promiscuity not only on the mistaken grounds that sex outside of monogamy or celibacy necessarily increases the risk of HIV infection, but also on the equally mistaken grounds that promiscuity always represents a reductive pre-occupation with sex (making 'fucking around your be-all and end-all') that is excessive ('sharing . . . [your sexuality] with the entire world') and creates a 'childish' and 'unhealthy' barrier to authentic adult identity and culture. While the word 'promiscuity' is not actually spoken out loud in all of these examples, their sentiments are consistent with Kramer's direct denunciations of the 'unhealthy' consequences of gay promiscuity, which is vaguely equated with having 'too much' sex beyond a single consistent partner. In a retrospective afterword to a 1985 article reprinted in *Reports from the Holocaust*, Kramer underlines that he 'was against promiscuity long before [writing] *The Normal Heart*; I believe being gay offers much more than that.'[45] And again, in the 1992 *Arena* documentary, he is particularly explicit about his belief during and since the years of Gay Liberation that gay male promiscuity is emotionally unhealthy:

Kramer: [In the 1970s,] the gay political leaders . . . were out there saying it's okay to have as much sex as you want wherever you want, and don't let anyone tell you it's wrong, and be proud, and all that, and I felt in my dis-covery, not that it was physically unhealthy, because we didn't know that yet, but that it was emotionally unhealthy, and that having so much sex made finding love impossible. . . .
Unidentified interviewer: But for many people, that period of [gay] sexual liberation was very important in discovering their sexuality, in being able to do what they'd always wanted to do but had been repressed. Don't you take their point that it was important for them?
Kramer: Most of them are dead now.
Interviewer: . . . But without AIDS, if AIDS had not happened, do you still think that the lives they were living then [were] wrong?
Kramer: Most of them are dead now. Yes I do, very much so, I feel very strongly and felt strongly at the time . . . for psychological reasons.[46] There are ways of coming to terms with your sexuality without sharing it with the entire world.

In one sense, of course, Kramer is right that promiscuity can have restrictive or even destructive psychological effects in some contexts.

Like anyone else, gay men know first-hand that while some of us embrace promiscuity as a means to sexual empowerment and self-expression, others endure or look back with regret on their promiscuity: as a response to peer pressure to exhibit personal success through sexual conquest; as an alienating form of sexual commodification, wherein certain younger 'masculine' body and character types reap the main rewards; as a lonely consequence of the culturally ingrained belief that you are unentitled to expect long-term love and commitment; as an inadequate substitute for conversation, and so on. Writing in 1982, Dennis Altman uncharacteristically echoes Kramer's far from solitary cynicism towards the post-Stonewall rhetoric of sexual freedom when he punctuates his discussion of the benefits of gay promiscuity with the proviso that 'at least amongst male homosexuals, . . . there is often a real fear of commitment and a quite unrealistic level of expectations that dooms many men to never finding a satisfactory relationship.'[47] In some other instances, the considerable range of opportunities men have to cruise for sex in general public spaces, and in specifically gay environments, coupled with the low levels of monogamous presumption in gay culture, can lead to debilitating forms of gay sexual compulsion.

Clearly, though, none of these negative experiences of promiscuity are in any way confined to gay culture. Nor, importantly, are monogamy or celibacy any less likely to prove emotionally unhealthy for those who practice either under repressed protest. In his 'Notes on Celibacy' (accompanying his 'Notes on Promiscuity'), Andrew Holleran compares safe-sex advice given to a friend by his doctor in 1982 – '"You cannot have sex anymore." *This* seemed awful: celibacy' – to that given to another friend by his doctor in 1987: '"You *must* continue to have sex." Safe sex – for his mental and emotional health.'[48]

In one respect, Kramer's concerns about the relationship between promiscuity and AIDS might also be seen to hold some significance. Given that maintaining some kind of control over our sexual practices has been all the more complicated since AIDS by the need for safe/r sex precautions, it would be overly optimistic, and simplistic, to reject outright the notion that these complications are often multiplied for those who variously negotiate a number of sexual partners. This potential further complication is clearly one central motivation behind many of the supposedly 'well-intentioned' warnings against multiple partners that continue to dominate mainstream heterosexual, and sometimes gay and lesbian, discourses on safe/r sex.

The crucial missing issue here, though, is of course the particular context wherein any given promiscuous sexual encounter takes place. Hence, alongside heat-of-the-moment unsafe slip-ups and deliberately unsafe encounters, many promiscuous gay men have obviously become attuned to negotiating and practising safe/r sex – however difficult it is becoming to maintain these standards as the epidemic persists. Douglas Crimp has suggested that '*it is our promiscuity that will save us*' as gay men in the face of AIDS because promiscuity has 'taught us ... not only about the pleasures of sex, but about the great multiplicity of those pleasures,' allowing 'many of us to change our sexual behaviors ... very quickly and very dramatically' in response to safe/r sex requirements.[49] After all, negotiating safe/r sex in new, or even established, monogamous relationships is usually just as problematic as in one-off or occasional encounters. In fact, in some respects, discussing how to balance personal sexual needs with safety becomes all the more fraught in familiar and emotionally intimate circumstances, and for that reason may be avoided. Echoing the findings of many studies of gay men's sexual practice, Alison Redick has summarised that:

The problem of maintaining safer sex practices in the context of monogamous relationships is one of the greatest obstacles that prevention research has encountered. A common response to GALHPA's [Gay and Lesbian HIV Prevention Activists] demand that cubicle doors be removed from commercial sex establishments has been to question the assumption that unprotected sex will take place behind these doors but not bedroom doors. Indeed, current research indicates that the pressures to engage in unprotected anal sex are much higher in the context of a long-term relationship than at a club, because sex without latex barriers tends to operate symbolically as a measure of trust and commitment.[50]

In brief, the reasons for gay, or any, sexual promiscuity becoming emotionally unhealthy are never inherently to do with promiscuity in its many forms *per se*, but relate instead to an intricate web of unanswered personal needs and cultural pressures, impinging upon specific circumstances. To return to Kramer's judgementalism, then, we cannot anticipate the experience and effects of promiscuity for all, or even most, gay men – and this is equally true whether that promiscuity amounts to occasional encounters with known or unknown partners, or lots of sex with strangers every week. As Altman underscored in 1982, despite frequent distancing interpretations of queer sexual experimentation by 'straight [and, I would now add, conservative and many liberal gay and lesbian] critics as an obsession with sex,' promiscuous and otherwise sex-positive gay and lesbian cultures have 'more accurately [had] a preoccupation with constructing relationships that can meet our needs for both security and independence, commitment and variety.'[51] In other words, these cultures have often – if by no means always – attempted to consciously and openly accommodate those integral complexities of desire that more unbending cultural traditions tend to allow non-punitive expression of only at the level of fantasy (whether publicly represented or personally internalised).[52]

GAY MARRIAGE: UNTYING THE KNOT

If I risk overemphasising the incommensurability of promiscuous experiences and desires here, my caution is partly symptomatic of the insidiously powerful influence of monogamy-mandating and promiscuity-pathologising discourses – an influence that extends, if not as pervasively, then still substantially, to many aspects of gay and lesbian culture. Thus, despite abundant historical evidence against the oft-professed ethical superiority of (actually or purportedly) monogamous culture, Kramer has often supported his hasty dismissal of promiscuous gay culture in his non-fictional statements by suggesting that the standard of domestic monogamy and marriage set by normative heterosexual culture is, if not exactly a guarantee of ideological integrity, then at least a move in the right direction towards 'respectable' and 'responsible' adulthood. Kramer interprets the prevalence of gay male promiscuity – whether outside, or consensually within, a primary relationship – as a direct effect of gay men's structural exclusion from the sociojuridical acknowledgement and benefits attending traditional heterosexual monogamy, epitomised by the authenticating stamp of marriage. In 'Report from the holocaust', he argues in relation to gay men that:

Had we been allowed to marry, many of us would not have felt obliged to be promiscuous. (While we may not see much to emulate in heterosexual marriages, this does not preclude our desire to try it ourselves. It wouldn't be the first time we've demonstrated to the straight world that we can do something better.)[53]

In this representative statement, Kramer upholds the notion that marriage is not only something gay men 'can do ... better', but also represents 'something better' for gay culture as a whole. If promiscuity is a 'childish' and 'unhealthy' diversion from more pressing sociopolitical matters, making the process of 'finding love impossible', then by implication, the more 'mature' maintenance of normalised monogamous cultural structures will assign sexual practice and desire to their properly ordered places, enabling us to finally '[find] love', leaving sufficient room to agitate for more significant queer social rights.

Several key misconceptions coalesce in this comparison between monogamous marital maturity and promiscuous irresponsibility that I think are important to outline briefly here – not least because they recur time and again across the currently burgeoning range of marriage-oriented popular gay discourses, most prominently on display in two bestselling conservative gay male meditations on the social function of the gay subject, Bruce Bawer's *A Place at the Table: The Gay Individual in American Society* (1993) and Andrew Sullivan's *Virtually Normal: An Argument About Homosexuality* (1995).

At the most general level, Kramer's argument for marital/monogamous 'respectability' relies upon an insupportable equation between sexual and political practice: the presumption of a monogamous social order versus promiscuous social disorder. Any such attempt to stabilise, and even permanently weld together, the sexual and the sociopolitical (whether for monogamous or promiscuous purposes) ignores the instability of desire itself; its continual promiscuous mutability within and between the competing logics of consciousness and the unconscious. As Karla Jay notes, in a 1975 essay that firmly warns against assuming any stable alignment between sexual activity or desire and social ideology:

It's been my experience that sex is the last area in which we reconcile the differences between our political ideals and our personal actions. And in no [other] area have I seen such hypocritical dichotomies between what people preach and what they actually do [or, we could add, fantasise about].[54]

Perhaps the most culturally prominent examples of such hypocritical dichotomies can regularly be found in the disjunction between public figures' support for normatively monogamous heterosexual 'family values' as political ideals, and their secret pleasures with (same or cross-sex) extra-marital lovers and sex workers in their personal actions.

Perhaps more precisely, Kramer's belief in the potentially superior cultural benefits of naturalised monogamy works, in part, to de-eroticise marriage and monogamy. For as well as conflating the sexual and the social, Kramer's grandiose claims for marriage submerge the specific monogamous sexual arrangement underpinning the marital contract beneath an ennobling 'ideological framework which is able at any point to draw instant analogies between the individual family [and couple] and the nation, understood as a familial [and monogamous] entity.'[55] The more mundane question of differing erotic pleasures and relationships is thus strategically displaced on to a cultural contest between (monogamous) meaning and (promiscuous) chaos.

Equally, Kramer's optimism about translating marriage into gay culture lacks any contextual consideration of the profoundly distressed history of this dominant model for sexual and intimate relationships; a model that, to quote Michèle Barrett and Mary McIntosh, 'is sanctified by tradition, not justified by rational social debate'.[56] Moreover, whether explicitly tied to religious ideals or otherwise, that tradition has been overwhelmingly one of patriarchal privilege: in the most conventional terms, which nevertheless retain considerable traces throughout its many revised forms, marriage is:

A contract not only about the sexual fidelity, cohabitation and mutual support mentioned in the wedding ceremony but also: sexual availability at
will, housework, financial support even after marriage breakdown, a relation
between a citizen head-of-household and a secondary dependent [who nevertheless maintains the domestic space through full- or part-time unpaid
labour; the privatised transmission of property and wealth, usually between
male relations] and so on to indeterminate terms.[57]

However, at the centre of this cultural concern to preserve male dominance through a patrilinear family tree, there has also often existed an
overt as well as covert licensing of married men's promiscuity, at the
expense of married women's sexual agency and pleasure. John D'Emilio
and Estelle B. Freedman observe that in mid-nineteenth-century
America:

Despite the prescriptive literature that recommended male continence, a
persistent double standard acknowledged men's 'natural' lust and their need
for sexual gratification. . . . For men, the double standard allowed extramarital
relationships to develop without necessarily disrupting marriage.[58]

Unsurprisingly, then, these writers also document that marriage rates
have generally dropped and divorce rates risen in direct proportion to
improvements in the social standing of women, including the greater
leniency of divorce laws. For as with any other cultural fantasy, the
maintenance of dominant cultural beliefs in the organic stability and
necessity of marriage-based monogamy has always been substantially
dependent upon highly idiosyncratic legal interventions. Or as Barrett
and McIntosh argue (in a statement that could equally be applied to the
cultural naturalisation of heterosexuality):

Those who defend marriage as what people want and need must explain
why it has to be so massively privileged by social policy, taxation, religious
endorsement and the accolade of respectability. . . [I]f marriage is the basis
of the family, then this supposedly individual and freely chosen form has a
state instrument at its heart.[59]

Kramer's argument for the resignification of marriage within gay terms
certainly finds support in the continuing diversification of cultural
meanings and expectations surrounding marriage. The ripple effects of
the birth of the Pill and 1960s 'permissiveness', amongst other things,
have helped to relativise marriage, making the marital option 'both
romantic and companionate . . . – certainly a less stable form than the
older, overtly male-dominated and more prosaic tie.'[60]
Such historical increases in female pleasure and mutual agreement
within marriage mask the overriding fact, however, that the (differing)

social gains that heterosexual women and men obtain through marriage are always at the expense of all publicly promiscuous sexualities.
More than this: without the abjected spectacle of promiscuity, there
can be no sense of marriage (or other conventionally condoned forms
of monogamy) as the 'civilised' subject's inevitable destiny or choice;
to adapt Barbara Creed's formulation:

Although the subject must exclude the abject, it must, nevertheless, be tolerated, for that which threatens to destroy life [and/or shared cultural meaning]
also helps to define life [and/or shared cultural meaning]. . . . [T]he activity
of exclusion is necessary to guarantee that the subject take up his/her proper
place in relation to the symbolic.[61]

In short, marriage nurtures itself on the promiscuous.

What arguments for implementing lesbian and gay marriage fail or
choose not to account for, therefore, is the *foundational* devaluation
and exclusion of promiscuous, 'unattached' and 'unwed' monogamous
sexualities on which the marital authentication of (at least officially)
monogamous relationships rests. Hence the categorisation of 'illegitimacy' (applied to erotic bonds and children 'born out of wedlock'),
'living in sin', and the supposedly arrested development of those
unwilling or unable to 'settle down'. Regardless of any diversification
of the meanings of marriage, this structural devaluation and exclusion
of the 'unwed', and the concurrent quasi-deification of those who
strive to embody a church/state-ordained model of monogamy, will
persist largely unchanged. For as the mainly accepting mainstream
media coverage of professional gay couple Bob Paris and Rod Jackson's
marriage exemplified (as just one example of many straight cultural
assimilations of willing queers in the 1990s), monogamy – especially
when authenticated within dominant cultural terms – can serve to
sugar the pill of homosexuality for liberal heterosexual constituencies
in a way entirely inaccessible to publicly promiscuous gay men.[62]
Thus, Kramer's call for legalised gay marriage, as a means of obtaining
'the right to tax advantages and employee benefits that married couples
enjoy,'[63] can only advance the social security and recognition of gay
men to the same extent that it distances and discredits the innumerable
promiscuous and 'single' ranks within queer cultures. In this sense, it
is marriage and normalised monogamy, not promiscuity, that seriously
undermines any maturely democratic or socialist political project.[64]
Moreover, such a cultural focus on narrowing the range of acceptable
sexual practices and intimacies frustrates the attempts being made
within gay culture, against all odds, to keep encouraging and sustaining safer sexual practice through experimentation.

ABJECTION AND PROMISCUOUS DESIRE

Yet there has also been a considerable amount of ambivalent self-implication, and even fascination, within Kramer's resentment and reproach of gay promiscuity. In a 1979 interview, for instance, he declared that:

Having so much sex available makes love impossible. It is so *easily* available and I don't think that any relationship can sustain the kind of extra-marital exuberance that goes on.[65]

The implication here is that the mere availability of sex is enough to make 'love' (generally equated with monogamy by Kramer) 'impossible'. In this repressive scenario, it is only by making sex, or even the possibility of sex, less readily available that the fragility of monogamous love can sustain itself against ever-lurking and ever-potent promiscuous desires: in the above interview, Kramer also argues that 'if two people have a relationship and go down to The Mineshaft [a bar known for its obsessive ultra-raunchiness (sic!)] it's going to jeopardize that relationship.'[66]

So aside from implying sexual uncertainty at the centre of much monogamous coupling, this telling complaint about the lure of promiscuity is also one example of the many ways in which disgust or disapproval are often intimately interrelated with – and, indeed, ambivalent expressions of – a preoccupation or fascination with, or desire for, the expelled object: in this case, promiscuous sexuality.[67] To reiterate, the will to cultural self-elevation through monogamy depends heavily upon a puritanical projection of promiscuous sexuality outwards on to marginalised individuals and groups. But in turn, those receptacles for normative cultural discomfort with sexual diversity become perpetual sources for anxious, yet thrilled, warnings against the seductive powers of the margins. Such warnings necessarily implicate the voyeuristic objector, and their less than purely monogamous desires, in the construction of numerous promiscuous 'others', whose fantasised sexual powers and prowess belie the purported moral and cultural supremacy of marriage and monogamy.

In Creed's description of the psychical ambivalence surrounding abjection, for example, such apparently divisive forms of 'ritual [become] a means by which societies both *renew their initial contact with the abject element* and then exclude that element.'[68] However, Creed then goes on to suggest that through such social 'ritual, the demarcation lines between human and non-human are drawn up anew and presumably made all the stronger for that process.'[69] I would argue instead that as these dominant 'demarcation lines ... are drawn up anew' again and again, the persistent movement between renewed contact and exclusion that recurs each time remains far less linear and resolved than Creed presumes (at this point in her discussion). The repetition enacted by each reorganisation of an already established interdependence can have no finite completion; can never be seen to reproduce an entirely identical hierarchical division 'all the stronger for that process' of renewed contact.[70] The 'fascinating, seductive aspect of abjection'[71] not only endlessly colours such hierarchical relations, but is integral even – often especially – to those moments where the act of exclusion is at its most forceful. As Creed later underscores, 'abject things are those which highlight the "fragility of the law"'[72]: 'the subject is constantly beset by abjection which fascinates desire but which must be repelled for fear of self-annihilation.'[73] (This latter comment is especially suggestive in relation to cultural fears about the 'destructive' properties of promiscuous sexuality, and of sexual abandonment in general.) As we saw in the previous chapter, Julia Kristeva similarly notes that that which is culturally abjected 'is above all [an] ambiguity' which is 'inseparable' from dominant order in its ever-proximate location 'at the boundary of what is assimilable . . . [and] thinkable',[74] where it endlessly bespeaks the culturally 'contaminated . . . [and] condemned.'[75]

My point, then, is not that promiscuous sexualities and desires are inherently more potent, real or diverse than 'truly repressive' monogamous ones. Nor am I suggesting a necessary progression from the seemingly universal occurrence of sexual fantasies about diverse objects of desire (the unbounded promiscuity of fantasy) to the desire to carry those fantasies through into actual promiscuous sexual practices. Instead, to requote Altman's words, 'our needs [are] for both security and independence, commitment and variety', to differing degrees at different times, and often all at once. This is a core paradox of desire; or rather, paradoxical within dominant conscious, rational, social terms. So it is the proscriptive cultural insistence upon absolute continuity and linearity in our desires – whether in terms of monogamy, promiscuity or otherwise – that heightens the lure, as well as the fear, of inconsistency and difference. Equally, the ubiquity of promiscuous fantasies and desires, even within those who are most vehemently anti-promiscuity, implicitly calls into question the dominant moral distinction between 'reassuringly familiar' monogamous sexual culture and an 'utterly alien' promiscuous minority.

Hence, as Kramer's writings repeatedly illustrate, not only does anti-promiscuous ideology lean strenuously upon demonising promiscuity in order to explain the ostensibly 'natural' benefits of monogamy, and the existence of cultural rewards for married/monogamous couples. At the same time, the almost ritual return to dissections and indictments of promiscuity within these repressive discourses often provides an indirect means of expressing desire for, and fascination with, the self-imposed 'forbidden' realms of promiscuous fantasy and activity. (It cannot help but do so, for, of course, the disturbingly alien originates within the same human psyche as the stabilisingly familiar.)

FAGGOTS: 'MY FANTASIES RUN WILD, JUST LIKE YOURS'

This repeated movement between sexual proscriptiveness (directed at oneself and others) and shifting, contradictory desires is all the more pronounced throughout Kramer's fictional works. Unlike the pointedly conclusive public statements encountered so far, the relative indirectness of Kramer's (lightly) fictional representations – wherein competing accounts of gay life must, necessarily, be juxtaposed more extensively for dramatic and intellectual impetus – means that his novels and plays generally provide a far more complex, and often self-reflexive, interpretation of contemporary urban American gay sexual history. Nowhere is this considerable ambivalence in relation to promiscuous practices and desires more in evidence than in the Chinese-boxed narrative of Faggots.

As with Andrew Holleran's simultaneously published Dancer from the Dance (with which it was often unfavourably compared),[76] the commercial success of Faggots in relation to other 1970s gay fiction made Kramer's interpretation of gay male sexuality widely available for gay and non-gay audiences to a degree unmatched by most other gay cultural perspectives of that era, whether fictional or factual: by 1978, the novel had sold more than 440000 copies.[77] As a satire, 'very much influenced by Evelyn Waugh',[78] Faggots necessarily deals in hyperbole and partiality, seeking to puncture the sometimes glamourised mythology of 1970s urban American gay sexual practices.

Dennis Altman situates Kramer's narrative within the context of a dominant 'tension present in contemporary gay male writing [that] stems from the attempt to reconcile the traditional image of romantic love and the reality of present-day sexuality, with its demands for constant variety and performance.'[79] While many gay critics rejected the anti-promiscuous tenor (and stylistic shortcomings) of Faggots,[80] for Altman in 1982, it was 'the most explicit discussion' of this dilemma to date in gay literature, which 'poses ... very real questions.'[81] Although the novel's 'traditional romantic' message may well be 'quite unrealistic', its critique of gay promiscuity is 'not necessarily ... homophobic ...; Kramer just wants the sort of relationship that is less and less possible even outside the rarefied world of Fire Island.'[82]

Yet the naturalisation of main protagonist Fred Lemish's disgust at gay promiscuity in *Faggots* can be seen to increase almost in exact proportion to his, and often the novel's, growing displacement of the complex conflicts within his own monogamy-centred sexuality. On the one hand, the novel does offer various (largely critically overlooked) moments of self-consciousness concerning Fred's hypocritical denunciation of a promiscuous culture in which he also actively participates. Yet on the other hand, the novel's conspicuous simplification and silencing of promiscuity-centred characters, and often promiscuous desires generally, contradicts Kramer's contention that in *Faggots*, 'you saw every possible gay aspect of living in New York at that time.'[83]

More generally, though, this hypocrisy and partiality also stem from the contradictions inherent in satire as a literary form; contradictions that echo the disavowed interdependence of subject and abject discussed earlier. For the satirist's denunciation and exposure of their chosen target require that they immerse themselves, however tentatively, within that denigrated environment – hence producing a familiarity, and even fascination, on the part of the ostensibly impartial 'outsider' towards their object of ridicule. Equally, the satirist's frequent claim to distanced insight is dependent upon a quintessentially partial, condensed, and often caricatured, representation of figures and events to produce satire's comedy of superiority (although this extreme partiality can be complicated somewhat by the multiplication of characters juxtaposed within a narrative). Thus, while the term 'satire' is derived from the Latin *satura*, meaning a medley (or mixture) and recurring 'in the phrase *per saturam* . . . indiscriminately'[84] – shades of promiscuity's origins – nevertheless, in the true spirit of literary satire, Kramer's descriptively and narratively promiscuous text[85] is a sexual melting pot where erotic variety is almost always being stirred by a firm and steady authorial hand, rather than being allowed to remain a more complexly dispersed mixture.

Faggots focuses on Fred Lemish – a thinly fictionalised Kramer[86] – 'your average, standard, New York faggot obsessive kvetch. Nice though,'[87] who is, as the narrative opens:

single, still, though for many years he had claimed to want a lover. He had had one or two before, perhaps nine or ten; he often had trouble defining precisely what constituted a lover and not just a trick he had turned a couple of times . . . But, by any definition, none had lasted beyond a vague introductory offer. He usually blamed it on the other fellow and still maintained that he was alone against his will.[88]

Already, there is some uncertainty about Fred's distinction between brief and more significant sexual encounters, and a hint that his publicly stated desire for a monogamous partner may not always have been entirely accurate. But his immediate intentions are clear: 'Fred had, at thirty-nine, hoped love would come by forty. He had only four days to go.'[89] The novel proceeds to trace Fred's pursuit of his current, multiply unfaithful, object of desire, Dinky Adams, while also detailing Fred's, and many others', exploits in and around Manhattan's most popular commercial clubs, sex parties and bathhouses. The narrative concludes with the frenzied sexual festivities over Memorial Day weekend on Fire Island, where Fred turns forty. Having finally separated from Dinky, Fred declares to the reader that he will now abandon the promiscuous realms of 'faggot' culture to search for monogamous sexual moderation.

The novel's discrediting of gay promiscuity through a progressively valourised monogamy-oriented perspective takes several forms. For instance, the most central of the novel's various depictions of gay promiscuity concerns Fred's endlessly thwarted attempts to stabilise a monogamous relationship with Dinky (pun of course intended), his 'tall, dark, bright, gorgeous' lover of three months, who continues to be prodigiously – but more importantly, dishonestly – promiscuous throughout the narrative. True, we do learn early on that 'Fred had been amazed ... to discover in his address book's rear that he and Dinky had met and tricked seven years ago, a one-nighter.'[90] Yet that forgotten incident belongs to a past (and present) promiscuous life that Fred is striving to relinquish: he panics that he has just 'spent a whole year (not to mention all the preceding ones!) with a faceless group of sex objects! ... Talk about using the body as a thing!'[91]

Instead, by and large, Fred's repeated betrayal by his 'Great Love' can be seen as a small-scale mirroring, and reinforcement, of the novel's surrounding vision of gay promiscuity as a betrayal of gay culture in general (despite the contradiction of an ongoing essentialising omniscient message that *all* 'faggots ... think primarily with their cocks'[92]). Two moments that introduce metaphors of a 'turning against nature' exemplify this contrived connection between personal and cultural 'disloyalty' to a 'more honestly human' monogamy.

At one point, the third-person narration wisecracks that 'if Dinky Adams spent half as much time legitimately planting and fertilizing as he did scattering his seeds to the winds, he'd be New York's leading gardener.'[93] Note the normative/marital association between monogamy and legitimacy here, which, through the notion of 'wasted seeds', also bears obvious traces of an older, even more restrictive, Biblical reproductive norm. In *The Invention of Heterosexuality*, Jonathan Ned Katz comments that although 'the twentieth century witnessed the decreasing legitimacy of that procreative imperative, and the increasing public acceptance of a new hetero pleasure principle ..., only in the mid-1960s

would heteroeroticism be distinguished completely from reproduction.'[94]
As the preceding quotation from *Faggots* illustrates, traces of that preceding 'procreative imperative' clearly continue to lurk within more
conventional late twentieth-century sexual discourses.

Earlier in the novel, a comparable third-person passage locates supposedly unnatural promiscuous activity at the wider level of New
York's commercial gay culture:

Later, it would be recollected as the False Summer. Everything had blos-
somed too quickly. Fire Island, this Memorial Day, would be like the Fourth
of July. Too much too soon. . . . All cups runneth over.[95]

As with Dinky at the micro-level, promiscuous gay pleasure-seeking
'ruins the crops' of all of New York gay culture: 'Everything had
bloomed too quickly'.

Like many other gay (and less often, lesbian) critics and historians
of Euro-American gay societies, Altman noted in 1982 that whereas
'until recently most homosexual men and women sought to duplicate
traditional heterosexual marriage', since liberationist reappraisals of
that model and of heterosexually implanted queer sexual guilt:

There is in the gay male world a strong stress on sexual adventure, which is
not seen as necessarily incompatible with relationships. . . . The crucial
point, true also for a number of gay women, is that gay relationships are not
based upon an assumption of monogamy.[96]

(This is obviously an over-generalisation: even within the period in
which Altman was writing, the influence of dominant monogamous
presumption was never absent from gay culture.) Similarly, Pat Califia,
in her 1984 celebration of '*un*monogamy' amidst the first misdirected,
AIDS-inspired stages of an ongoing lesbian and gay rejection of
promiscuity, remarks that:

enjoying other people intensifies my relationship with my lover . . . Still, I
preserve a very rigid line between my lover (my heart- and house-mate) and
everybody else with whom I have sex. That line is romantic love.[97]

In *Faggots*, however, the governing representation of widespread gay
promiscuous renegotiations of coupledom is structured according to
the dominant marital (and, again, Biblical) concept of adultery, as well
as other (non-marital) relationships that, as Altman argues, hastily con-
fuse 'monogamy and love . . . because of certain social pressures',[98]
rather than because monogamy is necessarily what really suits each
partner's needs.

Hence, for the first half of the novel, Dinky's infidelities are echoed in a tragicomic subplot of deception. Patty – 'tall, thin, balding, hyper-active'[99] – gets a seven-year itch in his relationship with Maxine – 'hefty, bouncy, . . . sharp . . . [and] addicted, in moments of stress, to dressing up as Elizabeth Taylor'[100] – and secretly plots to 'move in with Juanito, Cappricio's Puerto Rican d.j. with the skin of velvet, tasting of honey and maple sugar'.[101] (Rather like the Puerto Rican boys fetishised by wealthier white gay men throughout Holleran's *Dancer from the Dance*, Juanito appears only as a fabric and a flavour.) Again, the emphasis is on betrayal, although in this instance, symbolic punishment is at hand. Running off together, the new couple perish in the real-life Everard Baths fire of 25 May 1977; they 'had elected to . . . spend their wedding night' there.[102] The combination of treacherous 'honeymooners' and gay promiscuity is proven to be fatal, in a moment that might be seen as the dominant narrative strain's unconscious wish-fulfilment – not because a number of bathhouse patrons were in reality accidentally burned to death, but because the betraying couple are fictionally included in that list of victims.

Faggots also makes strategic use of female figures to reinforce its hostile view of gay promiscuity. Amidst the packed crowds at the opening night of The Toilet Bowl club, we are introduced to Nancellen Richtofen, whom we later learn to be – unusually enough – 'one of those dykes who do not like the company of other dykes. And since she certainly wasn't keen on straight men either, . . . this left only faggots or solitude.'[103]

Nancellen's preference for gay male company is certainly convenient for a novel that critiques gay male sexuality without ever exploring promiscuity on the lesbian scene. (Although Kramer has claimed that 'most of *Faggots* was true',[104] it seems not a little curious that it should only home in on this dyke-disliking dyke.) However, Nancellen 'knew how to cruise. . . . [and] was not one to beat around the bush, or rather, was one to do just that.'[105]

Yet in the very same moment we learn of her cruising capabilities, her promiscuous desires begin to fade:

She was also, at thirty, feeling the pressures of advancing age. Most of her Lesbian friends [– despite her disliking other dykes –] were now settled down, as opposed to most of her faggot friends, who never seemed to roost, and she was tired of being the single woman at all those dinner parties. . . . So perhaps she was ready for a relationship.[106]

Of course, the desire for erotic/emotional dependability and familiarity often increases with age – though nowhere nearly as often or as entirely as monogamy-oriented discourses generally assume. More to the point, the only sign of Nancellen's considerable cruising powers arises as she meets and flirts with an interested middle-aged heterosexual woman who only awakens Nancellen's monogamous desires all the more. The nature metaphors we encountered earlier return to faintly normalise this shift towards monogamy: as Ephra Bronstein, her object of desire, becomes flustered at Nancellen's advances:

Nancellen, sensing that such seeds planted must be harvested, or at least watered, as soon as possible, . . . otherwise the drought sets in, winter comes, love dies, stood up with Ephra.[107]

But more significantly, the nature imagery here also accurately represents the instigation of potentially monogamous relationships as a fragile and threatened process: 'the drought sets in, winter comes, love dies.' This denaturalisation of monogamous sexuality is mirrored in Nancellen's culturally pressured search for monogamy in order to escape being the promiscuous 'single woman at all those dinner parties'. As Pat Califia has described this state of affairs:

[Lesbians who] think of themselves as single and avoid any appearance of being coupled . . . encounter some prejudice based on the notion that refusing to form permanent relationships is a sign of immaturity. . . . When you feel lonely and depressed, it's easy to get suckered in by the myth that couples always take good care of each other and keep each other perfect company.[108]

On the other hand, this meeting constitutes the staid Ephra's first lesbian awakening, suggesting a wealth of sexual possibilities beyond married life: 'I am an old lady who wants some Number One Good Times before I die. And was God not giving her a last clue on what she'd been missing all these years?'[109]

Ultimately, though, this pick-up between two women in a gay male nightclub is used to discredit an essentialised 'faggot' sexuality. The following night, as New York's richest and chicest gay men indulge all across Fire Island, Ephra visits Nancellen at her home on the Island to consummate their cruise. The latter's ambiguous movement between scene vamp and secret romantic is reiterated as she swooningly reflects: 'was there nothing so perfect as a trick sighted, wooed, captured, won, was this the love she had sought so many years and never found?'[110] Yet finally, she tearfully embraces her new lover in proud defiance of the 'trick' mentality of her previously preferred gay male environment (just as Fred will relinquish gay culture shortly afterwards): 'do you see me all you men and faggots?,[111] dykes are not the same as faggots, we can love!, we can make commitments!'[112] Nancellen's ascendance to the monogamous state normatively presumed to signify a 'real' lesbian only takes place in order to explain away her previous promiscuity as an effect of her male surroundings. (The question remains how she was able to be a promiscuous lesbian while *in* those all-male surroundings.) The representation of women here therefore functions solely as ammunition against promiscuous gay men.

The unstably privileged equation between promiscuity and gay men implied in Nancellen's rejection of her gay bar past is reiterated in Kramer's 1988 essay, 'Report from the holocaust'. There he supports his continuing preoccupation with critiquing gay male promiscuity in particular by citing:

Dr Richard Isay, a practicing psychoanalyst and Clinical Associate Professor of Psychiatry at Cornell Medical College, [who] writes in his . . . book, *Being Homosexual*: 'Human males in general are more interested in variations of sexual partners than females.' To which Dr Kinsey's words can be added: 'This is the history of his anthropoid ancestors, and this is the history of unrestrained males everywhere.'[113]

A 'practicing psychoanalyst', quite possibly (if not necessarily) steeped in the male-oriented assumptions of that frequently normalised discipline, is perhaps a less than ideal commentator on erotic differences between the sexes. More to the point, though, Kramer's quotation from Kinsey unknowingly begs a vital, equally unconsidered, question: since we are so dramatically different from our anthropoid ancestors in almost every other way, why should we assume their forms of sexual behaviour even approximate, let alone exactly match, the diversity of subsequent human sexualities?[114] Most importantly, neither of these secondary sources considers the cultural reasons why women might generally be, or seem to be, less interested in multiple sexual partners.

As in the patriarchal privileging of married men's promiscuity discussed before, 'a persistent double standard'[115] favouring male sexual pleasures over those of women has been, and still continues to be, shakily supported by unprovable, pseudo-scientific references to men's stronger sexual needs, as a result of their supposedly greater 'animalistic virility'. Looking back at the emergence of self-naturalising heterosexual 'scientific' discourses, Jonathan Ned Katz cites Richard von Krafft-Ebing's declaration in his 1886 'Medico-Legal Study' of the *Psychopathia Sexualis* that, 'undoubtedly, man has a much more intense sexual appetite than woman'[116] as a particularly influential example of 'a dominant, though not universal, nineteenth-century notion'[117] that has carried through in conventional, and also many marginalised, subsequent sexual discourses.

It is this notion that 'human males in general are more interested in variations of sexual partners than females' that enables Kramer's – and many, many others' – over-generalising construction of gay men as pre-eminently promiscuous: the logic runs that if most men 'naturally' want and/or need more sex than most women, then men who desire other men have far less of an obstacle to their sexual gratification, and will therefore be even more likely to be sexually 'unrestrained' together (the normative interpretation of promiscuity). The complementary implication of this logic is that the less male involvement there is in sex, the less likelihood there will be of 'intense sexual appetite', and hence less desire for 'variations of sexual partners'; so lesbians would generally be seen as 'naturally' the least sexual, and certainly the least promiscuous, of all. In 'Report from the holocaust', Kramer's reference to Isay's and Kinsey's biological beliefs about male virility, even as he argues for the *cultural production* of gay male promiscuity ('had we been allowed to marry, many of us would not have felt the obligation to be promiscuous'), exemplifies the ambivalence and inconsistency that trouble the widespread cultural recourse to this rigidly male-centred vision of sexual difference.

For this masculinist model of promiscuous desire is easily exposed as incoherently lopsided. In the case of heterosex, as the saying goes, 'it takes two to tango': although an unknowable number of straight men occasionally or regularly take secret male sex partners, they are, for the most part, not sexually active without the involvement of women. Of course, rape and less obvious male sexual coercion are both highly common (and commonly trivialised). Many heterosexual men also keep many female sex workers in business, most of whom are unlikely to be doing it simply for sexual gratification. But none of this male-instigated sexual activity is evidence of a biological sex drive difference between the sexes. Instead, these central types of straight male-driven sexual practice are primarily examples of the far wider range of culturally encouraged opportunities for men to actively choose to have 'variations of sexual partners', or just sex in general.

To take only one of countless counter-examples of resistant women's potent and preferred promiscuity, in a 1995 newspaper interview, queer photographer Della Grace recalls her confidently non-conformist sexual journey through the early 1970s. In her heterosexual early teenage years, she 'started becoming promiscuous':

'Between the ages of 14 and 18 [from 1971–75], I must have slept with more than 100 men.' But Grace was far from confused. 'Because my mother had injected me with feminism from an early age, I just thought that was the way to do things – to treat men as casually as they treated women. I was never emotionally involved with them. I just liked sex.'[118]

Grace's memories of approaching her early sex life through her mother's egalitarian version of sex education highlights the pivotal role that cultural messages play in shaping women's sexual perception of them-selves, their partners, and the male = sex/female = love dominant moral dichotomy.[119]

Notable literary examples of female promiscuity include: Audre Lorde's recollection of her experimentation with a three-way relation-ship during the sexually restrictive 1950s – 'We were certainly the first to have tried out this unique way of living for women, communal sex without rancor... None of the gay-girl books we read so avidly ever suggested our vision was not new, nor our joy in each other... [T]hat meant we had to write it ourselves, learn by living it out'[120]; Rechy's observation in *City of Night* of heterosexual women's freedom to be sexually open and promiscuous during the New Orleans Mardi Gras of the late 1950s: 'Emancipated of their restrictive sex for the length of this one liberating day, women like scavengers will prowl the streets, in and out of the shadows... their bodies flung, given easily'[121]; Maureen Duffy's fictionalisation of the 'incorrigibly plural' lesbian sex culture of 1960s London in *The Microcosm* (1966); and Jane DeLynn's unabashedly promiscuous picaresque novel, *Don Juan in the Village*, whose bluntly honest lesbian hero complains of 'the cowardice and hypocrisy of women – so desirous of the amenities of conversation and a nice clean bed, a history for a face that would somehow provide Romantic justi-fication for that utterly simple desire to explore the wet insides of another's body. For I had taken the promise of our liberation seriously, and thought that, with the right attitude, anybody could be perceived as the most desirable in the world – at least for one night.'[122]

Faggots includes another major instance wherein gay male promis-cuity is represented from an acutely distorting and unself-consciously partial perspective. While Ephra Bronstein is first being cruised by Nancellen at The Toilet Bowl, her ex-husband, Abe, is wandering with bewilderment through the backrooms of the same club. To a small degree, Abe's ex-husband status implicitly signifies the frequent provi-sionality of marriage, even as he arrogantly bemoans his impersonally promiscuous surroundings: 'Tell me, how do you meet people when no one talks?'[123] Yet while clumsy, pompous Abe is partly a figure of fun, the narrative also naturalises his particular type of heterosexual outsider perspective on gay promiscuous sexual codes.

Meeting Fred and Dinky in the club, he asks for an explanation of the humourless, wordless erotic interactions he sees around him. Fred – a movie scriptwriter (like Kramer at the time) who is in the process of convincing Abe to finance his vision of 'the first respectable faggot movie',[124] centring on a monogamous gay couple – is eager to answer the request:

Dinky said: 'You don't talk to people when you cruise. The secret is just to look mean.'

'What please is a cruise?'

Fred answered, waving his hands about in his best screenwriter's descriptive way: 'Think of this place as a great big store, with lots of merchandise on display. But you don't really look too closely, because you don't feel like shopping today. You look at it . . . obliquely. You give it a little look, pretending not to look, but being able to see, out of the corner of your eye only, if anyone else is pretending not to look back at you. If you see someone else pretending not to look, you look the other way. Only after a few moments do you look back, to see if he's still looking. And if your eyes look, at the same moment, you'll only let it happen for a second, and then you'll look away again.'

'It's very complicated. You want to write a movie about this? The pace will be very deadly.'[125]

At one level, this exchange functions as part of the novel's rightful satiric debunking of the more utopian elements of pro-sex liberationist discourse, particularly its more masculinist pretentions. (Earlier, the novel's Everard bathhouse sequence leading up to the fire provides a more sustained and successful corrective to the sometimes utopian myth of the gay bathhouse as 'the great leveler'[126]: 'Earlier arrivals, the younger ones at any rate, would by now have ejaculated in some manner or another, approximately three to six times, while older soldiers, passing thin-walled moans and groans, would by now have received approximately forty-one rejections as they heaved pasty white frames from cubicle to cubicle.'[127])

At the same time, though, Fred and Dinky's gay male exposition of cruising for a voyeuristic heterosexual patriarch bestows a false homosexual specificity upon that practice, serving to reassure Abe's sense of distance from a commonplace ritual that he nevertheless feels so superior to.[128] Here the novel supports a disingenuously 'rational' heterosexual dissociation from the universal disorder, self-contradiction and indirectness of desire and its cultural articulation. As with Kramer's attempt to equate sexual practice with ideological perspective discussed earlier, Abe's incomprehension — and the novel's willingness to humour his incomprehension at this point — stem from a failure to perceive of desire as predominantly irrational (within the framework of conscious logic) and defensive, not only because of, but also regardless of, the specific context of its conscious expression: in Jacqueline Rose's pithy phrase, 'the persistence of the question of desire *as* a question.'[129]

In defiance of Fred's apologetic rendition of gay desire, we can adopt a less subservient and more accurately attentive gay/queer perspective on heterosexuality, which uncovers the conventionally disavowed connections between gay and straight male cruising patterns. Such a perspective can be found, for example, in Mark Rappaport's 1992 queer deconstructionist documentary, *Rock Hudson's Home Movies*. There, an openly queer 'Rock Hudson' (played by Eric Farr) looks back at the homosexual innuendoes littered throughout his movies. However, one particular montage of actual clips where Hudson eyes and then approaches women leads 'Queer Rock' to reflect on the previously unspoken similarities between his onscreen heterosexualised, and off-screen gay, deployment of cruising codes. Unlike Fred's self-denigrating exposition for Abe, Queer Rock's speech directly addresses a gay audience:

Before . . . [heterosexuals] appropriated the word 'cruising,'[130] it was called 'flirting,' 'making a pass at,' 'coming on to,' 'showing an interest in.'[131] The tell-tale signs: discreet or indiscreet glances and a dumb ice-breaker or two.

Rappaport's script serves as a reminder that heterosexual cruising is both a naturalised everyday occurrence, and often characterised by precisely those 'discreet glances' that Abe finds so incomprehensible in the gay club and backroom. After all, the reason that cruising is, in Abe's terms, so 'very complicated' is substantially to do with the necessarily oblique interaction of the desires and fantasies of both (or more) desiring subject/objects.

Yet in another sense, Abe's perplexity at the 'very complicated' mechanics of gay cruising also stems from his position within a normalised heteropatriarchal tradition wherein men are encouraged to 'uncomplicatedly' cruise and court women, and women are in turn culturally positioned as receptive to the male gaze and proposition; the two-way indirectness of much gay cruising translates in normative heterosexual terms into straight men simply staring and staking claims. However, the humourlessness and indirectness that Abe observes between gay men cruising one another certainly illustrate a similar – albeit mutually reflected – display of masculinity in many ways (as well as illustrating the general ambivalence of desire).

Most importantly, though, those particular impenetrably exchanged gay glances that Abe witnesses clearly do not make cruising a practice that is exotically specific to, or originating from, gay men. Rather, that mirroring machismo is specific to a particular sex/gender dynamic frequently (not always) at work when masculine-oriented gay men cruise one another, just as the often normative power relations circulating when masculine-identified heterosexual men cruise, and when feminine-identified heterosexual women are cruised, signify another, more culturally validated, model of cruising.[132]

I want to turn now to the novel's repeated diversion from its own disdain for the seeming ubiquity of gay promiscuity – a diversion that, like the 'straying' of promiscuous desire itself, may be seen to take place both consciously and unconsciously.

At a conscious level, *Faggots* incorporates several sequences that telescope together opposed, often multiple, perspectives on gay culture – especially on sex and desire – without privileging a dominant point of view. The most overt of these is a chorus of unnamed 'Everygayman' voices that provides a prelude to the novel's concluding scenes on Fire Island. Like the bathhouses, that island's mythical status within gay discourse, particularly in the 1970s and 1980s, as a shorthand for all the possibilities and problems of gay culture, gives this passage a far wider resonance:

'If the Outside World is ugly and not many laughs and doesn't want us any-way, what's wrong with making our very own special place, with our dancing and drugs and jokes and clothes and music and brotherhood and fucking and our perfectly marvelous taste!'

'You are absolutely right. There is simply nothing that is ugly at Fire Island Pines. The eyes are bathed in constant delights. Uglies and ugliness are simply not tolerated. Go away! Shoo!'

'We have created our own aesthetic!'

'You mean our own Ghetto.'

'This place is all about belonging, the love of friends, Togetherness!'

'And the Quest for Beauty.'

'And the search for Mr. Right.'

'Oh, I don't know about that.'

'We play here too much.'

'Never too much.'

'I think we come here to be hurt and rejected.'

'Oh, I don't know about that.' . . .

'What does it all mean?'

'Oh, stop it!'

Yes, everyone talked about its essence endlessly. Such a complicated place.[133]

Unlike much of the surrounding narrative, this snapshot of contesting viewpoints allows for unresolved differences of opinion about the common bonds of gay life on Fire Island, and by extension, in gay culture beyond. These explicit differences trouble the novel's broader drive towards denouncing those gay men who 'play here too much' in their 'Quest for Beauty'. Here, 'faggot' culture remains 'a complicated place' for all concerned. This gay Greek chorus also contrasts favourably with the more conventionally Krameresque romantic polarisation of gay ghettoism and heterosexual small-town 'Happiness' at the start of Holleran's more widely championed *Dancer from the Dance*; there, the narrator remembers a mournful journey to Fire Island via a mainland traditional small town, accompanied by the novel's tragic hero, Malone:

It was the sort of scene Malone always turned sentimental over. He always passed through Sayville with a lingering regret for its big white houses and friendly front yards with picket fences and climbing roses. He always looked back as he went through, saying this might be that perfect town he was always searching for, where elms and lawns would be combined with the people he loved. But those summer taxis drove inevitably through it, like vans bearing prisoners who are being transferred from one prison to another – from Manhattan to Fire Island – when all we dreamed of, really, in our deepest dreams, was just such a town as this, quiet, green, untroubled by the snobberies and ambitions of the larger world; the world we could not quit.[134]

Earlier in *Faggots*, back on the island of Manhattan, the use of third-person narration combined with first-person stream-of-consciousness draws attention to the competing perspectives on promiscuity within the individual gay man. Like the unfaithful lover he eventually denounces, Fred has an impromptu sexual encounter 'in the basement toilet of his beloved West Side Y'[135] while Dinky is out of town. Despite Kramer's repeated condemnation of gay promiscuity as personal and cultural betrayal elsewhere, here we find that Fred's 'orgasm . . . [is] summoned hastily by the excitement of this Forbidden Moment, . . . sending him through the roof in a way that no ordinary licit encounter had in recent memory'[136] – yet he also begins to fantasise that his unknown partner is Dinky. This visceral experience of the absolute concurrency of contradictory desires leads him to reflect anew on the inexorable lure of the illicit and unknown, and also on the persistent psychical rupture and movement between consciously structured sexuality and the surrounding *de*formative effects of desire:

Intelligent human beings do not go around doing it in public johns. . . . Or do they? Anyway, this one just had. Come on, Fred, admit it felt good. He recollected, from . . . [a] seminal volume . . . : 'The warring conflict in man between the intellect and the libido shall never be twinned.' From this he now took comfort.[137]

My earlier reference to Karla Jay's 1975 comment on 'the differences between our political ideals and our personal [sexual] actions' stood in direct opposition to Kramer's Enlightenment-descendent belief in monogamous 'rationality'. Here, by contrast, we find a more complex reinforcement of her sentiment.

Meanwhile down at the docks, the novel also pauses repeatedly on the contradictory thought processes of Fred's best friend, Anthony Montano, as he cruises the disused piers and warehouses along the

river. As Anthony arrives at the docks, his stream-of-consciousness
interior monologue becomes an ambivalent, yet heartfelt, ode to semi-
public cruising that (as with Fred in the Y tearoom) suggests a complex
alternative to his pessimistic complaint earlier in the novel that 'it's
not possible for two men to get it together'[138] in a monogamous relationship:

Ah, home away from home, ah black hole of Calcutta, ah windswept, storm
toss'd, fire-ravaged skeleton of former grandeurs! That you are still standing! . . . What a fantasy trip, I don't have to see you and you don't have to
see me, you are John Wayne with real hair, . . . my heart's still beating, my tits
aren't sagging, my pecker's hopefully still pecking, I've made it through
another winter, now I deserve a break today, go out, go up, show them that
I'm still Alive! . . . and while I may be going down the tubes, I'll go down
getting my cock sucked as I start another year of my life![139]

Here his monologue serves to prise apart his publicly upheld monogamous identity at the psychical level.

Equally, though, the juxtaposition of deathly metaphor and life-
affirming eroticism here refers not only to the darkness and decay of
the cruising ground; nor entirely to the actual threat of homophobic
murder there;[140] but also to less consciously articulable erotic anxieties
and ambivalences – impelled both by cultural pressures and by that
(self-)destructiveness sometimes known as the death drive[141] – in the face
of apparent sexual 'freedom'. Thus, to return to an observation from the
previous chapter, if desire's inherent inconsistency problematises the
dominant disparaging definition of 'promiscuity', then, conversely,
Anthony's oscillation between dread and exhilaration illustrates that
avowedly promiscuous sexuality is also persistently disrupted by
un/conscious psychical conflict.

At the same time, within specific cultural terms, Anthony's and Fred's
fumbling negotiations of semi-public promiscuity also function as
unusual correctives to the dominant masculinised gay cultural narrative
of cruising. Instead, we find an all too rare representation of gay promiscuity not from the usual point of view of the muscularly/culturally
empowered John Rechy-type all-American sex icon, but rather from
the perspective of the more culturally discredited, less conventionally
masculinised, gay man who cruises and fantasises *about* such a gay
'John Wayne with real hair'. Kramer's decidely deromanticising focus
on his characters' paranoid thoughts here takes account of precisely
the diversity of 'faggot' identities and desires that his novel will later
renounce. Hence, the following uncomfortable pier sex scenario can
be read directly against Rechy's macho 'outlaw images' of 'hard limbs,

hard muscles, hard stomachs, strong bodies, male and male'[142] under a decaying Santa Monica pier the same year in *The Sexual Outlaw*:

Oi, do I have to come to this cesspool and pass out every time I want to get it up? Why have I been so impotent? . . . come on Anthony, *stay hard*, fuck this gorgeous number, oh shit why can't I get it over with and come!, . . . I'm going to jerk off in a corner, how do you find a corner in the dark?[143]

But for the purposes of my argument, perhaps the most relevant implication to be drawn from these contradictory interior monologues is their deliberate depiction of the internally divisive influence of the unconscious and subconscious upon sexual activity. Ironically, if *Faggots* ultimately offers a crudely binarised view of monogamous 'order' versus promiscuous 'disorder', the numerous glimpses it offers into its purportedly monogamy-inclined characters' internalised sexual paradoxes cause the narrative to keep returning (almost compulsively) to a more complex understanding; returning, that is, to the largely disavowed knowledge that, regardless of its particular consciously manifested form, all desire is unsatisfiable in its very excessiveness and – in Freud's famous phrase – because of the strong 'possibility that something in the nature of the sexual instinct itself is unfavourable to the realization of complete satisfaction.'[144]

Indeed, the novel's descriptive promiscuity, and its inclusion of so many promiscuous scenarios that delay the finalé of Fred's 'escape' from gay culture, keep conspicuously re-enacting the *deferral of satisfaction* on which all narrative pleasure, like desire in general, depends: as Elizabeth Cowie concisely argues in relation to the structure of fantasy underpinning desire, 'the pleasure is in how to bring about the consummation, is in the happening and continuing to happen; in how it will come about, and *not* in the moment of *having happened*, when it will fall back into loss, the past.'[145] The same might be said of the multiplicity and inconclusiveness of promiscuity: while every promiscuous encounter 'will fall back into loss, the past', those numerous 'consummations' also represent a deferral or rejection of the monogamous/ marital 'moment of *having happened*.'

Hence, in its incessant 'straying from the path' before Fred finally claims to abandon the New York gay scene to find a monogamous 'something better',[146] *Faggots* is a mostly (but not always) unintentional example of the fascination and temptation of the *un*consummated – the cruise and the brief encounter, versus monogamy and marriage – that energises society at large. Cowie clarifies this ambiguous pull in two diametrically opposed directions, which takes place at both the narrational and wider social level: 'though [at one level, like Fred] we all want the couple to be united, and the obstacles heroically overcome, we don't want the story to end.'[147] It is the novel's representation of promiscuity that leaves desire enticingly unfulfilled and inconclusive, deferring that always anti-climactic closure.[148]

Finally, *Faggots* problematises its own governing demonisation of promiscuity through its conscious and subconscious depiction of Fred's paradoxical desires on Fire Island. As he catches up with and confronts the unfaithful Dinky in his Fire Island apartment, Fred's despairing rant against, amongst other things, 'using my body as a faceless thing to lure another faceless thing, I want to love a Person!' and the fact that 'faggots have to fuck so fucking much'[149] is – rather like his tearoom encounter – pointedly sidetracked by his own wandering eye and desires:

So talk, Freddie, Fred-chen, talk. You're here. God damn it, talk! That g-string is very sexy. It carries his cock and balls nicely. It fits around his waist nicely. It fits into his crack in his ass nicely. I am shivering nicely. I think I am getting off my course.[150]

Kramer suggestively underlines the draw towards objectification of the sexual object that is central to the fracturing effects of fantasy and desire, regardless of 'Person'-centred liberal sexual discourse. Hence, Fred's desires, necessarily manifested through an objectification of the sexual object and erotic partialisation of the object's body, are repeatedly shown to uncoil and 'lead astray' the thread of his argument, and – like the novel's promiscuity-studded narrative so far – to defer and compromise his denunciation of Dinky's wayward ways: 'Oh, Fred. When are you going to say No?,' he asks himself.[151]

As the novel closes, Fred reasserts his essentialising view of all gay men as exceptionally promiscuous by declaring to the reader his new status as a resolutely monogamy-bound and magically degayed 'enlightened' individual:

I'm not gay. I'm not a fairy. I'm not a fruit. I'm not queer. A little crazy maybe. And I'm not a faggot. I'm a Homosexual Man. I'm Me. Pretty Classy.[152]

Accordingly, his parting observation of those gay Fire Island revelers 'sitting on the sand . . . under disappearing stars and moon, and the rising sun', enjoying one anothers' 'narcotic beauty',[153] evokes Tennyson's 'Lotos-Eaters', who 'have had enough of action, and of motion we' (l. 150), and so in drugged sensuous bliss 'sat them down upon the yellow sand,/Between the sun and moon upon the shore' (ll. 37–8) to 'ripen toward the grave' (l. 96).[154]

Yet those numerous self-conscious moments that have complicated gay promiscuity throughout the narrative remain unrecuperable into the principal monogamy-privileging drive towards closure; 'the question of desire' persists. For if the allusion to Tennyson implies that faggots have a 'fatal' fascination with sex, physical beauty and desire, then as the narrative ends, Fred's self-ennobling belief in 'something better' beyond promiscuity can clearly be seen to rise in direct proportion to his active suppression of the 'narcotic beauty' of 'hundreds, thousands, passing the message of love from body to body' on the beach[155]: 'It's hard to leave you,' he intones melodramatically, 'yes, it's hard to leave.'[156] (We saw a similar ambivalence earlier in the conclusion of Rechy's *Rushes*, where Endore remains drawn to SM gay culture even as he pompously rejects it.) The point, then, is not that monogamous desire is shown to be merely a transparent mask for deeper promiscuous needs; this would merely constitute a reversal of the normative representation of promiscuity as 'false consciousness'. Rather, the novel's closing scene unintentionally hints that the insistent reification of monogamy over promiscuous sex and desire produces an abiding concern with promiscuity in the (gay) subject that continues to pull them in both directions at once.

The notion of abjection as 'a composite of . . . condemnation and yearning'[157] is apt again here, if we recall Creed's observation that 'the subject is constantly beset by abjection which fascinates desire but must be repelled for fear of self-annihilation.' Thus, while he is at his most forceful in asserting the superiority of his sexual preferences and ostentatiously severing himself from a supposedly destructive promiscuity, the monogamy-naturalising gay man finds that his desire for the unfamiliar, the multiple and the unknown ('hundreds, thousands, passing the message of love') – in short, his love of the seemingly alien – cannot but continue to resurface and recirculate. As Fred himself expresses it: 'My fantasies run wild, just like yours.'[158]

THE NORMAL HEART: SPEAKING FOR 'THE PEOPLE'?

In a sense, *The Normal Heart* picks up almost exactly where *Faggots* left off: the action is set in New York three years later, between July 1981 and May 1984. Yet unsurprisingly, given Kramer's worldview, the play also polarises the relationship between monogamy and promiscuity all the more in the light of the emerging AIDS crisis. According to Kramer, AIDS has 'proved his point' about the purported need for monogamy and greater sexual restraint in order to combat the 'destructiveness' of gay promiscuity: in a 1986 interview, for instance, he argued that in the 1970s and early 1980s:

The gay political platform – especially in the USA – was promulgated by a very few people who did *not* speak for the people. They were sounding off, but they were only expressing *their* point of view. Until very recently their message was 'promiscuity is all.' They did not speak for the mass of people. But when I wrote *Faggots*, I didn't think what I was screaming about was going to lead to death.[159]

Not only does Kramer's now familiar causal link between promiscuity, death and destruction return here; there is also a very strong suggestion that 'the mass of people' are resistant to promiscuity. Hence, Kramer's own espousal of an anti-promiscuity perspective from 'the gay political platform' since the early 1980s apparently constitutes not one person 'only expressing *their* point of view', but a public figure who *does* 'speak for the people', and is further justified by the 'evidence' of AIDS.

This universalisation of a very particular anti-promiscuous gay position by simplifying the range of surrounding and preceding debate on sexual practice within gay culture is inconsistent with *The Normal Heart*, which instead casts Kramer's stand-in,[160] Ned Weeks, in the role of Ibsen's misunderstood 'Enemy of the People', Dr Stockmann. As Douglas Crimp comments:

For Kramer, being defined by sex is the legacy of gay politics; promiscuity and gay politics are one and the same . . . [In this way,] Kramer's ignorance of and contempt for the gay movement are demonstrated throughout the play . . . [which] is very largely directed against other gay men.[161]

Thus Ned continues, like Fred before him, to distinguish himself from the 'deluded' gay multitude – particularly his fellow founders of GMHC, who eventually exclude him from the organisation:

NED: Must we all be reduced to becoming our own murderers? Why couldn't you and I, Bruce Niles [the clean-cut spokesperson for GMHC] and Ned Weeks, have been leaders in creating a new definition of what it means to be gay?[162]

Apart from the broader issue of whether having wealthy, masculine-identified, white male 'leaders' could ever be beneficial for gay culture as a whole, the answer to Ned's question – 'Why can't we join together as cutting-edge leaders?' – lies largely in his weakness as an intracultural negotiator of the many complexities of the emerging gay health crisis, and especially in his inability to incorporate the validity of other, often less blaming, gay male understandings of the crisis.

However, like *Faggots*, *The Normal Heart* is at once both normatively motivated and more un/consciously contradictory than the many 'for or against' critical responses to the play often suggest. On the one hand, for example, I agree with Douglas Crimp that it represents 'the view of someone who did not participate in the gay movement, and who has no sense of its history, its complexities, its theory and practice.'[163] In the following exchange between Ned and his soon-to-be-lover, Felix, we are reminded of how Kramer's ostensibly all-encompassing image of gay New York in *Faggots* similarly shied away from the diversity of gay politics amongst the promiscuity:

FELIX: Do you ever take a vacation?
NED: That's the great goal, isn't it. A constant Fire Island vacation. Party, party; fuck, fuck. Maybe you can give me a few trendy pointers on what to wear.[164]

Yet on the other hand, the play does deliberately dramatise the challenge that the experiential insights of long-term gay political workers present to inexperienced Ned's project of monogamy-based leadership:

MICKEY: I've spent fifteen years of my life fighting for our right to be free and make love whenever, wherever . . . And you're telling me that all those years of what being gay stood for is wrong . . . and I'm a murderer. We have been so oppressed! Don't you remember how it was? Can't you see how important it is for us to love openly, without hiding and without guilt? We were a bunch of funny-looking fellows who grew up in sheer misery and one day we fell into the orgy room and we thought we'd found heaven. And we would teach the world how wonderful heaven can be. We would lead the way. We would be good for something new. Can't you see that? Can't you?[165]

Admittedly, Ned ultimately argues that the health crisis has made promiscuity murderous, in a statement that supposedly undercuts political issues; and he also contends that anyway, regardless of AIDS, 'the only way we'll have real pride is when we demand recognition of a culture that isn't just sexual,'[166] conflating promiscuity with sexual excess and depoliticisation once again. Nevertheless, in GMHC member Mickey's speech above and at other key isolated moments, Kramer's use of dramatic form (as with the Fire Island chorus of voices in *Faggots*) enables a more open-ended debate to take place between opposing gay discourses of promiscuity.[167] Within this debate, Ned's voice – despite being clearly privileged – remains one amongst several viewpoints for the spectator (as opposed to the omniscient third-person narration of *Faggots*, which largely works to recuperate a diversity of opinion). While Ned almost always gets the last word, we should be careful to remember that closure is never omnipotent; it cannot erase all the traces of unresolved complexities clean from the stage, particularly when each competing viewpoint has been seen physically embodied in performance.

Such productive incoherence is all the more apparent in a play that deals with the confusion and absolute uncertainty of the very earliest years of AIDS awareness – an uncertainty that prevents Ned's conviction (via the equally bewildered Dr. Emma Brookner) that his friends are dying purely from promiscuity from becoming fully conclusive. (Kramer has since continuously sought to verify this conviction, however, in his quest to film *The Normal Heart* since its initial success in 1985, immediately after the actual events it dramatises. While the conflation of promiscuity and AIDS was still in debate in 1985, even with the unlikely addition of a thorough historical contextualisation in the screenplay, Kramer's film version can only serve to perpetuate pre-safe/r sex anxieties about promiscuity in the late 1990s.)

If the play mainly privileges Ned's personal background over that of his fellow activists, in focusing there it also problematises his role as the 'lone voice of reason' by suggesting that his cut-and-dried political pronouncements are, to an extent, a diversion from more messy immediate personal issues. Witness Ned and Felix on their first date:

FELIX: God you are relentless. And as cheery as Typhoid Mary.
(NED *comes over to Felix and sits beside him. Then he leans over and kisses him. The kiss becomes quite intense. Then* NED *breaks away, jumps up, and begins to walk around nervously.*)
NED: The American Jew knew exactly what was happening, but everything was downplayed and stifled. Can you imagine how effective it would have been if every Jew in America had marched on Washington? Proudly! Who says I want a lover? Huh!? I mean, why doesn't anybody believe me when I say I do not want a lover?[168]

As this scene takes place in 1981 prior to safe/r sex awareness, Ned may well be anxious about a potential health risk in kissing Felix here. But more immediately, this moment indicates that Ned's demands for unified cultural responses to catastrophe – deploying an essentialising ethnic analogy to 'streamline' the actual diversity of gay identities along the way – are, in part, a means of overriding deeper psychical anxieties about his sexual/emotional relationships with other men. Therefore, Ned/Kramer's moral certainty in demanding that gay culture unite as one against anti-gay indifference to AIDS fails to take into account his own very particular conceptualisation of that struggle, which is shaped by his unconscious and subconscious, as much as by his specific conscious political agenda. Moreover, that fervent political agenda is also called into question. For if Ned/Kramer resolutely insists that monogamous relationships should be the cornerstone of gay political 'responsibility', then his ambivalence and defensiveness towards being in a stable relationship when he asks, 'Why doesn't anybody believe me when I say I do not want a lover?', stresses a more wavering and vulnerable uncertainty in the face of erotic and emotional intimacy.

Nevertheless, the play ends with Dr. Emma Brookner performing a variation on the marriage ceremony for Ned and Felix, who is dying from an AIDS-related illness:

EMMA: We are gathered here in the sight of God to join together these two men. They love each other very much and want to be married in the presence of their family before Felix dies. . . . Do you, Felix Turner, take Ned Weeks . . . to be your . . .
FELIX: My lover. My lover. I do.
NED: I do.
(FELIX *is dead.* EMMA, *who has been holding Felix's hand and monitoring his pulse, places his hand on his body. She leaves. The two orderlies enter and push the hospital bed, through all the accumulated mess, off stage.*)[169]

The intended image is of a poignant commitment to marital monogamy that comes too late: a warning for gay audiences to fight AIDS by relinquishing promiscuity, and ideally, getting married. Yet equally, the couple's marriage at Felix's death bed, followed immediately by his death, can be seen unintentionally to symbolise the actual ineffectiveness of gay marriages (or any other cultural authentication of monogamy) as a response to the AIDS crisis. As subsequent years have shown time and again, focusing on culturally condoned monogamy not only does nothing to diminish HIV/AIDS or political apathy and hostility – it actively marginalises all the more the many promiscuous gay men who are living or dying with AIDS.

Like *Faggots*, then, *The Normal Heart* produces both knowing and unknowing contradictions that frustrate its foregrounded defence of monogamy and marriage. Unlike the shorthand, soundbite polemics of his speeches and essays as an AIDS activist, Kramer's use of fiction requires and allows a somewhat more fluid representation of factual events from differing perspectives; a deployment of what Toni Morrison calls the fiction writer's 'ability to imagine others and . . . willingness to project consciously into the danger zones such others may represent' for the author.[170] In Kramer's case, these often brief excursions into the psychical and cultural 'danger zones' of promiscuity necessarily complicate his most consciously upheld public allegiance to a politics of monogamy. Having entered and even loitered in these promiscuous zones, his fictional works reach more ambiguous and uncertain conclusions than either Kramer or his audiences may have anticipated or acknowledged.

POLITICS AND GAY PROMISCUITY

As we have seen, both the deromanticised scenes in *Faggots*, and Ned's fury at gay men who only 'party, party; fuck, fuck' in *The Normal Heart*, bypass simplistic celebratory accounts of the commercial gay sex scene (rather like Rechy's novels, which are in other ways diametrically opposed to Kramer's anti-promiscuous perspective). Moreover, in doing so, they also raise the frequently dismissed issue of gay male preoccupation with the right to sexual pleasure over broader questions of structural oppression.

   In many ways, as I began by arguing, this gay male focus on sex is vital, given that much discussion of sexual politics, in academia as elsewhere, has tended to marginalise the crucial importance of sexual practice in shaping and articulating sexual identities and cultures. But equally, the reduction of sexuality solely to the issue of sexual pleasure within much of commercial gay discourse ignores the ways in which homosexuality is experienced and perceived diversely, depending on equally integral differences in race, ethnicity, sex, class, region, and gender affiliation, amongst other formative factors. As one example (which we already encountered in the introduction), black gay critics have often been especially attuned to the limitations of that gay male 'concern with sexuality in an individualistic sense' that Kramer rejects. This phrase comes from Isaac Julien and Kobena Mercer, who argue that the notion of 'sexual libertarianism is itself based on certain ethnic privileges as it is their whiteness that enables some gay men to act out this "freedom of choice," which itself highlights the consumer-oriented character of the metropolitan gay subculture.'[171] In a very important sense, Kramer's own emphasis on the need for gay men to fight homophobia and AIDS on each others' behalf also challenges normative gay culture's focus on enjoying the benefits of increased access to commercial spaces and sex, as exemplified in the following quotation from an otherwise complex study of *Sex, Gay Men and AIDS*: '[Some queers] have been known to bewail the dissipation of the political energy of the early years in disco dancing, while not recognising that, in many ways, that is what it is all about.'[172]

   Kramer makes the mistake, however, of suggesting that his belief in marriage and monogamy is an inevitable aspect of challenging the apolitical gay man's preoccupation with erotic pleasure. For on the contrary, it is partly Kramer's culturally privileged status – as a wealthy ex-film scriptwriter and producer, who had no involvement in gay politics prior to the AIDS crisis – that leads him to sidestep 'the sexual, racial, and economic dimensions of the AIDS epidemic'[173] and instead yoke his activist aims to the institutional 'respectability' of monogamy.[174] (I say 'partly' because sociopolitical perspective is, though largely, not entirely determined by one's social status.) Far from 'rising above' sex in order to tackle 'more serious' issues, Kramer's insistently monogamous approach to AIDS activism is as thoroughly entangled in questions of sexual practice as the work of those (pro-)promiscuous activists he dismisses for their supposedly 'childish' and 'unhealthy' sexual plea- sures. Furthermore, while Kramer represents those pro-promiscuity activists as apolitical individualists, their acceptance and encourage- ment of sexual diversity is thoroughly political and, in fact, directly opposed to Kramer's own highly individualistic emphasis on marriage as an act 'against AIDS.' Yet when (pro-)promiscuous activists answer Kramer's call to political involvement while also addressing the reality of sexual diversity, he – and other conservative and liberal critics like him – can only criticise them for not subscribing to his own restrictive sexual agenda.

There might be a further, concurrent explanation for insisting so relentlessly on the perils of promiscuity. Prior to AIDS (as in the pier scenes in *Faggots*), deathly representations of sex have always partly functioned as indirect articulations of the dissolving and disrupting effects of desire upon subjectivity. Yet since the early 1980s, the more immediate and relentless confusion surrounding HIV and AIDS has, of course, produced an inextricable psychical overlap between sexual pleasure, illness and death, especially for gay men. Writing of his conflicting feelings towards a potential new lover in 'Report from the holocaust', Kramer recalls:

I find I've made this note in my diary after he left, after our fifth night together. When we hold each other, there are three people in bed and one of them is Death. I confide in no one, not even Rodger, who was my former lover and with whom I share everything. In one of our many daily phone conversa- tions, he volunteers, 'I think Jesus would have to carry me in his arms to Paris for me to put out.'[175]

The extreme difficulty in resisting a conflation of death and desire expressed here may be another reason for Kramer's movement between fearing and rejecting sex, and especially promiscuity – a response that is symptomatic of many gay men's responses to a daily environment of illness and death, to some extent regardless of their HIV status: in Eric Rofes' words, 'whether HIV positive, HIV negative, or unaware of anti-body status, significant numbers of gay men in America appear to be experiencing confusion, dysfunction, impotency, and deep ambiva- lence about sexuality and intimacy between men.'[176] Within this context, the politics of sexual practice can seem rather remote and tangential.

But such psychical confusion cannot account for Kramer's consistently anti-promiscuous view of gay sexuality since at least the mid-1970s,

and his belief that AIDS 'proves' his preceding viewpoint (rather than
in fact complicating everyone's relationship to sex). Nor do I believe
that Kramer's tireless and rightly influential commitment to AIDS
activism should be used to overlook or excuse the consistency with
which he has pathologised gay promiscuity in his public pronouncements – although even Simon Watney, who has publicly advocated
safer sexual diversity with equal consistency, has argued for such a
glossing over of ideological contradictions:

> Over the past few years I have had a few differences of opinion with Larry
> on some issues . . . But these are not issues concerning which we should, as
> it were, go to the Cross . . . It is surely far more important to recognize that in
> relation to the vast majority of the many topics on which he has written over
> time he has been consistently right on target, and only too correct.[177]

Such an argument wrongly places this most hard-working and famous
of activists virtually beyond criticism, exacerbating the widely sustained notion that Kramer's gay cultural prominence and wider media
success make him a 'popular expert' on the relationship between the
AIDS crisis and gay sexuality.

Kramer has also repeatedly defended his words by arguing for the
necessity of oversimplification and overamplification in order to get
mass media and public attention:

> Of course I speak in hyperbole. Of course I speak in broad strokes. I'm here
> to tell you that if I didn't, no one would have heard a thing I have said over
> all of these years.[178]

Yet his 'hyperbole' is clearly intended to draw attention in part to a very
specifically anti-promiscuous agenda, which is – despite Kramer's own
claims – quite discrete from actual life-and-death issues concerning
AIDS treatment, care and research. Far from diluting a more intricate
underlying understanding of sex since AIDS, therefore, Kramer – like
a number of other mainstream gay spokesmen – has continued to
broadcast a restrictive marital/monogamous message, while underesti-
mating or discrediting the actual complexity of gay (and for that
matter, all other) sexual behaviour.

As his fictional work simultaneously admits and unwittingly implies,
however, those psychical and cultural complexities attending desire
invariably resurface to trouble the un/conscious of a universalised
'orderly' model of gay sociosexual relations. Both *Faggots* and *The
Normal Heart* un/willingly attest to the fact that attempts to cancel out,
or negotiate around, the fact of promiscuity require a suppression of the
promiscuous unpredictability of desire itself; an always incomplete

suppression, moreover, that necessitates the censor's ambivalent continuing interconnection with their own conflicting desires.

Approaching the third decade of the AIDS crisis, with rising levels of homophobic and anti-gay activity to arm oneself against, it is easy enough to perceive the question of defending promiscuity to be a diversionary, or at best, marginal one, to be pursued after more immediate struggles have been diffused. In some ways, this is of course true: while sex will flourish whatever the predicament, survival must come first.[179] But as Kramer's marrying of AIDS work with idealised monogamy exemplifies, to devalue or disregard the importance of sexual practice is to ignore its insidiously shaping influence throughout (even supposedly unrelated) political work – and, of course, nowhere more so than in naturalised cultural equations between promiscuous sex, death and destruction in relation to AIDS.

In response to Kramer's increasingly fashionable defence of an assimilatory marital model of gay desire, then – and against all the unabated scaremongering surrounding sexual pleasure, HIV and AIDS – I want to reaffirm the restlessness, contradiction and uncertainty permitted us, and demanded of us, by our desires. Indeed, in Kramer's paradoxical fictional explorations of promiscuity, we can sometimes decipher a struggle to face and even 'love the "alien"' within oneself and others. On the one hand, this struggle requires that we socially acknowledge and integrate conventionally alienated conscious promiscuous desires. But at the same time, and more ambiguously, it requires that we learn to accept that desire also persists as an *un*socialisable promiscuous sway, within the always contrary and unresolvable realms of the subconscious and unconscious.

Notes

1. The first part of my title comes from the David Bowie song 'Loving the Alien' (*Tonight*, EMI, 1984).
2. Quoted in Laermer, 'The real John Rechy', p. 51.
3. Laermer, 'Rechy on AIDS', p. 52.
4. Ibid.
5. See, for example, Rechy's withheld thoughts during an interview in *The Sexual Outlaw* (p. 47).
6. King, *Safety in Numbers*, p. 1.
7. Ibid., p. 21. The end of this quotation has been spliced on from an earlier sentence.

8. Ibid., p. 89. See especially Chapter 3 of King's book, 'Promoting safer sex', for a succinct overview of key methods of community-based safe/r sex interventions during the 1980s.
9. Ibid., p. 109.
10. The phrase 'revisionist thinking' is obscure, but presumably refers to the notion that promiscuity is not the cause of HIV transmission.
11. Rechy, *Sexual Outlaw*, p. 285.
12. Ibid., p. 71.
13. Rechy, *City of Night*, p. 245.
14. Schulman, *My American History*, p. 11.
15. Davies et al., *Sex, Gay Men and AIDS*, p. 32.
16. Sullivan, 'Larry Kramer', p. 40.
17. In *Reports from the Holocaust: The Story of an AIDS Activist*, Kramer records his rapid disenchantment with GMHC for 'concretizing ... into ... a social service organization, rather than an advocacy one' (p. 57), resulting in his pressurised resignation in 1983. Nevertheless, Kramer also partly apologises for his frustration with the group at that time – 'I was furious and hurt and probably burnt out' (p. 59) – and reflects that 'it dawned on me that now I couldn't even criticize this organization – which I had come to look upon as my child – and certainly not publicly, without inadvertently hurting it, perhaps stunting its growth in these early years of its development' (p. 65). This last statement, which acknowledges that the price paid for presenting a unified political front is the marginalisation of internal dissent and difference, becomes ironic later in this chapter, given Kramer's own frequent demand for a quelling of gay sexual diversity in the interests of a 'greater' political cause.
18. Callen and Caviano, 'Sex After AIDS', p. 42.
19. Kramer, afterword to 'Some thoughts about evil' (1993), in *Reports*, p. 454.
20. Ibid., p. 16.
21. 'Letters to the editor', p. 6.
22. Tucker, 'Ivory towers', p. 26.
23. Collard, 'Wanna be in my gang?' p. 10.
24. For instance, whereas in the 1986 'Rechy on AIDS' piece, he cites 'the astonishing, amazing courage' of gays in response to AIDS, a decade earlier in *The Sexual Outlaw*, he envisages the promiscuous 'outlaw' existing on the edges of a 'gay world' where 'we reduce "gaypride" to a matter of holding hands in public' (p. 245), and where, as in heterosexual culture, 'even so-called liberals condone ... [the promiscuous sexual outlaw's] persecution' (p. 28). On the other hand, Rechy's texts deflect heterogeneity by recurrently chastising gay SM sex.
25. Quoted in Koehler, 'Normal Heart', p. 20.
26. Kramer's first play, *Sissies' Scrapbook* (1972), remains unpublished; the others are *Just Say No: A Play About a Farce* (1988) and *The Destiny of Me* (1992). Prior to his avowedly gay writing career, his screenwriting credits include adaptations of Hunter Davies' novel, *Here We Go Round the Mulberry Bush* (1967), and of D. H. Lawrence's *Women in Love* (1969). Kramer has been at work on his magnum opus, a novel entitled *The American People*, for a number of years.
27. Kramer, *Reports*, p. 273.
28. Kramer, quoted in Zonana, 'Kramer vs. the world', p. 48.
29. Kramer, *Reports*, p. 273.

30. Boswell, *Christianity*; page unspecified.
31. Kramer, *Reports*, p. 273.
32. Ibid.
33. Ibid., pp. 274–5.
34. Needless to say, contrary to Kramer's 'broad strokes', this is not a characteristic shared by all straight men.
35. Holleran, *Ground Zero*, p. 113. However, 'slut' is clearly a word applied to almost *any* promiscuous woman, regardless of her age.
36. Tucker, 'Larry Kramer's ghetto', pp. 1–8.
37. Zonana, 'Kramer vs. the world', p. 46
38. Kramer, 'Sex and sensibility', p. 59.
39. Califia, 'Slipping', p. 87. A comparable AIDS-era perspective on the history of sexual practice was expressed elsewhere in the same year, in James V. Hart's screenplay for Francis Ford Coppola's version of that classic novel of 'dangerously' transformational bisexual promiscuity, *Bram Stoker's Dracula*. In that film (but not in Stoker's novel), Dr Van Helsing amuses a lecture theatre of young scientists by observing that 'civilisation and syphilisation have advanced together.'
40. Rotello's thesis – that gay male culture is a uniquely structured ecological system where sexually transmitted diseases are being bred in ever-growing and ever-mutating numbers through promiscuity – has been concisely dismantled by two progressive critics. Michael Warner has observed that Rotello's use of the metaphor of sexual ecology 'is never more than a metaphor, since sexual cultures have neither the boundedness nor the co-ordination of functions that define ecosystems.' (Warner, 'Media gays', p. 15.) Joshua Oppenheimer has criticised 'Rotello's . . . direct equation of the fast-paced and mutation-prone replication of HIV. . . [with] the replication of other viruses and micro-organisms (such as herpes simplex). HIV replication is unique because the virus attacks the very apparatus that would otherwise prevent unfettered reproduction: the immune system itself. This is no small mistake, because it is the lynchpin for Rotello's ominous prediction that unless the gay community completely reconfigures its sexual life, other viruses as devastating as AIDS will surely emerge in the communal petri dish in the near future. He forgets that all other viruses and bacteria meet an awesomely powerful match in the human immune system.' (Oppenheimer, 'Unforgiving errors', p. 41.) As with Kramer's direct linking of promiscuity with disease, 'Rotello refuses to acknowledge . . . that if the vast majority of gay men would use condoms correctly, whenever they have anal intercourse – with as many partners as they choose, as often as they like, anonymously or in the context of a relationship – this would be a genuine and dramatic ecological change. The gay community would not remain a healthy niche for HIV transmission' (p. 43). Oppenheimer perhaps overestimates the potential effects of complex, non-sloganeering AIDS education in halting unsafe sex, given the diverse and long-term psychical difficulties that can lead gay men to forego safe sex. Yet Rotello's call for monogamy and/or marriage is far less attuned to these psychical difficulties than such non-judgemental AIDS educational strategies.
41. Holleran, *Ground Zero*, p. 114.
42. Of course, promiscuity *has* frequently been used to explain personal and cultural catastrophe.

43. Giteck, 'Larry Kramer', p. 27.
44. From an interview in the BBC *Omnibus* documentary *Larry Kramer* (1992, dir. Brian Skeet).
45. Kramer, *Reports*, p. 94.
46. My elision here only removes the words 'as I said', rather than any qualifying remark.
47. Altman, *Homosexualization*, p. 190.
48. Holleran, *Ground Zero*, p. 122.
49. Crimp, 'How to have promiscuity', p. 253.
50. Redick, 'Dangerous practices', p. 97.
51. Altman, *Homosexualization*, p. 187.
52. And of course, even within those public representations, non-normative sexual desires and practices are often hypocritically punished by narrative's end.
53. Kramer, *Reports*, p. 274.
54. Jay, 'The spirit is liberationist', p. 211.
55. Watney, *Policing Desire*, p. 48.
56. Barrett and McIntosh, *The Anti-Social Family*, p. 55.
57. Ibid.
58. D'Emilio and Freedman, *Intimate Matters*, pp. 79 and 81–2. D'Emilio and Freedman's observation clearly resonates variously throughout twentieth-century popular discourse as well. On the 'double standard', see also Gibson, *Dissolving Wedlock*, pp. 76–7; and Barrett and McIntosh, *The Anti-Social Family*, pp. 71–6.
59. Barrett and McIntosh, *The Anti-Social Family*, p. 56.
60. Ibid., p. 54.
61. Creed, 'Horror and the monstrous-feminine', p. 65.
62. However, cultural understandings of sexual practice are obviously also tightly bound up with other factors, including gender identification. Bob and Rod's butch bodybuilding image, for instance, further endows them with the cultural privilege of 'masculinity'. Ironically, the couple divorced in 1996, revealing that they had privately separated some time earlier, but had remained together in order to sustain their public images as models of gay monogamy.
63. Kramer, *Reports*, p. 274.
64. However, while Leo Bersani has argued that queer reworkings of existing normalised familial terms in unconventional circumstances are 'too closely imbricated in the norms they continue' (Bersani, *Homos*, p. 51), I would argue that, unlike marriage, the concept and practice of 'the family' need not always be quite as tightly dependent upon normativity-privileging ideology. The notion of the 'chosen' or 'extended' family might best symbolise the needs and experiences of non-assimilatory lesbians and gays (and, indeed, many others): such a family is extended outwards in diverse directions from the primary supportive nucleus, and hence remains relatively open to incorporating new members, whether as occasional lovers, long-term partners or non-sexual friends (unlike the dominant model, which privileges a very small range of internal interrelationships, and only authenticates new members through marriage or long-term monogamous coupledom). See also Weston, *Families We Choose*.
65. Howes, 'Where love has gone', p. 28. Note the slippage between 'relationship' and marriage here ('extra-marital exuberance'). Ironically, marriage is being used as the model for deceitful non-monogamy.

66. Ibid.
67. This notion of the mutuality of disgust and desire is explored more fully in Stallybrass and White, *The Politics and Poetics of Transgression*.
68. Creed, 'Horror and the monstrous-feminine', p. 64; emphasis added.
69. Ibid.
70. My understanding of the impossibility of an identical 'reproduction', given the *re*-constructive process of producing and sustaining ideology, is indebted to the work of Judith Butler.
71. Creed, 'Horror and the monstrous-feminine', p. 66.
72. Ibid.
73. Ibid., p. 67.
74. Kristeva, *Powers of Horror*, p. 9.
75. Ibid., p. 18.
76. In fact, Holleran's novel was originally entitled *Letters from an American Faggot*, but his publisher 'insisted that something less likely to cause embarrassment at the nation's cash registers be chosen.' Howes, 'Where love has gone', p. 27.
77. Getlin, 'Kramer vs. Kramer', p. E3.
78. From an interview in the BBC *Larry Kramer* documentary.
79. Altman, *Homosexualization*, p. 188.
80. Scott Tucker wrote: 'The novel is a patch-and-paste job of free association, and what passes for characterization and insight could have been lifted from a sophomore's psych notes.' (Tucker, 'Ivory towers', p. 26.) Kramer recalls that 'even though the book was a best-seller, at the time I was wounded and frightened by the criticism. I found myself actually shunned by friends. My best friend stopped speaking to me, even to this day. People would cross the street to avoid me.' (Kramer, *Reports*, p. 6.) New York's Oscar Wilde Memorial Bookshop refused to stock the novel for several years (ibid., p. 19), and George Whitmore in *The Body Politic* even asked readers to boycott it. (Whitmore, 'Beer, baloney and champagne', p. 13.) Perhaps because of cultural distance, the European gay press was more favourable towards, and even championing of, *Faggots*.
81. Altman, *Homosexualization*, p. 188.
82. Ibid.
83. From an interview in the BBC *Larry Kramer* documentary.
84. 'Satire' entry in the Oxford English Dictionary.
85. *The Advocate*'s reviewer of *Faggots* complained of 'the built-in promiscuity... [of its] long lists [,with e]very item being equal to every other item.' Maves, review of *Faggots*, pp. 28–9.
86. In an *Advocate* interview coinciding with the novel's publication, Kramer was reminded that 'you've said that Fred Lemish and Larry Kramer are basically the same person.' Giteck, 'Larry Kramer', p. 28.
87. Kramer, *Faggots*, p. 28.
88. Ibid., pp. 24–5.
89. Ibid., p. 30.
90. Ibid.
91. Ibid., p. 29.
92. Ibid., p. 224.
93. Ibid., p. 125.
94. Katz, *The Invention of Heterosexuality*, p. 86.
95. Kramer, *Faggots*, p. 16.
96. Altman, *Homosexualization*, p. 175.

97. Califia, *Public Sex*, pp. 200–3.
98. Altman, *Homosexualization*, p. 176.
99. Kramer, *Faggots*, p. 36.
100. Ibid.
101. Ibid., p. 43.
102. Ibid., p. 194.
103. Ibid., p. 325.
104. From an interview in the BBC *Larry Kramer* documentary.
105. Kramer, *Faggots*, p. 232.
106. Ibid., p. 232.
107. Ibid., p. 233.
108. Califia, *Sapphistry*, p. 56.
109. Kramer, *Faggots*, p. 232.
110. Ibid., p. 326.
111. 'Men' and 'faggots' are apparently mutually exclusive categories here.
112. Kramer, *Faggots*, p. 327.
113. Kramer, *Reports*, p. 273.
114. On a related note, contrary to the naturalisation of cross-sex desires within conventional theories of animal behaviour, a recent study conducted on a chimpanzee group in the Ivory Coast suggests that 'half of all chimpanzees may be conceived on the sly when females sneak off for risky trysts with males outside of their social group.' While 'evolutionary biologists often treat females as a prize to be won by the most deserving male,' Professor Pascal Gagneaux of the University of California at San Diego, involved in the Ivory Coast study, argues that 'females are not some sort of resource that just wait there like fruit to be picked.... Females have their own agenda.' (Crenson, 'Chimpanzees sleep around', p. A17.) On myths of female animal and human sexual desires, see also Angier, *Woman: An Intimate Geography*.
115. D'Emilio and Freedman, *Intimate Matters*, p. 79.
116. Krafft-Ebing, *Psychopathia Sexualis*, p. 13.
117. Katz, *The Invention of Heterosexuality*, p. 31.
118. Orr, 'Say grace', p. 14.
119. A similar 1970s scene featuring a family lesson on promiscuity takes place in Rita Mae Brown's *Rubyfruit Jungle* (1973). Interestingly, promiscuous wisdom is here exchanged back and forth between teenage dyke Molly and her father, albeit with a more conventional warning against public openness about one's sexual practice. Father: '"It'd kill me to see you buckle under to anyone, especially a husband." "Well, don't worry about it 'cause it'll never happen. Besides, why should I buy a cow when I get the milk for free? I can go out and screw anytime I damn well please." He laughed. "People are silly about sex. But if you'll take a word of advice from your old man – do it all you want but be quiet about it"' (p. 92).
120. Lorde, *Zami*, p. 213.
121. Rechy, *City of Night*, p. 337.
122. DeLynn, *Don Juan in the Village*, pp. 236–7.
123. Kramer, *Faggots*, p. 261. Similarly, Ephra's agreement to let Abe move back in while finalising his divorce from his fourth wife, 'not ... [because she] either wanted him or was forgiving' but because her 'large Park Avenue apartment ... was in his name and he still like to live in it' (p. 47), represents the passionless complications that can arise from marital, or ex-marital, economic interdependence.

124. Ibid., p. 21.

125. Ibid., p. 261.

126. The phrase comes from Bruce Mailman, who opened both the Saint and New St Marks Baths in New York; quoted in Holleran, 'Steam, soap, and sex', p. 100.

127. Kramer, *Faggots*, pp. 173–4.

128. This apologetic address of a self-distancing straight onlooker is reproduced at the wider level of the novel's third-person narration. As Fred humours Abe to gain finance for his monogamy-centred film, so Kramer's clearly authorial narration occasionally attempts to gain mainstream heterosexual approval for his monogamy-centred novel by directly addressing its didactic view of gay promiscuity to a normative straight readership: 'Of the 2,639,857 faggots in the New York City area, 2,639,857 think primarily with their cocks. You didn't know that the cock was a thinking organ? Well, by this time, you should know that it is' (p. 224). Apart from re-emphasising that Fred is amongst these cock-centred 'faggots', this echo of the novel's opening sentence ('There are 2,556,596 faggots in the New York City area': p. 15) appears to serve mainly as an assurance for Kramer that the range of gay characters introduced up to this point have not clouded outsiders' understanding of the novel's monogamous stance on gay sex.

129. Rose, *Sexuality in the Field of Vision*, p. 46.

130. One prominent institutionalised example of this appropriation can be seen in the American 'No Cruising' signs that warn kerb crawlers away from picking up sex workers: cruising in your car has shifted into also signifying cruising for sex.

131. I would, however, disagree that flirting is synonymous with cruising; both in gay culture and elsewhere, flirting offers a less goal-oriented range of thrills.

132. George Chauncey similarly notes, in relation to early twentieth-century New York City, that 'the purposes and tactics of gay men out cruising resembled those of young men and women out looking for a date in many respects. The casual pickups men made on the streets were hardly unique to male couples in this era, for many young women depended on being picked up by men to finance their excursions to music halls and amusement parks.' Chauncey, *Gay New York*, p. 202.

133. Kramer, *Faggots*, pp. 283–4.

134. Holleran, *Dancer*, pp. 24–5. I am not suggesting that such nostalgia and desire for an idealised 'stable' life – heterosexual or otherwise – should not be acknowledged or explored. Yet while *Dancer from the Dance*'s invocation of such ambivalent, sometimes self-loathing, rarely discussed gay longings is one of its many strengths, it also tends to portray promiscuous homosexual desire as inherently tragic and doomed; an aspect of the novel that is often overlooked or 'excused', given its stylistic excellence, frequent complexity, and precision in evoking ambivalent emotions and moods.

135. Kramer, *Faggots*, p. 103.

136. Ibid., p. 104.

137. Ibid.

138. Ibid., p. 23.

139. Ibid., pp. 137–8.

140. He passes and tries to 'ignore [a] handpainted flourescent warning: LAST JULY A GUY WAS MURDERED HERE AND ROBBED OF HIS CARTIER WATCH AND

STABBED IN THE GUTS with under-scrawling: "Glad to hear someone's got guts"' (p. 138).

141. 'By making all violence external, pushing it to the outside and objectifying it in "enemy" institutions and individuals, we deny its psychic articulation, deny that we are effected, as well as affected, by it. . . . [B]y ignoring the death drive, . . . we fail to confront ourselves, to acknowledge our ambivalence, to comprehend our misery is also self-inflicted.' Crimp, 'Mourning and militancy', pp. 242–3.

142. Rechy, *The Sexual Outlaw*, p. 27.

143. Kramer, *Faggots*, p. 195.

144. Freud, 'On the universal tendency to debasement', p. 258.

145. Cowie, 'Fantasia', p. 80.

146. Kramer, *Faggots*, p. 382.

147. Cowie, 'Fantasia', p. 80.

148. *The Advocate*'s reviewer of the novel asked, teasingly: 'Does Larry Kramer himself believe . . . that "Our sexual fantasies are ruining us"? Or is that just lip service to some fashionable ideal so that the lips may more freely service quite other ideals in the raunchier portions of *Faggots*?' Maves, review of *Faggots*, p. 29.

149. Kramer, *Faggots*, p. 335.

150. Ibid., p. 332.

151. Ibid., p. 339.

152. Ibid., p. 381.

153. Ibid., p. 382–3.

154. Tennyson, *Tennyson*, pp. 73–5.

155. Kramer, *Faggots*, p. 382.

156. Ibid., pp. 382–3.

157. Kristeva, *Powers of Horror*, p. 10.

158. Kramer, *Faggots*, p. 380.

159. Interview in Burton, *Talking To* . . . , p. 82.

160. In the BBC *Arena* documentary, the author comments that 'of everything I've written, *The Normal Heart* is probably the most factual.'

161. Crimp, 'How to have promiscuity', pp. 247–9.

162. Kramer, *The Normal Heart*, p. 115.

163. Crimp, 'How to have promiscuity', p. 247.

164. Kramer, *The Normal Heart*, p. 51.

165. Ibid., p. 103.

166. Ibid., p. 114.

167. Kramer has argued that 'I tried to make Ned Weeks as obnoxious as I could. He isn't my idea of a hero. He fucks up totally. . . . I was trying, somehow and again, to atone for my own behavior. I tried to make Bruce Niles, . . . [based on GMHC member] Paul Popham . . . , the sympathetic leader he in fact was.' Kramer, *Reports*, p. 93.

168. Kramer, *The Normal Heart*, p. 52.

169. Ibid., p. 122.

170. Morrison, *Playing In the Dark*, p. 3.

171. Julien and Mercer, 'Race, sexual politics and black masculinity', pp. 132–3.

172. Davies et al., *Sex, Gay Men and AIDS*, p. 32.

173. Tucker, 'Larry Kramer's ghetto', p. 8.

174. Although Kramer regularly draws analogies between the treatment of queers or people with AIDS and the Nazi persecution of Jews (and queers), Lawrence D. Mass observes that 'he is silent about anti-Semitism in the world today. In terms of his current work – his novel

The American People, which is very much about Jews and American history – Larry's stance can be appreciated as being parallel to his position *vis-à-vis* gay people at the time he wrote *Faggots*: as a critic who had extremely important and valuable things to say but who did so from a standpoint of detachment, of not yet entering the fray himself.' Mass, 'Larry versus Larry,' p. 17.

175. Kramer, *Reports*, p. 273.
176. Rofes, *Reviving the Tribe*, p. 98. In a 1992 article, Michael Callen similarly noted that, unsurprisingly, 'many people with AIDS go through a period of abstinence.' Callen and Caviano, 'Sex after AIDS', p. 41.
177. Watney, Foreword to *Reports*, pp. xxviii–xxix.
178. Zonana, 'Kramer vs. the world', p. 48.
179. Or perhaps not. In a 1997 *Advocate* article, the (since deceased) Scott O'Hara explained his decision, as an HIV-positive man, to stop using condoms: 'I may die at a younger age than my gay brothers who are more cautious, [and] who limit the number of their sexual contacts . . . And you know something? I decided a long time ago that it was worth it. There may be safety in reduced numbers, but safety has never been my goal.' O'Hara, 'Safety first?,' p. 9.

'A Landscape for Drifting':
Promiscuity, Fantasy and Travel
in the Memoirs
of David Wojnarowicz

It was a landscape for drifting, where time expands and contracts and vision is replaced by memories; small filmlike bursts of bodies and situations, some months ago, some years ago.

David Wojnarowicz, *Close to the Knives*[1]

In the summer of 1995, *Out* magazine interviewed Jim Lyons, star of the newly released film *Postcards from America*, based on the life of gay artist, AIDS activist and writer David Wojnarowicz, who had died from AIDS-related illness in 1992. In this brief interview, the actor who had portrayed Wojnarowicz's life recalled his own past:

It was, as Jim Lyons likes to put it, 'the tail end of the clone thing.' It was 1978, and the actor and film editor had left Port Jefferson on Long Island to study English at New York University. 'When I got to school, I read the book *Faggots*,' he says. . . . 'It set my coming out back five years.' We are both laughing, but not really. 'I found myself very alienated from gay culture. I hated the apolitical bit of it.'[2]

In an uncanny way, Lyons's words might be seen to echo the sentiments of David Wojnarowicz himself (with whom Lyons also shares a remarkable physical resemblance). Like Lyons, Wojnarowicz 'hated' – or at best, expressed antipathy towards – 'the apolitical' or socially myopic aspects of gay culture, and culture at large: his 'life and work were driven by a desire for justice more than by any particular political agenda; he insisted upon challenging and dismantling what he termed a "pre-invented existence," which discriminates and imposes hierarchies on the bases of sexual preference, race, ethnicity, . . . gender' and class.[3]

Indeed, in his fervent and increasingly public attacks on diverse American manifestations of apathy and inhumanity from the late 1980s until his death, Wojnarowicz could also be compared, momentarily, to Larry Kramer. And for differing reasons, his status as a perpetual 'outsider who refused to be taken in'[4] echoes Kramer's (more condescending) frequent sense of alienation from gay culture, and also Rechy's earlier ambivalent cultural affiliation: while he was gay-identified, Wojnarowicz 'never felt kinship with the gay community, at least the visible gay community, except for what we all have to endure. I just can't relate.'[5] This similarity between all three prominent gay male writers and cultural figures also suggests the ambiguous, 'non-monogamous' relationship that so many of us have towards our inclusion within the always shifting parameters of gay (or any other) culture and identity.

Yet beyond these superficial comparisons with Kramer, Wojnarowicz, like Lyons, is unlikely to have admired Kramer's novel, not only because of its 'apolitical' qualities, but also because of its largely antipromiscuous tone. In a 1990 interview with New York photographer Nan Goldin, he reflected back on the complexity and diversity of his sexual history, commenting that although 'after my [HIV] diagnosis I had to rearrange *how* I have sex,' throughout his life:

an element of my sexuality had always been fantasy, or in . . . anonymous sex. . . . It's something I . . . loved about growing up in the seventies, and going over to the warehouses occasionally, or in the parks, or in the subways, or four o'clock in the morning on a train going to Brooklyn.[6]

Elsewhere, Wojnarowicz expressed his continuing defence of promiscuous desires, as well as multiple 'anonymous' sexual encounters, in a characteristically angry response to:

a recent review of a[n unspecified] novel in the *new york times book review*, [where] a reviewer took outrage at the novelist's descriptions of promiscuity, saying, 'In this age of AIDS, the writer should show more restraint . . .' Not only do we have to contend with bonehead newscasters and conservative members of the medical profession telling us to 'just say no' to sexuality itself rather than talk about safer sex possibilities, but we have people from the thought police spilling out from the ranks with admonitions that we shouldn't *think* about anything other than monogamous or safer sex. I'm beginning to believe that one of the last frontiers left for radical gesture is the imagination.[7]

These statements encapsulate two central aspects of Wojnarowicz's life and his highly autobiographical texts: his pleasure (as an adult) in promiscuous sex and desires, and his conceptualisation of sex/uality as centrally informed by, and experienced through, fantasy. In the above interview with Goldin, for example, he notes that in his brief sexual encounters, 'I would project . . . [a "created biography"] on to the other guy that I was engaging in sexual activities with – the sum total of desires.'[8] Moreover, his first memory of sexual desire concerned the erotic associations aroused in him by a magazine image; a childhood precursor to adolescent masturbation fantasies:

I was sitting on the couch looking at a *TV Guide* and I came across a soap advertisement with this guy under a stream of running water, lathering himself up. And there was something about his face, his lips, his arms, the bicep – I went into a trance. It must have lasted an hour and a half.[9]

And both of these comments are summarised in the writer's reflection that 'it is the appearance of a portrait, not the immediate vision I love so much.'[10] For Wojnarowicz, then, it was clear that fantasy not only articulated, but also constructed – brought into being and shaped – 'the sum total' of his desires.

While much insightful criticism has appeared on Wojnarowicz's art-work, photography and (somewhat reluctant) status as 'probably the most acclaimed of all the East Village artists'[11] who rose to prominence during New York's mid-1980s art scene boom,[12] almost none of the existing work has addressed his writings, and their central concern with gay sexual practice, in any detail.[13] In this chapter, I examine the complex and lyrical accounts of promiscuous sex and desire in Wojnarowicz's writings, and the significance of their repeated return to the cultural 'value of unrestricted fantasy, unrestricted thought.'[14] Wojnarowicz's emphasis on fantasy can be seen to produce a more sustained depathol-ogising exploration of psychical mobility and ambivalence in relation to gay male promiscuity – and specifically, gay sex during the AIDS crisis – than we found in Kramer's, or even Rechy's equally autobio-graphical fiction. This concern with psychical reality and mobility is also externalised, in the recurring form of Kerouac-like travel scenarios 'on the road' across America, which in turn lead to a greater diversity of erotic fantasies and encounters – as the author/artist underlined: 'all my work sprang out of travel.'[15] I therefore also investigate the rela-tionship between promiscuous travel, sexuality and desire produced in these narratives, and also their wider cultural resonances and implications.

These Kerouac-informed coast-to-coast journeys also share Rechy's erotic restlessness. On the whole, however, Wojnarowicz's poetic pleasure in the fleeting details and lasting psychical traces of brief encounters arguably produces a more consistently complex rendition of gay male promiscuity than Rechy's fiction. To be more specific, although both writers express an erotic fascination with butch (and/or straight) men, unlike Rechy's variously defensive and self-conscious machismo, Wojnarowicz only ever indirectly identifies with conventional forms of 'masculinity'. (More on this later.)

Wojnarowicz's accounts of 'bottom-line, sidewalk lust'[16] can also be seen to complicate dominant notions of 'compulsory' monogamous romantic love. Yet they often express a co-existent desire for an idealised, romantic 'coastal dream . . . of . . . some timeless place where the past was forgettable and there was just some guy with a tough stomach to lie against, and I could listen to his heartbeat sounding through his trembling skin.'[17] Hence, in contrast to my discussion of the varied forms of promiscuity that invariably recur within monogamous structures in the previous chapter, I now explore the frequent romanticism of apparently unattached promiscuous sexuality as well, and what that promiscuous romanticism suggests about the nature of romantic fantasy in general.[18]

A SOLITARY LIFE (?)

Wojnarowicz's sense of distance from 'the visible gay community' is relatively unsurprising within the context of his early life experiences. These past events resurface repeatedly throughout his published writing, whether in the diaristic juxtaposition of memories, fantasies and dreams in *Close to the Knives: A Memoir of Disintegration* (1991), *Memories That Smell Like Gasoline* (1992) and *In the Shadow of the American Dream: The Diaries of David Wojnarowicz* (1999); in the 'tragicomic comic book'[19] based on his youth, *Seven Miles a Second* (1996); or scattered amongst the monologues of various people he encountered while travelling and later transcribed from memory, collected in *Sounds in the Distance* (1982) and *The Waterfront Journals* (1996).[20]

While the revisiting of past events is obviously the basis for all personal experience-based literature, it is especially pronounced in Wojnarowicz's quintessentially autobiographical texts. Elizabeth Hess has noted that 'Wojnarowicz shatters his narrative[s] and displays the shards as if they were competing with each other for attention.'[21] Yet at the same time, these fantasmatically splintered narratives of actual and imagined events are also characterised by a confrontationally direct prose style, which frustrates any attempt on the reader's part to separate the content of the text from its surrounding personal and wider cultural context. A speculation offered up by art critic Carlo McCormick in relation to Wojnarowicz's art work might also be applied

to the artist's written texts: their 'immediacy and directness . . .
induces – even demands – a rare degree of personal introspection.'[22]
These writings therefore actively demand a materialist response that
takes account of the writer's (and, by implication, the reader's) own
subjectivity and cultural location, as well as the broader sociopolitical
questions being raised.[23]

Like *City of Night*, Wojnarowicz's writings partly record his childhood physical, and also sexual, abuse by his father. The details given
in his 'Biographical dateline' (1990), a short year-by-year chronicle of
his life, reappear across the other texts. After his parents divorced in
1956 when he was two years old, his sailor father alternately neglected
and terrorised David and his siblings: 'He would shoot guns off in the
livingroom missing us and sometimes put the guns to our heads,'[24] or
he would 'beat [them] with dog chains and two-by-fours.'[25] As with
Rechy, and so often generally, this physical and psychological patriarchal
violence was also eroticised by his father. On one occasion, after the
seven-year-old Wojnarowicz responded to a masochistic nineteen-year-
old bully's sexual demands by wrapping 'a handful of insulation . . .
around his dick and [pulling],' Wojnarowicz's father was summoned to
the boy's house:

After two hours of sitting on the driveway my father took me home and beat
me. He pulled out his dick at some point and told me to play with it. I said
no and he beat me some more.[26]

At 'a very young age[,] about eight or nine,'[27] Wojnarowicz began hustling in Times Square, and continued hustling, on and off, to survive
on the streets (in between attending and dropping out of art school)
until he was seventeen and began travelling across North America –
and later, went on to become an internationally acclaimed artist.[28] In
his writings, Wojnarowicz underlines the direct psychical links
between his confusingly violent sexual initiation by his father (and by
older boys), the general absence of affection from his parents, and his
initial entry into prostitution: in *Close to the Knives*, he recalls 'walking around times square looking for the weight of some man to lie
across me to replace the non-existent hugs and kisses from my mom
and dad.'[29] As with the young narrator of *City of Night*, though, it is the
ambiguously erotic psychical imprint left by his father's sexual hostility
that remained the strongest:

I have always been attracted to dangerous men, men whose gestures inti-
mated the possibilities of violence, and I have always seduced them into
states of gentle grace with my hands and lips. I have loved the sweetness of
their blushing long after our body fluids stopped their arcing motions and

settled onto the sheets; the sweet flush of their embarrassment at the real-ization of the tenderness of their momentary gestures.[30]

This eroticisation both of 'masculine' power and its momentary disrup-tion exemplifies Pat Califia's observation that one important – though not always conscious – 'strategy for dealing with oppression is to eroti-cize certain signs which symbolize it and transform them into signs imbued with meaning supplied by the [marginalised individual or group].'[31]

Of course, the un/conscious shaping of sexuality in response to actual (as well as fantasised) familial interrelationships is far from spe-cific to Wojnarowicz, or homosexual or promiscuous desires generally. In the same closing section of *Close to the Knives* that the above passage appears in, Wojnarowicz highlights this point as he reflects that traumatic childhood familial experiences are a (largely heterosexually instigated) cultural commonplace:

I sat in the park in Merida [while visiting Mexico,] wondering how much heterosexuals really love each other. Everyone I know has come from a childhood where they suffered some element of abuse at the hands of their parents. They watched the marriages of their parents turn into ugly battle-grounds whose parameters were defined by the four sides of a house.[32]

Even when these early traumas or abuses are not explicitly sexual or physical, they cannot help but have a formative – if also unpredictable – effect upon the youth's subsequent sexuality (just as any early, or later, significant experiences may impact upon sexuality, and on sub-jectivity as a whole). At the same time, Wojnarowicz's own specific fantasmatic search for a placatory 'union' with 'dangerous men' also reminds us that sexuality and desire are always as much predicated upon the eroticisation of that which is withheld (in this case, paternal affection), as upon the eroticisation of that which is directly experi-enced and enforced.

At a more general level, Wojnarowicz's alienating early experiences of being moved between – and often neglected by – his parents and relatives, and then surviving on the streets of New York, ultimately produced a pleasurable yearning for that initially enforced state of isolation and transition: 'I've always loved being anonymous and moving around, travelling. . . . that's the most powerful state for me to be in. Away from any references. . . . That's where my life makes sense.'[33] Hence, that sense of nomadic anonymity imposed upon him by cir-cumstances later became a conscious source of empowerment.

Moreover, as the memoirs and monologue pieces clarify, these expe-riences of rootlessness and neglect also led Wojnarowicz to an unusually acute awareness of a broad range of cultural interconnections, which are conventionally disavowed and made separate within dominant social 'pyramids of power and confinement'.[34] As David Cole comments in relation to Wojnarowicz's visual art, 'David's theme was often solitude (the underside of independence), but nothing exists in isolation' in his work.[35] Core cultural binarisms are repeatedly questioned and blurred in his collages, paintings and photography, as well as in his writings – especially dominant divisions between reality/fantasy, culture/nature, human/animal, life/death, present/past, urban/rural, private/public and rich/poor. (I'll return to some of these later.)

In particular, Wojnarowicz's working-class background, long-term homelessness, and subsequent sense of affiliation with the socioeconomically disenfranchised 'tribe I had left'[36] on the streets, all made the notion of a primary allegiance to visible gay culture highly problematic for him – and all the more so in the case of the affluence-oriented commercial gay scene. Just as Rechy's early narratives of hustling and diverse street lives 'want to talk to everybody,'[37] so Wojnarowicz's distance from socioeconomic security throughout his youth partly led him to produce complex representations of multiple marginalised cultural experiences and struggles (principally, but not exclusively, related to AIDS, class, sexuality and gender) that 'have attracted a sizeable audience made up [perhaps] equally of gays and non-gays.'[38] Thus, while his self-declared literary touchstones were Burroughs, Genet and Rimbaud,[39] the frequent foregrounding of class dynamics in his erotic narratives also links him to gay filmmaker/writers like Fassbinder and Pasolini, and lesbian and gay writers like Dorothy Allison, James Baldwin, Jane DeLynn, Audre Lorde and Sarah Schulman. In more general terms, although Wojnarowicz resisted categorisation, his self-reflexive representation of sexuality as relative to, and interdependent with, other cultural factors intersects with the more progressive strands of queer subjectivity and thought.[40]

SEXUAL AND INTELLECTUAL PROMISCUITY

Wojnarowicz's transformation of his imposed rootlessness into narratives of cultural interrelatedness and diversity was also centrally influenced by his promiscuous sexuality. On the one hand, that sexuality was initially an effect of his family life and class position: abuse and neglect led him to homelessness and hustling, in a search for 'nonexistent hugs and kisses' as well as sustenance. But on the other hand, in his late adolescence, promiscuity became 'something . . . [he] loved about growing up in the seventies' – a pleasure that also continued to shape, and broaden, his cultural perspective throughout his adult life. In several very important ways, then, Wojnarowicz's sexual promiscuity may be seen to have informed, and in turn been informed by, his intellectual promiscuity.

By this I mean that throughout his writings, his interest in cultural diversity and mutability, at both the psychical and material level, is closely bound up with the wide range and short-lived nature of many of his sexual (and other social) encounters. In *Close to the Knives*, for instance, he expresses his desire for difference through the example of a momentary sexual partner:

I found him sexy because I love difference. An unbearably handsome face bores me unless something beneath its surface is crooked or askew: even a broken nose or one eye slightly higher than the other, or something psychological, *something unfamiliar.*[41]

Of course, as we have already repeatedly seen in this study, any individual's sexual desires and practices never simply reflect their subjectivity and ideological perspective. (Hence, I will also address Wojnarowicz's partly identificatory desire for 'masculine'/straight men later.) Yet in this particular case, sex and ideology can often be seen to shape one other: promiscuous sexual practice influences promiscuous thought, and vice versa.

Wojnarowicz's work therefore refutes the dominant cultural overvaluation of supposedly 'permanent' forms of subjectivity and experience, both sexual and otherwise. As Edmund White summarises:

In conventional, straight America, people honor only the permanent and dismiss, even forget (or at least forget to mention) the transitory. Only what lasts is good. This prejudice in favor of what endures is unfortunate, I'd say, a concession to social institutions rather than a recognition of human experiences.[42]

Wojnarowicz's desire and respect for 'the transitory' exemplify a widespread – if by no means universal – queer sexual and political resistance to the dominant normalisation of 'permanence'. As in Wojnarowicz's (and Rechy's) case, this common queer embrace of transience often stems from a first-hand experience – enforced by homophobic/heterocentric culture – of the dispersed, unstable nature of 'home', and of any sense of sexual and emotional belonging. But at the same time, as Wojnarowicz clarifies, that queer knowledge of contingency and change is often gained to a considerable degree through promiscuous sexual experience.

'THE EXTENDED SECONDS OF A CRUISING NATURE': PROMISCUITY AND FANTASY

More specifically, Wojnarowicz's remembered narratives of promiscuous sexuality are largely articulated through the constantly shifting realm of fantasy. In contrast to Rechy's often perfunctory and mainly graphic descriptions of his sexual encounters, Wojnarowicz recounts his own sexual experiences amongst the ruins of Manhattan warehouses and piers, in parks and in rural highway rest stops, as much – if not more – for the associations and fantasies they stir up, as for the physical pleasure that, according to conventional wisdom, is supposedly the sole effect of promiscuous (yet, conveniently enough, not also monogamous) sexual practice.

My aim here is not to reproduce a normative value judgement, whereby the intricacies of Wojnarowicz's sex narratives are privileged over and above Rechy's sometimes complex, but often more straight-forwardly descriptive accounts. That prevailing distinction between 'worthy erotica' and 'base pornography' hypocritically attempts to place shame upon the physical pleasure, and frequent intellectual abandonment, of sex. Instead, as will become clear, my main intention here is to problematise dominant discourses that devalue and dismiss promiscuity, by focusing on Wojnarowicz's fascination with the effects of fantasy upon promiscuous sex in particular, and upon sexual practice in general.

In the notes accompanying his 1989 exhibition, *In the Shadow of Forward Motion*, Wojnarowicz recalls:

back when I was seventeen years old hanging out in central park and this cute guy was standing around the park entrance and we kept locking eyes and I felt this sexual flush because the eye signals we exchanged had the extended seconds of a cruising nature[43]

This description of a sudden pick-up, translated into 'extended seconds' by the 'sexual flush' within and between the two men, outlines one of the complex psychical effects of cruising and promiscuous sex that are relayed throughout Wojnarowicz's memoirs. Here, the focus is on a sense of time expanding during the exchange of erotic 'eye signals', as the two gazing men create a circuit of desire that arouses the circular, self-regarding timelessness of the unconscious.

In this and every other description of promiscuous desire and sex in Wojnarowicz's texts, the brief erotic encounter with a stranger,[44] far from being inconsequential, is a particularly potent site of interweaving fantasies and memories that also ultimately produces its own signifi-cant, lasting psychical traces. In 'Losing the form in darkness' – one of

the opening sections of *Close to the Knives* – the ebb and flow of cruising figures inside a derelict building at dusk, and Wojnarowicz's own
meandering path and obscured vision amongst those other men, stimu-
late the author's imagination. He glimpses a passing figure:

He was moving in with the gradual withdrawal of light, a passenger on the
shadows, . . . passion lining the folds of his shirt . . . one eye like the oceans
in fading light, the other a great vacant yawn shadowed black as the image
of his leather jacket, all of it moved with mirage shivers over his heavy
shoulders. . . . I was losing myself in the language of his movements . . .
Outside the windows the river light turned from blues to grays to flashes of
rain. A serious dark veil ran the length of the horizon; there's a texture to it,
a seediness like dream darkness you can breathe in or be consumed by. . . .
The stranger turned on his heel in the gray light and passed into other rooms,
passing through layers of evening, like a dim memory, faceless for moments,
just the movements of his body across the floor, the light of doorway after
doorway casting itself across the length of his legs.[45]

In this passage, the delicate descriptions of a fleeting object of desire,
and of the darkening night outside the decaying building, exemplify
the simultaneously disconcerting and pleasurable disruption of conventional, self-assured vision and logic that can take place within the
roaming activity of cruising (and particularly so when that act of cruising
also inverts the authorised non-sexual function of a public space): 'I
was losing myself in the language of his movements.'
    The recurring reference to twilight and approaching darkness simi-
larly suggests a movement deeper into the realms of fantasy and
memory, as the cruising narrator progresses through a disorienting
'maze of hallways'[46] in search of sex. From this perspective, 'the gradual withdrawal of light' that accompanies the stranger's entry into the
room signals an increasing blurring and warping of consciousness in
direct proportion to the growing possibility of sexual contact. Hence,
as the narrator watches the handsome stranger's meandering movements,
a troubling, yet also fascinating, 'serious dark veil' covers 'the horizon'
of his perception, and the passing stranger invokes 'a dim memory';
and finally, the 'gray' twilight that had tenuously distinguished consciousness from fantasy is subsumed by the sexual 'seediness' of a
'dream darkness you can breathe in or be consumed by.' This particular
promiscuous subject chooses to 'breathe in' and embrace that disruptive 'dream darkness'.
    At the same time, the image of the stranger as 'a passenger on the
shadows', disappearing and reappearing in 'other rooms, passing through
layers of evening', also functions as a metaphor for any promiscuous
gay man cruising outdoors, alternately seeking sex and retreating (into
the dark; into bushes or cubicles; into a stranger's bedroom) from

hostile or sneering surveillance within the overwhelmingly heterosexualised sphere of 'public' space.

It is also significant that this passage is itself a memory, pieced
together 'later, sitting over coffee and remembering the cinematic
motions as if witnessed from a discreet distance,'[47] and then later
again, as it is recorded on the page. These progressively distant resig-
nifications of the dream-like cruising experience enact a variation on the
conscious secondary revision of dream and fantasy material, illustrating
the continuing resonance of that initially half-registered and disorienting brief encounter for Wojnarowicz. Thus, contrary to normative
notions of the 'indiscriminate wastefulness' and 'self-destructiveness'
of promiscuous sex and cruising (pace Kramer), Wojnarowicz's private,
and later public, journal records of his promiscuity work to underscore
the frequent psychical and intellectual importance of those experiences
for avowedly promiscuous gay men.

Moreover, these narratives also repeatedly imply that, in Peter
Burton's words, 'because of the casualness and anonymity of the contact, fantasy can be more easily fulfilled.'[48] Burton's remark refers
specifically to the auto-erotic projection of imaginary identities on to
brief sexual partners – what Wojnarowicz calls his own 'created
biography' for each unknown man. But in Wojnarowicz's texts, these
particular fantasies about individual partners are only one element
within a broader promiscuous engagement with fantasy, which becomes
heightened within the destabilising unfamiliarity of 'anonymous'
sex.[49] In these accounts, sexual promiscuity is therefore envisioned as
intellectually and imaginatively productive, rather than – as normative logic would have it – inherently empty and even destructive:

He had a tough face. It was square-jawed and barely shaven. Close-cropped
hair wiry and black, handsome like some face in old boxer photographs. . . .
He had a nose that might have once been broken in some dark avenue bar-
room in a distant city invented by some horny young kid. There was a
wealth of images in that jawline. . . . I lean down and find the neckline of his
sweater and draw it back and away from the nape of his neck which I gently
probe with my tongue. . . . In loving him, I saw men encouraging each other
to lay down their arms. . . . I saw a hand in prison dragging snow in from the
sill. In loving him, I saw great houses being erected that would soon slide
into the waiting and stirring seas. I saw him freeing me from the silences of
the interior life.[50]

Apart from the shared romanticism of these images, their seemingly
random relationship to one another at first sight belies another significant link: the images of a resistance to war and imprisonment emerge
beside a symbol of mutability at the heart of social structures (the

erosion of the 'great houses'). In other words, here promiscuous sex causes an intense conscious surfacing of fantasy material ('freeing me from the silences of the interior life') that could be seen to express a resistance to oppression: the 'men encouraging each other to lay down their arms'; the solitary prisoner craving freedom; the decline of 'great houses' of privilege. In this sense, promiscuous sex is seen to trigger promiscuously overlapping fantasies of social interdependence and change.

However, the fantasies within Wojnarowicz's original pier encounter may well have undergone a secondary revision in his written account, superimposing a greater degree of order on to the promiscuous scattering of his actual thought processes during that less-than-fully-conscious sexual experience. The resistance of the unconscious to notions of social progress would contradict the mutually reinforcing flow of utopian imagery between the author's subconscious and conscious in the above passage. (Hence, one alternative reading of this ambiguous chain of fantasised images might be as a less ideologically congruent juxtaposition of structure or restraint – war, prison, great houses – against the melting of structure, mirroring the melting and merging sensations of the sexual intimacy accompanying these fantasies.)

Furthermore, even at the manifest level of the narrative, there is a tension between Wojnarowicz's romantic fantasy of his sex partner as a 'tough' boxer, and the resistance to 'masculine' violence that the writer may be seen to momentarily fantasise during their sexual encounter. (We might compare this to Jim's tension between desiring, and being repulsed by, macho stud Steve during his threesome in *The Sexual Outlaw*.) So – to complicate my opening argument in this section – while Wojnarowicz's promiscuous sexuality does interact closely with his promiscuous intellectual insight into cultural diversity and change, that intellectual promiscuity cannot be presumed to be fully coherent or progressive. Instead, un/conscious desires and surrounding material circumstances constantly make competing claims upon his conscious politicised subjectivity, producing conflict and ambivalence.

Thus, in the passage above as elsewhere in his writing, Wojnarowicz's desire simultaneously *to placate* and *to have* the violent patriarch, through loving sex with a tough brief partner, is symptomatic of a continuous interplay between his promiscuous sexual practice, desires, un/conscious fantasies and ideological perspective that is, inescapably, complexly contradictory as well as mutually reinforcing. In short, the psychical mobility displayed in Wojnarowicz's accounts of promiscuous sex is necessarily constrained by material cultural parameters (here, the dominant privileging of masculinity within patriarchy), by the specific ingrained psychical traces left by personal history (here, a violent/absent patriarch during childhood), and by the unconscious (universal primal incestuous fantasies, made all too real by his father's sexual abuse).

But, if psychical reality is inseparable from personal history and cultural context, then, conversely, Wojnarowicz's sexual narratives may be seen to denaturalise conventional understandings of sexual activity by underlining that fantasy is not merely a decorative appendage to desire, but rather the basis for all conscious sexual desire and practice. As in the previous examples, the following scenario from 'Into the drift and sway' (a short narrative in *Memories That Smell Like Gasoline*) symbolises the writer's especially sharpened understanding of the structuring influence of fantasy within the defamiliarising environment of his promiscuous encounter.[51] At a highway rest stop, he sees 'a silhouette of a man in worker's pants'[52] step down from a truck. The writer/narrator[53] follows him into the bathroom, and enters the adjoining cubicle:

I . . . pulled down my pants and sat on the cold toilet and looked down to my sides and there was a puddle of water between the two stalls under the dividing panel and it reflected light from the overhead ceiling fixture and through its transparency was the squared outline of gray floor tiles and as I looked at it I realized that I could see the overhead-lit features of this truck driver and the pale wash of his eyes and jawline and cheek bones . . . and the puddle moved a bit breaking the image into wavy lines and pieces of light and when his face came back into focus and the water was still I held my breath so as not to disturb it.[54]

As the narrator watches 'a silhouette of a hard dick which . . . [the trucker] waved back and forth in the reflection',

his image for a moment looked like it was floating upside down beneath the surface of the floor and I was therefore floating right side up and from his vantage point I was floating upside down and he right side up.[55]

The narrative concludes as the two men end up together in the trucker's rig, with the narrator sucking the driver as 'his fingers and face scattered into shards of light.'[56]

This scenario provides a particularly apt metaphor for the mediation of sexual desire and practice through the promiscuous instability of fantasy. The aroused narrator observes his potential 'trick' through an image that, like the play of fantasy within psychical reality, disrupts the seeming 'transparency' of sexual perception and experience through its destabilisingly uncertain visualisation of the object of desire. Moreover, the crucial role of fantasy in *stimulating* (not just expressing) desire is indicated in this scenario, as the greater the narrator's erotic intensity becomes, the greater the fantasmatic disruption of his consciousness: as he sees 'a silhouette of a hard dick . . . in the reflection', the image momentarily appears to be 'floating upside down beneath the surface' (of the floor; but symbolically, also beneath the surface of consciousness). Thus, the narrator's attempt to fix the image of the masturbating trucker – or metaphorically, to fix his psychical perception of the erotic encounter – is complicated by the fantasmatic fracturing and multiplication of the image/encounter, which can only be momentarily stilled: 'when his face came back into focus and the water was still I held my breath so as not to disturb it.'[57]

Indeed, attempting to override the 'floating' psychical influence of fantasy (by searching for a static, 'true' image/experience) is here seen as a restrictive and artificial process that disrupts the *always fantasmatically produced* psychosomatic pleasure of the sexual encounter – just as holding one's breath prevents the physiologically necessary act of breathing. This suggestion of the innate production and perception of sexual desire and practice within the sphere of fantasy is repeated once again in the final description of the narrator's orgasm with the trucker, where the earlier fantasmatic 'breaking' up of his eroticised visual perception into multiple 'wavy lines and pieces of light' in the toilet cubicle is now climactically 'shattered into shards of light'.

On the one hand, as I noted before, this scenario (like Wojnarowicz's others) suggests that the non-naturalised setting and relative anonymity of semi-public promiscuous sex, and the comparative absence of attachment within most once-only promiscuous encounters generally, can enable a sharper insight into the governing influence of fantasy upon sexual desire and practice (alongside the fear of unwanted onlookers, arrest, or the potential threat of the unknown sex partner[58]).

On the other hand, Wojnarowicz's promiscuous insights also have a crucial general relevance, which relates equally to monogamous sexuality. For Wojnarowicz, the psychical structuring of perception through fantasy and memory is the principal bond between all forms of sexual subjectivity – 'the dislocation of familiarity'[59] as well as unfamiliarity. In the following passage from *Close to the Knives*, his conflation of vision and psyche highlights their inextricable interpenetration:

There really is no difference between memory and sight, fantasy and actual vision. Vision is made up of subtle fragmented movements of the eye. Those fragmented pieces of the world are turned and pressed into memory before they can register in the brain. Fantasized images are actually made up of millions of disjointed observations collected and collated into the forms and textures of thought.[60]

In this same narrative, he drives past a group of scantily clad highway workmen, and reflects that:

when I see the workers taking a rest break between the hot metal frames of the vehicles, it doesn't matter that they are all actually receding miles behind me on the side of the road. I'm already hooked into the play between vision and memory and recoding the filmic exchange between the two.[61]

Again, the emphasis in this scenario is on the production of conscious sexual desire through fantasy and memory; a recognition that, in Victor Burgin's words, 'there is no possible state of unambiguous and self-possessed lucidity in which the external world is seen for, and known as, simply what it is', given that 'sexual identity itself is produced through the agency of fantasy.'[62]

This concern with the destabilising effects of fantasy upon sexuality can be seen to have significant implications for the dominant normalisation of monogamy. Wojnarowicz's attention to the psychical merging of dreams and fantasies with memories and political commentary in his writing calls into question the dominant cultural fiction of the unified, 'self-possessed' desiring subject, and the presumed monogamous fixity of that ideal subject's sexual desires. For while the above quotations from *Close to the Knives* focus on the conscious collation of experience 'into the forms and textures of thought', without also considering the *un*conscious signification of that experience, Wojnarowicz nevertheless consistently stresses the promiscuous instability of desire *per se*. Thus, where normative sexual discourses construct a hierarchical distinction between the 'familiar order' of the authentic monogamous subject and the 'alien disorder' of the marginal promiscuous subject, Wojnarowicz recognises sexual subjectivity as 'a bundle of contradictions that shift constantly',[63] frustrating any claim to absolute erotic consistency or certainty.

Indeed, Wojnarowicz's central interest in his own fantasmatic responses to promiscuous sexual encounters, often over the physicality of the experience (seen most clearly in the retrospective fantasy of the road workers), points to the *auto-erotic* basis of all sexual desire, which, within the primal terms of the unconscious, 'is neither for a thing . . . nor for a person, but for a fantasy – the mnemic traces of a lost object.'[64] Conventional claims for the ethical correctness of 'stable' monogamous sexuality fail to comprehend this basic relativity and contingency of all object choice – monogamous or promiscuous – in comparison to the *unconscious* stability of the fantasised primary 'lost object' or objects[65] (alongside, of course, more individually specific profound 'mnemic traces').

To summarise, then, against dominant constructions of promiscuous desire as an alienating, destructive 'social problem', Wojnarowicz's sex narratives partly record the complex, lasting psychical (and immediate physical) effects and pleasures of multiple brief sexual encounters. As I have already noted, Wojnarowicz's texts indicate that psychical variability is at the centre of all forms of sexuality. Yet at the same time, Wojnarowicz's accentuation of his physical sexual promiscuity in his memoirs can be seen to contest dominant culture's schizophrenic split between policing and punishing diverse promiscuous practices on the one hand, and encouraging the persistent proliferation of promiscuous public fantasies on the other (for example, through popular narratives of infidelity, or through the fetishisation of innumerable unattainable 'sex symbols').[66] While public fascination with such promiscuous fantasies is obviously not always indicative of an actual desire to have promiscuous sex, nevertheless, dominant discourses and social practices seek to impose an incoherently rigid separation between promiscuous thoughts and activities.[67]

This uneasy split also recurs in many areas of marginalised cultures, as we saw in the previous chapter: Kramer's call for gay men to unite in marriage and monogamy stands in tension with his intermittent representation of the fluidity of desire, and of the powerful pleasures of non-monogamous sex. Hence the rapture of Fred's anonymous encounter 'in the basement toilet of his beloved West Side Y' in *Faggots*, with 'the excitement of this Forbidden Moment . . . sending him through the roof in a way that no ordinary licit encounter had in recent memory.'[68] Of course, it is (for the most part) precisely Fred's own stringent injunction against gay promiscuity that intensifies his guilty pleasure in transgressing that self-imposed limit.

By contrast, Wojnarowicz's account of his bathroom stall pick-up at the highway rest stop represents a more 'mutually supportive' relationship between promiscuous/anonymous sexual fantasy and activity. The 'drift and sway' both of fantasy in general, and of recurring fantasies specifically about promiscuous sex, is shown to interact productively with the transient intensities of brief sexual encounters – albeit in unpredictable and uneven ways. Wojnarowicz's memoirs therefore work to publicly affirm promiscuous fantasy *and* promiscuous sex, even as they throw into relief the psychical flux that defines monogamous and promiscuous sexuality alike.

UNCERTAIN PLEASURES: PROMISCUITY, AIDS AND AMBIVALENCE

Wojnarowicz also draws attention to the more problematic aspects of this psychical flux, however. Like Rechy and Kramer, he occasionally expresses a considerable ambivalence towards promiscuous public cruising and sex, and towards promiscuity in general. In a 1989 interview in *The Native*, a New York gay newspaper, he commented: 'I was a pretty promiscuous person most of my life . . . It's not something I feel bad about.' Yet he elaborates: 'I have journals of years of it, the fears and everything else. A lot of it is really extraordinary to me. I also know that it was a very difficult thing to stop, and how long it took me to slow down from experiencing my sexuality in that way.'[69]

This statement is partly about his sometimes life-threatening experiences while hustling 'at a very young age . . . in Times Square.'[70] But it also refers to his adult sex life, and in so doing, articulates an ambiguously contradictory attitude to promiscuous sex, rather similar to Rechy's mid-1980s contention that 'you have to *revise*' the promiscuity of youth in subsequent years.[71] Moreover, Wojnarowicz's suggestion here that his early promiscuity 'was a very difficult thing to stop' might momentarily also be seen to reinforce Kramer's (and many others') belief that gay men need to overcome their 'immature addiction' to promiscuity. This partial similarity between these otherwise opposed gay writers is all the more striking if we compare Kramer's representation of gay promiscuity as an effect of being marginalised by dominant culture with Wojnarowicz's remark, in a 1989 interview, that 'things tend to gain power by their denial; if my sexuality is denied, no wonder for a period of time I explore promiscuity.'[72]

Of course, Wojnarowicz's predominant representation of gay promiscuity not only as 'something I [don't] feel bad about,' but also as productively pleasurable, is directly opposed to the pathologisation of promiscuous sexuality by both conservative and, frequently, liberal gay men, as exemplified by Kramer. For Wojnarowicz, it is the dominant culture's innumerable prohibitions against queer sexual diversity that often increase the significance of sex in queer cultures – not, as Kramer would have it, because of the dominant prohibition against gay marriage.

Equally, unlike Rechy's insistence on a universal relinquishing of promiscuity (in the face of AIDS and growing older) in his own 1986 interview with *The Native*, Wojnarowicz's gradual move away from promiscuous sex can, in part, be specifically linked to his discovery of a supportive relationship with photographer Peter Hujar, a 'surrogate father, brother, briefly lover' who became 'the strongest and most positive influence of his life'[73]; and to his subsequent long-term relationship with Tom Rauffenbart (whom he met, however, 'in the basement of a porno theater'[74]). These and other shorter relationships answered Wojnarowicz's desire, alongside his brief encounters, for 'an encounter away from the park and in the warmth of a home and bed'; for 'the communication that isn't quite there in outlaw sexual encounters no matter how much sense is transferred.'[75]

Yet Wojnarowicz's shifting perception of, and relationship to, promiscuity is perhaps most significantly attributable to the psychological effects of the AIDS crisis, and of personally living with HIV and AIDS. While the influence that living with AIDS has upon Kramer's antipathy towards gay promiscuity remains largely implicit in his writings, Wojnarowicz directly records those psychical changes. In one of the memory narratives gathered together in 'Spiral' (in *Memories That Smell Like Gasoline*), the writer/narrator visits a porn theatre – 'a wet and dark bunker, a basement',[76] perhaps the one where Wojnarowicz met Rauffenbart. As he watches 'a clump of three guys' having sex, the intricately involved point-of-view deployed in the earlier sex accounts of *Close to the Knives*, and elsewhere in *Memories*, is replaced by a more distancing eye:

One of the guys, the one who looks like he's praying at an altar, turns and opens his mouth wide and gestures towards it. He nods at me but I turn away. He wouldn't understand. Too bad he can't see the virus in me, maybe it would rearrange something in him. It certainly did in me. When I found out I felt this abstract sensation, something like pulling off your skin and turning it inside out and then rearranging it so that when you pull it back on it feels like what it felt like before, only it isn't and only you know it. . . . Like I said, he wouldn't understand and besides his hunger is giant.[77]

As throughout Wojnarowicz's other narratives, he remains self-consciously situated and implicated within this sexual scenario; yet he also foregrounds the acute sense of psychical 'rearrangement' following his diagnosis, separating him from the overwhelming sexual 'hunger' of those customers intertwining around him.[78]

The caution and concern articulated here are, however, primarily related to the predominance of unsafe/r sexual practice. Wojnarowicz goes on to recollect an earlier visit:

I once came to this place fresh from visiting a friend in the hospital who was within a day or two of death and you wouldn't know there was an epidemic. At least forty people exploring every possible invention of sexual gesture and not a condom in sight. I had an idea that I would make a three minute super-8 film of my dying friend's face with all its lesions and sightlessness and then take a super-8 projector and hook it up with copper cables to a car battery slung in my bag over my shoulder and walk back in here and project the film onto the dark walls above their heads. I didn't want to ruin their evening, just wanted to maybe keep their temporary worlds from narrowing down too far.[79]

The juxtaposition of promiscuous abandonment and the relentless reality of AIDS here is, again, superficially familiar from Kramer's rhetoric. In this case, however, the contrast is made from a position firmly within the dilemma, rather than as an attempt to wish away diverse sexual pleasures from an ostensibly 'elevated' position. (Wojnarowicz reflects eloquently elsewhere that 'having this virus and watching guys having sex and ignoring the invitation to join in is like walking between raindrops.'[80]) He 'didn't want to ruin' the sexual pleasures of those other men; instead, his dismay specifically at their unsafe/r sexual practices indicates a limit to the 'mutually supportive' interaction of promiscuously unrestricted fantasy and promiscuous sexual activity found elsewhere in his writings.

Nevertheless, the ambivalence expressed towards promiscuity *per se* in the preceding *Native* interview is momentarily echoed in a narrative from Wojnarowicz's pre-AIDS journals of his waterfront promiscuity, in *Close to the Knives*:

I step away from myself for a moment and watch myself climbing around [the piers] and I wonder, what keeps me going? Why is it these motions continue over and over, animal sexual energy? The smell of shit and piss is overwhelming; everybody uses this place as an outdoor toilet, getting fucked in the ass and then letting loose in some spare corner. . . . Deep in the back of my head I wish it would all burn down, explode in some screaming torrent of wind and flame, pier walls collapsing and hissing into the waters. It might set us free from our past histories.[81]

In stark contrast to the romantically utopian imagery of the pier scenario we encountered earlier, here the writer/narrator's fantasy of a 'screaming torrent of wind and flame, pier walls collapsing and hissing into the waters', recalls Anthony's similarly morbid ode to the same Manhattan piers in *Faggots*: 'ah black hole of Calcutta, ah windswept, storm toss'd, fire-ravaged skeleton of former grandeurs!'[82]

However, where Anthony's exclamation is, for the most part, defiantly jubilant – 'go out, go up, show them that I'm still Alive!'[83] – and describes the actual worn appearance of the piers, Wojnarowicz's description articulates a fantasy of completely eradicating the already decaying cruising ground. This outward projection of the writer/narrator's intermittent pessimism about the relentlessness of desire – and about the often purely functional fulfilment of that desire in 'anonymous' sex[84] – comes closer to Kramer's more common public proclamations against the 'animalistic baseness' of gay outdoor promiscuity. Indeed, Wojnarowicz's fantasy of destroying the piers in a 'screaming torrent of wind and flame' is reminiscent of Kramer's own Biblical warnings of retribution for excessive sexual indulgence. If the alienation from promiscuity expressed in the porn theatre scenario above was a direct effect of AIDS, then in this chronologically earlier narrative moment, Wojnarowicz's usual defence of 'unrestricted fantasy, unrestricted thought' is momentarily seen to collide, in a more general way, with the less-than-romantic aspects of unrestricted physicality (underlined by the unceremonious use of the deserted piers simultaneously as cruising ground and open toilet).

At the same time, Wojnarowicz's nihilistic fantasy in this narrative echoes Rechy's difficult admission in *The Sexual Outlaw* that 'after a night of hustling and dark cruising alleys, I think of suicide.'[85] On the one hand, Rechy's comment is, as we saw, partly symptomatic of the ways in which his macho promiscuity was, to some extent, a response to his childhood sexual abuse (just as Wojnarowicz's multiple sexual encounters with masculine 'dangerous men' were clearly also partly influenced by his abuse by his father). This partial similarity between the two writers' relationship to promiscuity underlines the individually specific aspects of their experiences of gay male promiscuity: namely, their differing fantasmatic negotiations of the traces of paternal sexual violence.

On the other hand, though, Wojnarowicz's sense of entrapment in the repetitiveness of promiscuous desire, as he fantasises about becoming 'free from our . . . [sexual?] histories', serves to reiterate a more general proposition: namely, that the pleasures of avowedly promiscuous sexuality are, as much as those of monogamy, persistently disrupted by un/conscious psychical conflict. As Wojnarowicz commented polemically in a 1989 interview: 'We all carry contradictions, and by negating our contradictions we live lies.'[86] In those moments of ambivalence and antipathy towards his own promiscuity, his writings capture not only the profound pleasure, but also the disturbing confusion, that can arise from psychical contradiction.

'THE HIGHWAY . . . LETS THE HEART UNRAVEL': PROMISCUITY, 'MASCULINITY' AND TRAVEL

In Wojnarowicz's texts, 'moving around, travelling . . . [is] the most powerful state . . . to be in.' We have already seen this fascination with motion at the micro-level in his description of cruising amongst the other 'passenger[s] on the shadows' on the piers of Manhattan. Elsewhere in *Close to the Knives*, he describes how walking through the city streets similarly stimulates his memory and imagination:

Restless walks filled with coasting images . . . Old images race back and forth and I'm gathering a heat in the depths of my belly from them: flashes of a curve of arm, back, the lines of a neck glimpsed among the crowds in the train stations, one that you could write whole poems to. I'm being buoyed by these pleasures, walking the familiar streets and river.[87]

The flow of 'old images' here is, however, largely drug-induced: 'Sitting in the Silver Dollar restaurant earlier in the afternoon, . . . I dropped a black beauty,' enabling 'the flat drift of sensations gathered from walking and seeing and smelling and all the associations.'[88]

Yet Wojnarowicz also experiences a 'sense of regret' that 'washes over me . . . whenever I drop something, a sudden regret at what might be the disappearance of regular perceptions. . . . [S]omehow that feeling of beauty that comes riding off each surface and movement around me always has a slight trace of falseness about it.'[89] The 'trace of falseness' that accompanies these drugged wanderings through the city is replaced by a more intense feeling of hyperreality during his cherished journeys across America: 'I wish I was travelling in a disposable body through the landscape of the u.s.a. map and I was like a blinking light moving from state to state. . . . I could live forever in this drift.'[90]

These journeys – driving, hitchhiking and 'hopping freights'[91] across the country – were significantly influenced by Jack Kerouac's narratives of his life 'on the road', as Fran Lebowitz recalls in a 1994 interview:

I think of David like the Beat poets, whose work he loved. . . . I also think David liked that way of life. David loved to drive places. It was a real thing with him, but it was also a kind of Kerouac thing. He liked to have adventures, you know, and experiences. And he would drive, not because he couldn't afford a plane ticket . . . but because he just liked the road, the myth.[92]

Kerouac's influence can also be heard throughout Wojnarowicz's published accounts of his travels. The reconstruction of 'the voices of men and women you will encounter as you travel the highways and backroads of this land'[93] in *Sounds in the Distance* and *The Waterfront Journals* echoes Kerouac's fictionalised documentation of his fellow travellers' personal histories, particularly in *On the Road* (1957). Equally, Wojnarowicz's acute ability to evoke physical movement through the diaristic stream-of-consciousness, and shifting perspectives, of his travel narratives recalls Kerouac's formal innovations in conveying the sense of rootlessness and fleeting freedom that often come from 'leaving confusion and nonsense behind and performing . . . [the] one and noble function of the time, *move*. And we moved!'[94]

At a wider level, though, Wojnarowicz's pleasure in travel – particularly long-distance driving – is also closely interrelated with his promiscuous sexuality throughout the memoirs: 'The highway at night in the headlights of this speeding car is the only motion that lets the heart unravel . . . I hate highways but love speeding and I can only think of men's bodies and the drift and sway of my own.'[95] The emphasis here, as elsewhere, is on an indeterminate fast drifting, rather than a hurrying towards the end of the journey ('I hate arriving at a destination. Transition is always a relief. Destination means death to me'[96]) – a preference that mirrors Wojnarowicz's fleeting, multiple, unattached sexual encounters with 'unfamiliar' men, 'because I love difference'.[97]

This preference for perpetual change – whether in terms of physical location or sexual contacts – exemplifies once more a frequently heightened queer awareness of the contingency and instability of any finite sense of belonging, which is often considerably informed by promiscuous sexual experience. In an evocative essay on the physical and psychical mobility of 'the lesbian *flâneur*', for example, Sally Munt records her own appreciation of the ubiquity of transience through her wandering desires:

my eye follows a woman wearing a wide-shouldered lined suit. Down the street, she starts to decelerate. I zip up my jacket, put my best boot forward, and tell myself that 'home' is just around the corner.[98]

Munt relates her understanding of mutability and transition both to the psychical effects of cruising, and to the destabilising effects of movement in general: 'Margins and centres shift with subjectivities constantly in motion.'[99]

For Wojnarowicz, the magnified experience of transition while driving mirrors, and triggers, the psychical flow of fantasy. The defamiliarisation of vision and perspective in travel causes his erotic fantasies to proliferate all the more. Thus, the highway rest-stop encounter with a trucker described earlier is narrated as the writer/narrator drives down the highway, where he 'can only think of men's bodies'. Similarly, the detailed sexual fantasy that Wojnarowicz produces after driving by a group of highway construction workers is prefaced by his observation that 'driving a machine through the days and nights of the empty and pressured landscape eroticizes the whole world flitting in through the twin apertures of the eyes.'[100]

Again, as with those representations of fantasy and promiscuity explored earlier in the chapter, Wojnarowicz's emphasis on the erotics of travel is at once specific to his perspective as a promiscuous gay man, and indicative of a much wider cross-cultural reality. Within heterosexual culture, the sexual connotations of travelling to, and through, unfamiliar places are commonly acknowledged through paradigms such as the sailor, trucker or travelling salesman with 'a girl in every port',[101] or the summer holiday 'fling' (traditionally coded as romantic for women, and as a sexual 'conquest' – often, promiscuously, one amongst many – for men). While dominant culture remains overwhelmingly oriented towards upholding the mainstream 'invisibility of the myriad possibilities of sexual activity',[102] these largely non-monogamous cultural paradigms, however much rooted in masculinism, still overlap with the openly promiscuous queer traveller's eroticisation of physical transition and unfamiliar cruising grounds.

This overlap between heterosexual and queer travellers becomes all the more apparent if we situate Wojnarowicz's road narratives within the broader American cultural tradition of the 'romance of the road'. In the most conventional twentieth-century form of this popular trope, the nineteenth-century pioneers' belief in their 'manifest destiny' of conquering America for Christianity becomes translated into the normative heterosexual man's romanticisation of himself as a latter-day 'Ideal Male: the virile adventurer, potent, untrammelled man of action'[103] by driving across the land. His journey is characterised by homosocial bonding; his destination and rest spots offer opportunities for (hetero)sexual 'conquest' – often promiscuously multiple. The contemporary literary archetype of the romance of the road is, of course, Kerouac's *On the Road*, where travelling buddies Sal Paradise and Dean Moriarty share a patriarchal notion of male spiritual self-discovery through travel, while Dean (and occasionally Sal) juggles women *en route* and on both coasts:

The magnificent car made the wind roar; . . . Dean's rocky dogged face as ever bent over the dashlight with a bony purpose of its own.
  'What are you thinking, Pops?'
  'Ah-ha, ah-ha, same old thing, y'know – gurls gurls gurls.'[104]

On the one hand, as Fran Lebowitz's interview comment suggests, Wojnarowicz clearly identified with the Kerouacian straight male adventurer and his mythology of the road.[105] On the other hand, however, and more interestingly, Wojnarowicz's queer embodiment of that traditional mythology – his semi-spiritual quest on the highway, interspersed with sexual encounters with other men[106] – places the conventionally disavowed or downplayed homoeroticism and homosex that has always lurked within the heterosexual male version of the romance of the road firmly at the core of the narrative.

This homoeroticism is unsurprising, given that the heterosexual male road traveller/explorer resists 'his . . . shadow', the 'settled husband/father, dependable but dull',[107] precisely by escaping into the company of other men: while heterosexual possibilities lie ahead, the focus is largely on the close male-oriented environment of the long journey itself. In *On the Road*, for instance, the barely repressed erotics between Sal and Dean surface throughout the latter half of the novel: Dean asks Sal to 'work' his girlfriend, Marylou, while he watches, ostensibly because 'he wanted to see what Marylou was like with another man'[108]; later, as 'masterful' Dean drives wildly, Sal recalls, with curiously penetrative language, that 'all I could see was the road unwinding into me. . . . There was no escaping it. I resigned myself to all.'[109] And when Sal visits Dean in San Francisco, he contrasts himself with the women neglected by Dean and the other men on the road: 'they envied . . . my position at his side, defending him and drinking him in as they once tried to do. Then they looked at me. What was I, a stranger, doing on the West Coast this fair night? I recoiled from the thought.'[110]

More explicitly, the dominant mythology of the 'manly' heterosexual trucker traversing the land, which we have already seen undercut in Wojnarowicz's rest stop encounter, has been repeatedly appropriated and challenged in popular gay porn magazines like *18 Wheeler*, *T.R.A.S.H* (*True Revelations and Strange Happenings*) and *Straight to Hell*, which either devote themselves to, or frequently include, readers' 'true stories' of their promiscuous encounters at highway rest stops with truckers, as well as publishing truckers' accounts of their male pick-ups.[111] The former type of narrative, usually written by a gay-identified man, frequently trades on the alternately masochistic and sadistic/vengeful erotic charge of sexual contact with the supposedly 'unattainable' or 'disinterested' straight-identified trucker. Yet the latter type of narrative, along with many examples of the former type, also indicates a large number of gay, or bisexual, truckers alongside their occasionally 'curious' straight-identified counterparts.[112]

As I mentioned before, though, Wojnarowicz can be seen to partly identify with, as well as desire, the rugged, adventuring masculine man in his sexual experiences on the road and the piers:[113] 'it's . . . lawlessness and anonymity simultaneously that I desire, living among thugs.'[114] In *Close to the Knives*, this ambiguous identification with conventional masculinity is underlined when a brief encounter in the parked car of a 'square-jawed and barely shaven' man is repeatedly frustrated by 'some transvestites . . . going from car to car, leaning in the driver's windows checking for business'[115]; finally, 'we pulled our clothes back on and closed up the car, heading toward one of the abandoned structures.'[116] In his 'Biographical dateline', Wojnarowicz writes that in 1971, he 'ran with a gang of transvestities along the hudson river. We were their "men" and they took care of us for periods of time in welfare hotels and dive apartments on the lower east side.'[117]

However, whereas Rechy's early novels (knowingly and unknowingly) represent an uncertain attempt to embody the dominant cultural ideal of masculinity through bodybuilding, macho posturing, and often denigrating gay male 'femininity' during his promiscuous travels across America, Wojnarowicz's sexual encounters with 'masculine' men on the road (and in New York) are usually experienced from a perspective mostly at odds with conventional masculinity: 'I always considered myself either anonymous or odd looking and there is an unspoken bond between people in the world that don't fit in or are not attractive in the general societal sense.'[118] In *Numbers*, Johnny Rio vainly (in both senses of the word) reassures himself of the 'visible evidence' of his 'masculinity' by regularly pausing during his promiscuous rambling around LA's Griffith Park to check his mirror reflection in a nearby men's room, 'standing a distance back . . . so he can see more of himself' as he 'squares his broad shoulders . . . [and] smiles widely at himself.'[119] By contrast, in 'Into the drift and sway', Wojnarowicz observes the enticing performance of a masculine-coded trucker in another public bathroom, sharing Fred's and Anthony's non-normatively-masculine negotiation of the masculinised public cruising space in *Faggots*. And where Johnny Rio is increasingly 'disturbed by the increasing sense of drift'[120] as he defensively cruises in and around Griffith Park, Wojnarowicz's promiscuous travel narratives prefer to revel in 'the drift of it' all.[121]

ROMANTIC PROMISCUITY, PROMISCUOUS ROMANCE

Wojnarowicz's texts contain a further complexity, in their ambiguous relationship to romance. In the closing monologue of *The Waterfront Journals*, 'From the diaries of a wolf boy', the young homeless narrator voices his bitter distrust of traditional notions of romantic love: 'There was nothing ahead of me but a return to the streets of New York unless there's something called love but it probably doesn't exist except in the mythologies we're fed in the media or by lying to ourselves over time.'[122] Yet this suspicion of traditional notions of 'love' is complicated by the concurrent romanticism of most of Wojnarowicz's cruising narratives. Indeed, in her preface to the *Waterfront Journals*, Amy Scholder explains that Wojnarowicz 'felt that AIDS had so completely changed him that this evidence of his former self would surprise those who knew only his later work. He felt it revealed his romanticism, his idealism, his orientation to the world before rage and hopelessness set in.'[123]

In an equally autobiographical monologue that appears immediately before the 'wolf boy' narrative in *The Waterfront Journals*, the writer/narrator's late-night orgasm with a 'young tough'[124] on the Manhattan waterfront is represented as a moment of spiritual transcendence:

As we both came he fell back against the wall, his arms to the sides like he'd been crucified and was delirious in the last intoxicating moments of it like St. Sebastian pierced with the long reeds of arrows, silhouetted against a night full of clouds opening up, revealing stars and a moon. We felt like figures adrift, like falling comets in old comic-book adventure illustrations.[125]

Note the quintessentially romantic projection of an identically shared emotional response on to the 'tough' stranger here: 'We felt like figures adrift.' The combination of 'young tough' and quasi-religious ecstasy here echoes the romantic 'masculinity' of Genet's writings – a similarity reinforced in the narrator's post-climactic fantasy of a 'timeless' blissful union with his rough-looking sexual partner:

I led him up to the streets feeling dizzy, saw myself with him in the rough woods of that coastal dream I'd always had of losing myself from the general workings of the world: no Robinson Crusoe but some timeless place where the past was forgettable and there was just some guy with a tough stomach to lie against, and I could listen to his heartbeat sounding through his trembling skin.[126]

In the previous passage, the sharpened intensity of the brief sexual encounter is romanticised in its own right; here, that encounter is also shown to provoke a further romantic fantasy of eternal monogamous union. This daydream of resting upon a 'tough stomach' in the sanctuary of 'rough woods' recalls the lyrical woodland embraces between masculine lovers in Genet's classic film of promiscuous sexual fantasy, *Un Chant d'amour* (1950), and in so doing, also re-enacts Genet's characteristic conflation of sex and romantic transcendence.

Wojnarowicz's traditionally romantic fantasy of eternal union with a protective masculine man clearly can be seen to restage a desire simultaneously for the protection withheld by his violently sexual father, and for the paternal eroticism that his father enforced. Yet this continuous tension between promiscuous sexual practice and monogamous fantasy also resonates throughout gay male culture, regardless of specific familial histories, where a yearning for a permanent muscled protector often persists alongside pleasure in multiple brief partners (hence the abiding popularity of Holleran's romantically monogamous *and* promiscuous *Dancer from the Dance*). On the one hand, such fantasies may well articulate a desire for actual monogamous stability. On the other hand, however, they also reiterate the co-existence of contradictory desires that I have been stressing throughout this study, with no consistently predictable relationship to interpersonal sexual practice. Moreover, as *fantasies* of monogamy, they stage an idealised scenario of endless erotic and emotional fusion with an ever-arousing, ever-fascinating, ever-comforting, ever-reliable partner that is enticing precisely because it exceeds the possibilities of human reality.

Wojnarowicz acknowledges this impossibility of realising fantasies of romantic permanence when he reflects that:

I always tend to mythologize the people, things, landscapes I love, always wanting them to somehow extend forever through time and motion. It's a similar sense I have for lovers, wanting to somehow have a degree of permanence in my contact with them but it never really goes that way.[127]

However, as the momentary transcendence of that waterfront encounter with a 'young tough' above illustrates, promiscuity also often contains its own distinct romanticism apart from monogamous connotations, in keeping with the marginalised secondary definition of 'romance' as '[a] strong, usually short-lived attachment or enthusiasm.'[128] In *Close to the Knives*, for example, Wojnarowicz reconstructs the psychical intensity of a brief sexual encounter, sat in another man's parked car on a desert road, in words that echo the soaring ecstasy of the conventional romantic narrative:

He was whispering behind my closed eyelids. Time had lost its strobic beat and all structures of movement and sensation and taste and sight and sound became fragmented, shifting around like particles in lakewater. I love getting lost like this.[129]

In Wojnarowicz's tenderly romantic sex narratives, the dominant cultural equation between romance and monogamy can therefore be seen to be complicated. For in one sense, these accounts of being psychically transported – and even momentarily united in that transcendence – during 'anonymous' sexual encounters frustrate the dominant notion of promiscuous sex (especially with unknown partners) as emotionally empty, alienating and unrewarding. Instead, Wojnarowicz underscores the common occurrence in anonymous sex of passionate connections and lyrical or sentimental interpretations that are conventionally ascribed solely to monogamous romance.

In another indirect sense, though, the strong similarities between these promiscuous accounts and the conventions of monogamous romance can also serve to foreground the latent promiscuous charge of dominant romantic narratives, despite their manifest adherence to monogamy. Writing of women's popular romantic fiction, Ann Barr Snitow points out that 'romantic sexual fantasies are contradictory. They include both the desire to be blindly ravished, to melt, and the desire to be spiritually adored.'[130] While the latter romantic yearning usually centres around monogamous commitment, the former desire for passion often implies a privileging of spontaneity and unfamiliarity – as in the paradigmatic sudden meeting with the proverbial tall, dark and handsome *stranger* – over the uniqueness and familiarity of the sex partner.

Thus, in Janice Radway's classic reader reception analysis of romantic fiction, even though her sample group of women 'scrupulously avoid the work of authors like Rosemary Rogers and Judith Krantz who deal in what they call "perversions" and "promiscuity,"'[131] their persistent consumption of more normative, monogamy-oriented, novels can nevertheless be seen to allow them a vicarious pleasure in numerous, often interchangeable, handsome heroes. These monogamy-espousing readers' escapist fantasies about multiple men are therefore never entirely distinguishable from Wojnarowicz's own pleasure in 'getting lost' in romantic fantasies during his actual sexual encounters: despite differing conscious attitudes to sexual behaviour, in each case, the interaction with romanticism is in some way intertwined with promiscuous desires. Indeed, despite the studiously monogamous trajectory of the traditional romantic novel, Snitow cites Peter Parisi's argument 'that the books' formula allows both heroine and reader to feel wanton again and again while maintaining their sense of themselves as not that sort of woman.'[132]

On the one hand, then, Wojnarowicz's romanticism partly expresses a real desire for 'a degree of permanence', answered by his later long-term relationships. Yet on the other hand, its promiscuous context also complicates the prevailing cultural presumption of a clear distinction between romantic, 'person-centred' monogamy and alienated, 'inhuman' promiscuity.

IN AND OUT OF THE CITY:
PROMISCUOUS SEXUALITY AND SPACE

These romantically promiscuous journeys also take their writer beyond the traditionally eroticised spaces of the metropolis, out into rural areas that are conventionally characterised as mainly monogamously heterosexual – and hence homosexually barren and repressed – in gay male literature, as throughout contemporary urban-centred cultural discourses in general.[133] In these scenes of rural sex (seen already in the encounters at the highway rest stop with a trucker, and in a stranger's parked car in the desert), Wojnarowicz's texts disrupt the dominant homogenising view of gay male culture as a network of urban commercial social spaces, and instead stress those largely unrecorded anonymous sexual encounters on the road, or in the desert, where urban, surburban and rural dwellers briefly meet.[134] For as Lawrence Knopp points out, although 'the city, as a world of strangers in which people relate to each other as objects and surfaces, . . . [is] an archetypal space of modern sexuality,'[135] nevertheless, the erotics of 'anonymity, voyeurism, tactility, motion, etc. . . . bear no *necessary* relationship to the city.'[136] For Wojnarowicz in fact, sexual encounters with strangers while travelling through the country are often intensified by the vast natural beauty and comparative isolation in which they occur.

This heightened delight in non-urban sex is, however, also significantly influenced by Wojnarowicz's subject position as a visitor from the city, passing through and pausing for romantically fleeting sexual adventures. Although, as Kath Weston underlines, prevalent 'facile oppositions between city and country' tend to 'depict rural gays as exceptions or impossibilities'[137] with no local means of socialising together, nevertheless, in many instances, queers who live in rural and small town environments do remain constrained in their choice of places to meet one another (or meet interested non-queers) for sex and companionship. Within this context, the subterfuge of the highway rest stop or outdoor cruising ground may be the only readily available option, at once a source of pleasure and a frustrating compromise, in contrast to the urban gay man's opportunity to choose the public cruising ground over the bar, the nightclub, the social group, and so on.[138]

Having qualified Wojnarowicz's eroticisation of rural space, I want to return momentarily to that desert encounter in a parked car, with a man he met at a highway rest stop:

I saw nothing but empty space and earth and sky . . . and here we are, here I am, some fugitive soul having passed through the void of the cities, skimmed across the emptiness of landforms and roadways . . . to this one point in the dead road. . . . And to be surrounded by this sense of displacement, as this guy's tongue pulls across my closed eyelids and down the bridge of my nose, or to be underneath all that stillness with this guy's dick in my mouth, lends a sense of fracturing. It's as if one of my eyes were hovering a few feet above the car and slowly revolving to take in the landscape.[139]

While the 'sense of fracturing' mentioned here is traced directly to the dramatic 'emptiness' and 'stillness' of the desert landscape, Wojnarowicz's psychical 'fracturing' of that surrounding space – his movement between experiencing the immediate detail and imagining the wider bird's-eye view from above – is also symptomatic of his generally decentred perspective. And as we have already seen, this self-consciously unfixed perspective was influenced by the constant mobility both of his life hustling on the streets and of his pleasure in cruising and promiscuous sex. To reinvoke Munt's observation: 'margins and centres shift with subjectivities constantly in motion.'

The shifting perspective of this desert road narrative is therefore consistent with Wojnarowicz's other sex narratives, where his erotic preference for the fleeting and the transient intersects with, and in some ways also produces, his psychical resistance to rigid dominant cultural mappings and zonings of public spaces that discount the innumerable subjective codifications of space. Whether cruising the city streets, the piers or the country roads, these narratives repeatedly counter dominant spatial demarcations with – to borrow George Chauncey's phrase – 'a more finely calibrated sexual map of the city' and countryside;[140] a documented eroticisation of familiar and unfamiliar environments alike which affirms, in Chauncey's words, that:

Space has no natural character, no inherent meaning, no intrinsic status as public or private. . . . [I]t is always invested with meaning by its users as well as its creators, and even when its creators have the power to define its official and dominant meaning, its users are usually able to develop tactics that allow them to use the space in alternative, even oppositional ways that confound the designs of its creators.[141]

In one of the Manhattan sex narratives in *Close to the Knives*, for instance, Wojnarowicz can be seen to distinguish between his own fantasised bird's-eye view in the desert scenario above, and a more impersonally 'official' macro-perspective of the city – a perspective that, in literalising the rigid boundaries of the geographical map, and downplaying interaction and change, 'transforms the . . . [street-level] world by which one was "possessed" into a text that lies before one's eyes' to be 'possessed' by the gazer.[142] Against such attempts by the (usually solvent-to-wealthy, heterosexual, white, male) privileged urban subject to impose finite spatial definitions through distance, Wojnarowicz records his own subjective ground-level eroticisation of an ostensibly disused waterfront building where he is cruising:

If viewed from miles above, this place would just appear to be a small box-like structure like thousands of others set down along the lines of the rivers of the world; the only difference being that in this one the face of the kid [climbing a ladder to another level of the building] starts moving up the wall past a window framing the perfect hazy coastline with teeth of red factories and an incidental gas explosion which sends flowers of black smoke reeling up into the dusk. I could feel his lips against mine from across the room.[143]

Here, the writer/narrator's cruising movements through a 'boxlike structure like thousands of others' invest the space with new, fleeting, contextually specific meanings. Yet at a more broadly resonant level, his description of the inviting young man's ascent into a more 'private' corner of the building for sex, and his blurring of the inside and out-side of the decaying building, also exemplify the way in which desire perpetually dissolves, and redefines, the conventional boundaries between private and public spaces.

In the previous chapter, Kramer's normative focus on the private monogamous domestic space could be seen to construct 'public' promiscuous gay sex as abjectly excessive and inhuman – yet also, for that very reason, a site of extreme forbidden pleasure (again, monogamy-oriented Fred's thrilling encounter in an appropriately 'low' basement toilet is paradigmatic here). This troubled naturalisation of monogamous privacy is symptomatic of a preoccupation with 'the right to privacy' across conservative and liberal gay male (and lesbian) discourses alike that, as Scott Tucker stresses, 'orients the gay move-ment in a conservative direction'.[144]

Tucker notes that when liberal and conservative 'gay rights advocates' argue that *'sexuality is a private matter'*, they mean *'Let us live our lives in peace'* – whereas when 'anti-gay bigots' argue that sexuality is a private matter, they mean *'Get back into the closet.'*[145] Yet on both sides of this argument, the persistent prioritisation of the notion of 'privacy' ultimately precludes a systematic defence of those countless daily occasions where queers transgress the always nebulous bound-aries of the private realm. The effects of the pro-privacy argument are therefore as divisive as those produced by gay and lesbian arguments for marriage and naturalised monogamy – which are, of course, the legalised models for that 'respectably' hidden private sphere. In their scramble for individual or coupled safety 'behind closed doors', gay advocates preoccupied by privacy rights fail to reflect that 'there is no true autonomy which is purely personal. Autonomy exists *between* people and *within* a world which surrounds the individual. The right to be left alone is a poor right if we are denied the right to associate: the right to form *community'*,[146] and the right to use communal space – sexually or otherwise – on our own terms.

Wojnarowicz's accounts of his life on the streets, when he 'hung around a neighborhood that was so crowded with homeless people that I can't even remember what the architecture of the blocks looked like',[147] emphasise that the prevalent insistence in mainstream heterosexual and queer cultures upon privileging the supposedly private sphere over the public is grounded in class privilege.[148] Equally, like so many other gay male activists, his rejection of the cultural prioritisation of privacy arose from living with AIDS, and fighting homophobic cultural responses to AIDS: 'It's just too ridiculous to consider my own privacy in the face of mortality and death.'[149] Or again, in a 1988 diary entry: 'IT'S HEALTHY TO MAKE THE PRIVATE PUBLIC. . . . DON'T GIVE ME A MEMO-RIAL IF I DIE. GIVE ME A DEMONSTRATION.'[150]

In conjunction with these material factors, Wojnarowicz's writings repeatedly clarify that his sexual promiscuity (which was, of course, initially necessitated by his homelessness, and partly reduced in response to his AIDS diagnosis) led him to seek out and openly affirm the use of public spaces as rich, and sometimes even revelatory, settings for sexual pleasure. In this respect, Wojnarowicz indirectly follows on from Rechy, whose own outdoor sexual adventures similarly throw into relief the tenuousness of dominant public/private designations of social space. (In *The Sexual Outlaw*, for example, Jim reflects that he 'passes from day to twilight to night in moments' while cruising under a pier.[151] After having sex with several men there, he returns to his beach mat, as an 'old fisherman and his ragged wife continue obliviously staring toward the horizon vanishing in the rising mist',[152] which mirrors the blurred boundary between public and private on the beach itself.) Wojnarowicz's texts avoid the intermittent machismo of Rechy's novels, as well as *The Sexual Outlaw*'s utopian (and macho) 1970s contention that 'public' sex necessarily constituted 'a radical statement'.[153] Yet both writers' cruising narratives similarly foreground sexual pleasures beyond the privatised domestic sphere, which are simultaneously part of a predominantly gay male cultural tradition, and indicative of the pan-cultural promiscuousness of sexual desire, which, in its very formlessness and plurality, cannot help but exceed dominant physical and symbolic boundaries.

Against such finite boundaries, then, Wojnarowicz's sex narratives offer up a more complex and shifting textual 'landscape for drifting': a space that affirms the promiscuous gay man's conventionally vilified sexual practices, and unsettles the certainties of those heterosexuals and queers who would naturalise 'private' monogamy and pathologise 'inhuman' promiscuity, by dwelling instead upon the intrinsic contradiction and flux of sexual desire and fantasy. If the enforced rootlessness of Wojnarowicz's familial history and early poverty propelled his promiscuity in significant ways, his finely textured accounts of brief promiscuous encounters throughout his memoirs also illustrate the acute, and lasting, understanding of mutability and difference that can arise from physically fleeting sexual attachments.

Notes

1. Wojnarowicz, *Close to the Knives*, p. 47.
2. Chua, 'Lyons at the Gate', p. 34.

3. *Aperture*, p. 2.
4. Carlo McCormick, quoted in Lippard, 'Passenger on the shadows', p. 11.
5. Kuby, 'The art of David Wojnarowicz', p. 59.
6. *Aperture*, p. 58.
7. Wojnarowicz, *Close to the Knives*, p. 120.
8. *Aperture*, p. 58.
9. Ibid., p. 60.
10. Wojnarowicz, *Close to the Knives*, pp. 9–10.
11. Cooper, 'The East Village', p. 29.
12. Many of these pieces are collected in Blinderman (ed.), *Tongues of Flame*; the 1994 special issue of *Aperture*; and Scholder (ed.), *Fever*. See also Carr, *On Edge*; Deitcher, 'Ideas and Emotions'; and the bibliographies in *Fever* and *Tongues of Flame*.
13. Elizabeth Young's 1992 essay, 'On the road again', places Wojnarowicz largely in opposition to 'the more soft-focus, college-kid urban fictions' of many of his New York contemporaries. However, Young anxiously attempts to displace the crucial sexual impetus and content of his writing from her critical framework: 'Although much of *Close to the Knives* deals explicitly with [Wojnarowicz's] own homosexuality and the AIDS crisis, . . . the emphasis on sexuality in this case tends to lead us away from any crude definitions of people in sexual terms and towards an engagement with basic moral issues and human values' (pp. 217–18). This tactic is based in a misrecognition of those 'basic moral issues and human values' as being somehow 'beyond' sexuality. Worse, Young's confused and insufficiently close reading leads her to propose that 'it is impossible, within Wojnarowicz's book, not to see AIDS as having an apocalyptic edge, as seeming to arise from the corruption and mind-rot and dying of dreams in America that he has described in the early part of the memoir, as seeming to arise inevitably from his words to form a new language of pain and disaster' (p. 225). Young's conventional literary critical dissociation of *Close to the Knives* from its sociosexual context is reprised here, with AIDS transmogrified into a symbolic embodiment of the American popular imaginary. In her description of the health crisis 'as seeming to arise inevitably from . . . [Wojnarowicz's] words to form a new language', AIDS is finally rendered as a free-floating discourse of 'pain and disaster' that is actually *produced* by the author's 'apocalyptic' world view. In other words, Wojnarowicz becomes responsible for AIDS . . .
14. Kuby, 'The art of David Wojnarowicz', p. 59.
15. Ibid., p. 60.
16. Quoted in Lippard, 'Passenger on the shadows', p. 57.
17. Wojnarowicz, *Waterfront Journals*, p. 113. Most of the 'monologues' in this collection are attributed to particular 'strangers' whom Wojnarowicz met; however, some of them clearly borrow from the author's own personal experiences. (Compare, for example, pp. 26–9 and 72–4 with incidents in *Close to the Knives*.) Moreover, this particular quotation appears under an anonymous heading: 'The Waterfront 2.00 a.m. New York City'.
18. We saw a less willingly acknowledged interest in monogamous/mutual desires previously in Rechy's texts.
19. Hess, 'Last action hero', p. 28.
20. Some of the pieces included in *Close to the Knives* also appear together with other material by Wojnarowicz in *Tongues of Flame*.

21. Hess, 'Queer in normal', p. 98.
22. McCormick, 'Fables, facts, riddles, and reasons', p. 11. In a 1991 interview, Wojnarowicz, 'a little amazed', commented that 'whenever I do a reading, ... people take license to speak, to reveal personal things for the first time. I don't know how to handle it.' Quoted in Yablonskaya, 'Covering the slaughterfront', p. 81.
23. A recollection from Hess, an art critic who was also one of Wojnarowicz's friends, illustrates his governing desire for contextually specific and self-reflexive cultural production: 'I remember him explaining to me that he didn't want to make any image – ever – that could be plunked down in a gallery and removed from its ideological intentions. "That's impossible," I told him. "It's not," he said.' (*Aperture*, p. 33.) When Donald Wildmon of the American Family Association indirectly taught him otherwise, by circulating decontextualised 'pornographic' sexual images from Wojnarowicz's art work in a propaganda leaflet, the artist sued Wildmon and the AFA for $5 million in libel damages; he won the case, but was awarded only a symbolic $1. (David Cole, Wojnarowicz's lawyer, describes the case in *Aperture*, pp. 36–7.)
24. Wojnarowicz, 'Biographical dateline', p. 114.
25. Lippard, 'Passenger on the shadows', p. 18.
26. Wojnarowicz, 'Biographical dateline', p. 114.
27. Hirsh, 'Speed at all costs', p. 30.
28. Wojnarowicz, 'Biographical dateline', p. 117.
29. Wojnarowicz, *Close to the Knives*, p. 81.
30. Ibid., p. 271.
31. Califia, *Public Sex*, p. 211.
32. Wojnarowicz, *Close to the Knives*, p. 255.
33. Quoted in Lippard, 'Out of the safety zone', p. 133.
34. Wojnarowicz, *Close to the Knives*, p. 33.
35. *Aperture*, p. 42.
36. Blinderman, 'The compression of time', p. 54.
37. Rechy quoted in Pally, 'A visit with author John Rechy', p. 52.
38. Cooper, 'The East Village', p. 29. This 1985 comment relates to Wojnarowicz's visual art, but also holds true for the subsequent growing recognition of his writings; although the more consistent focus on gay sex and desire in the writings is likely to draw more of a gay audience. For one indication of the diverse audiences that the artist had begun to attract through his images, writings and highly performative public talks, see Hess, 'Queer in normal', pp. 97–9.
39. Wojnarowicz, 'Biographical dateline', p. 117; Lippard, 'Passenger on the shadows', pp. 8–9.
40. In saying this, I in no way want to imply that gay and lesbian identities and analyses are necessarily less self-conscious. Obviously, a considerable amount of cultural production and daily living done under those earlier categories overlaps with, and predates, the questioning aspects of queerness. For an introduction to this self-problematising branch of queer thought, see the 'Queer theory: Lesbian and gay sexualities' issue of *differences* (de Lauretis, ed.) – the title of which also encapsulates the murky distinction between 'old' and 'new' (homo)sexualities.
   Using a different – but equally applicable – definition of queerness, Gregory W. Bredbeck has situated Wojnarowicz within an emerging literary tradition of 'new queer narrative', including such writers as Dorothy Allison, Dennis Cooper, Gary Indiana and Kevin Killian. While

never thoroughly distinct from the gay construction of 'alternative nar-rativities that destabilise the hegemony of unitary cohesion', Bredbeck argues that the 'new queer narrative' (rather like the short-lived category 'New Queer Cinema') is nevertheless 'most prominently defined . . . by its unwillingness to engage in the second step of intervention that marks the gay critique. Queer narrative critique . . . seeks primarily to expose the perniciousness and pervasiveness of hegemony' without focusing on alternatives. (Bredbeck, 'The new queer narrative', p. 485.) Interestingly, he suggests that the reference to 'disintegration' in *Close to the Knives*' subtitle, 'A memoir of disintegration', 'may very well be the best critical term to describe the poetics of the new queer narrative,' given its dual connotations of 'falling apart' and '*dis*-integration, the process of extri-cating something from an integrated system' (p. 491). Wojnarowicz illus-trated the nihilism frequently implicit in this perspective when he declared, in his interview with Nan Goldin: 'If I could write a book that killed America, I would have done it.' *Aperture*, p. 61.

41. Wojnarowicz, *Close to the Knives*, pp. 49–50; emphasis added.
42. White, 'Paradise found', p. 153. White's proviso that 'conventional, straight America' may not 'forget . . . the transitory,' but instead often conveniently 'forget to mention' it, is important: as should become clear later in my discussion of the American 'romance of the road', it is the ambiguous *disavowal* – not the outright 'dismissal' – of 'transitory' sexual/cultural experience that is characteristic of dominant heterosexual American culture.
43. Note 28 on 'SPIRITUALITY for Paul Thek (photographic piece)' from 'Notes on the work', exhibition catalogue for *In the Shadow of Forward Motion* (8 February–4 March 1989, PPOW Gallery, New York City).
44. I am including that sexually charged sustained exchange of looks between the two cruising men, which may or may not lead to sexual contact, as a form of 'brief erotic encounter' in its own right.
45. Wojnarowicz, *Close to the Knives*, pp. 10–11.
46. Ibid., p. 9.
47. Ibid., p. 13.
48. Burton, 'Tearoom trade', p. 6.
49. Of course, as with anything else (including monogamy), the repetition of promiscuous sex – even with always unfamiliar patterns – will eventu-ally, or sporadically, produce its own increasingly predictable familiarity.
50. Wojnarowicz, *Close to the Knives*, p. 117.
51. But again, see my qualifying comment in n. 49.
52. Wojnarowicz, *Memories*, p. 9.
53. The description of 'diaristic studies . . . and dream-like memoirs' on the back cover of *Memories That Smell Like Gasoline* reiterates the collaps-ing together of narrator and author throughout Wojnarowicz's texts.
54. Wojnarowicz, *Memories*, p. 12.
55. Ibid.
56. Ibid., p. 13.
57. Of course, at the material level, the narrator's difficulty in engaging directly with the trucker is the result of normative cultural restrictions upon gay and promiscuous quasi-public sex.
58. Wojnarowicz' snapshot account of 'Being queer in America: A journal of disintegration' includes a memory of rape by a stranger. (*Close to the Knives*, pp. 75–7.) In 'Memories that smell like gasoline', the writer docu-

ments another rape, as a teenage hitchhiker, by an older man. *Memories*, pp. 15–26.

59. Wojnarowicz, *Memories*, p. 15. The original context in which Wojnarowicz uses this phrase is not applicable here, but the quotation nevertheless seems relevant to his notion of the psychical 'dislocation' of all forms of sexuality.

60. Wojnarowicz, *Close to the Knives*, p. 26.

61. Ibid., pp. 26–7. Gary Fisher makes a similar observation, inflected by fantasising in the present rather than through memory, in his posthumously published journals. Reflecting on a man he desired in a bar, he writes: 'He left with Susan (the brunette bartender). Oh well, I know and he knows. Some more mid-air sex. I stripped you down, buddy – had you in the sack – and never left my barstool.' Fisher, *Gary in Your Pocket*, p. 164.

62. Burgin, 'Fantasy' entry, *Feminism and Psychoanalysis*, p. 87.

63. Wojnarowicz, *Close to the Knives*, p. 117.

64. Burgin, 'Fantasy' entry, *Feminism and Psychoanalysis*, p. 84.

65. Laplanche and Pontalis help to clarify the ambiguous nature of that primary 'lost object': 'A problem much debated in psycho-analysis – that of whether we must assume the existence of a "primary love-object" or, alternatively, take it that the infant is initially in a state of auto-erotism or narcissism – is one to which Freud offers a solution more complex than is generally claimed. The sexual instincts obtain satisfaction auto-erotically before they embark upon the evolution that leads them to object-choice. But the self-preservative instincts have a relationship to an object from the start; consequently, in so far as sexuality functions in anaclisis with these instincts, it too must be said to have a relationship to objects; only after detaching itself does sexuality become auto-erotic. [Freud in the *Three Essays on the Theory of Sexuality*:] "At a time at which the first beginnings of sexual satisfaction are still linked with the taking of nourishment, the sexual instinct has a sexual object outside the infant's own body in the shape of the mother's breast. It is only later that the instinct loses that object. . . . As a rule the sexual instinct then becomes auto-erotic . . . The finding of an object is in fact the refinding of it."' (Laplanche and Pontalis, 'Anaclisis; anaclitic (or attachment)' entry, *The Language of Psychoanalysis*, p. 31.) Yet it is also important to consider the possibility of other primary sexual objects, and of more than one originary object, given variations in child-feeding and in familial structures, such as gay male parenting.

66. However, the relationship between these public forms of promiscuous fantasy and dominant sociojuridical injunctions against promiscuous sex is extremely complex and non-linear. Thus, fan desires for public sex symbols are often part of teenage sexual rebellion, and popular narratives of 'transgressive' sexual activity can serve as affirmation, as well as providing a means for sublimating promiscuous sexual practice.

67. Although, to reiterate from previous chapters, straight male promiscuity is commonly condoned and encouraged as 'evidence of masculinity' within heteropatriarchal culture.

68. Kramer, *Faggots*, pp. 103–4.

69. Hirsh, 'Speed at all costs', p. 30.

70. Ibid.

71. Quoted in Laermer, 'The real John Rechy', p. 51.

72. Blinderman, 'The compression of time', p. 50.
73. Lippard, 'Passenger on the shadows', p. 15. On the same page, Lippard quotes Wojnarowicz: 'My experiences with Peter were in a great way responsible for everything that I've done. He encouraged me in a way that I had never gotten.' Fran Lebowitz, who became Wojnarowicz's friend through Hujar, recalls in a 1994 interview that 'after a while, I started to think of . . . [David] as Peter's son. . . . And I think that David may also have had that feeling about him, in a way. . . . I think that Peter influenced David perhaps in a kind of paternal way.' *Aperture*, p. 73.
74. Contributor's note on Tom Rauffenbart, *Aperture*, p. 84.
75. Wojnarowicz, *In the Shadow of the American Dream*, pp. 62–3.
76. Wojnarowicz, *Memories*, p. 44.
77. Ibid., pp. 47–8.
78. He elaborates in the same narrative: 'The first minute after being diagnosed you are forever separated from what you had come to view as your life or living, the world outside your eyes. The calendar tracings of biographical continuity get kind of screwed up. It's like watching a movie suddenly and abruptly going in reverse a thousand miles a minute, like the entire landscape and horizon is pulling away from you in reverse in order to spell out the psychic separation.' Ibid., pp. 47–8.
79. Ibid., p. 48.
80. Wojnarowicz, *In the Shadow of the American Dream*, p. 244.
81. Wojnarowicz, *Close to the Knives*, p. 187.
82. Kramer, *Faggots*, p. 137.
83. Ibid., p. 138.
84. On the other hand – to shift the emphasis in my comment at n. 49 above – monogamous sexual gratification can obviously become purely functional as well.
85. Rechy, *Sexual Outlaw*, p. 71.
86. Blinderman, 'The compression of time', p. 53.
87. Wojnarowicz, *Close to the Knives*, pp. 12–13.
88. Ibid., pp. 11–12.
89. Ibid.
90. Ibid., p. 201.
91. Butterick, Foreword to *Sounds in the Distance*, p. 3.
92. *Aperture*, p. 79.
93. Butterick, Foreword to *Sounds in the Distance*, p. 3.
94. Kerouac, *On the Road*, p. 111. William Burroughs, himself closely connected to the Beat ethos, reiterates Wojnarowicz's link to that literary movement in a comment originally published on the back cover of *Sounds in the Distance*: 'David Wojnarowicz has caught the age old voice of the road, the voice of the traveller.' In turn, Wojnarowicz's dream/fantasy narratives and artwork are considerably influenced by Burroughs's fiction. On the back cover of *Close to the Knives*, a quotation from the *Publishers Weekly* review states: 'What Kerouac was to a generation of alienated youth, what Genet was to the gay demimonde in postwar Europe, Wojnarowicz may well be to a new cadre of artists.'
95. Wojnarowicz, *Memories*, p. 9.
96. Wojnarowicz, *Close to the Knives*, p. 62.
97. In another sense, however, this travelling *is* impelled by a desire to reach 'the end of the journey': Wojnarowicz partly traces his pleasure in speeding to 'a recurring [teenage] fantasy that began after my first motorcycle ride,' wherein 'I saw myself riding this machine faster and faster

and faster toward the edge of a cliff until I hit the right speed that would take me off the cliff in an arcing motion. . . . [O]nce my body and the motorcycle hit a point in the light and wind and loss of gravity, in that exact moment, I would suddenly disappear, and the motorcycle would continue the downward arc of gravity and explode into flames . . . [I]t is in that sense of void – that marriage of body-machine and space – where one should most desire a continuance of life, that I most wish to disappear.' (*Close to the Knives*, p. 41.) Here, then, the 'destination' of death is yearned for, both through the literal scenario of the fantasy and through its very repetition: as Laplanche and Pontalis note (in their discussion of Freud's 'Beyond the pleasure principle'), ambivalent or unpleasant 'repetition phenomena . . . are difficult to account for in terms of the search for libidinal satisfaction or as a simple attempt to overcome unpleasant experiences.' Rather, these phenomena imply 'an irresistable force which is independent of the pleasure principle and apt to enter into opposition to it.' (Laplanche and Pontalis, 'Death instincts' entry, *The Language of Psychoanalysis*, p. 98.) Wojnarowicz's fantasy also contains an obvious erotic element – 'I realised that the image of the point of marriage between body-vehicle and space was similar to the beginning of orgasm' (*Close to the Knives*, p. 41) – that echoes the psychoanalytic contention 'that a libidinal satisfaction, . . . [including] narcisstic enjoyment, can always be present, even in those cases where the tendency towards destruction of the other or of the self is most in evidence.' (Laplanche and Pontalis, 'Death instincts' entry, *The Language of Psychoanalysis*, p. 99.) Yet Wojnarowicz's material circumstances are most crucially significant here: this recurring fantasy arose amongst the literal threats against his life during his teenage years, at a time when his compensatory 'childhood dreams of autonomy in the form of hermetic exile were quickly becoming less possible.' *Close to the Knives*, p. 40.

98. Munt, 'The Lesbian *Flâneur*', p. 125.
99. Ibid., p. 118.
100. Wojnarowicz, *Close to the Knives*, p. 26.
101. Sailors are, of course, repeatedly linked to queer sexual activity as well throughout popular culture. Incidentally, a straight trucker's narrative that appears in *Sounds and the Distance* and *The Waterfront Journals* is interesting for its suggestion that, contrary to conventional expectations of male-male sex at truck stops, women may look for truckers there as well: 'You can meet some great women driving throughout this country at these truck stops.' *Waterfront Journals*, p. 12.
102. Wojnarowicz, *Close to the Knives*, p. 119.
103. Wood, *Hitchcock's Films Revisited*, p. 291.
104. Kerouac, *On the Road*, p. 192.
105. Yet Kerouac's fictional representative in *On the Road*, Sal Paradise, already partly complicates the macho trajectory of this mythology: unlike Wojnarowicz, he is nervous both about being the driver on journeys – 'I just wanted to follow' (p. 110) – and about making sexual contacts; while fascinated by travelling, he repeatedly yearns for long-term commitment: 'I saw myself in Middle America, a patriarch. I was lonesome' (p. 148). (However, as I clarify later, Wojnarowicz often shares this desire for stability.)
106. Wojnarowicz's journeys were often solitary, although Tom Rauffenbart recalls numerous trips the couple took together in Mexico, New Orleans and Puerto Rico. *Aperture*, pp. 50–2.

107. Wood, *Hitchcock's Films Revisited*, p. 291. As Wood details in his sum-
      mary of the conflict between these idealised types in classical
      Hollywood cinema, this scenario is most obviously central to the
      Western.

108. Kerouac, *On the Road*, p. 108.

109. Ibid., p. 193.

110. Ibid., p. 161. Most striking of all is Sal's outburst after the two friends get
      a lift from a gay man on the road: 'In the john of a restaurant I was at a
      urinal blocking Dean's way to the sink and I stepped out before I was
      finished and resumed at another urinal, and said to Dean, "dig this
      trick." "Yes, man," he said, washing his hands at the sink, "it's a very
      good trick but awful on the kidneys and because you're getting a little
      older now every time you do this eventually years of misery in your old
      age [sic], awful kidney miseries for the days when you sit in parks." It
      made me mad. "Who's old! I'm not much older than you! . . . I'm no old
      fag like that fag, you don't have to warn me about *my* kidneys"' (p. 175).

111. While a number of both types of narrative may well be fantasies, rather
      than based on actual events, the detailing of time, place and surrounding
      events in many others indicates the widespread occurrence of such
      encounters.

112. Other popular cultural examples of the overlap between homoeroticism
      and homosociality on the road include the recurrent bond between Bing
      Crosby and Bob Hope, despite the temporary heterosexual romantic
      interest of Dorothy Lamour, in their long-running series of road movies
      (*Road to Singapore* [1940]; *Road to Morocco* [1942]; *Road to Rio*
      [1947] . . .), and the emotional intensity between *Thelma and Louise*
      (1991), which climaxes in a kiss before their orgasmic ascent/descent
      over the canyon cliff, rather like Wojnarowicz's teenage clifftop fantasy.
      Other explicitly gay male reworkings of the romance of the road narra-
      tive include Gregg Araki's queer road movie, *The Living End* (1992), and
      Lars Eighner's memoir of his homelessness, *Travels with Lizbeth: Three
      Years on the Road and on the Streets*, wherein the writer echoes
      Wojnarowicz's desires when he is briefly tempted to travel with an
      attractively dangerous man: 'I cannot deny there is a romance of the
      road' (pp. 32–3). In Godfrey Hamilton's play, *Road Movie* (Starving
      Artists Theatre Company, Edinburgh/Toronto/British tour, 1995–6), the
      focus is on moving from promiscuity to monogamous (albeit ultimately
      unrealisable) love: the narrative follows a thirtysomething gay man's
      drive across America to California (like Sal Paradise returning to Dean
      in San Francisco) to reunite with his soulmate, who has died of an AIDS-
      related illness by the time he arrives. Yet the play also shares strong sim-
      ilarities with Wojnarowicz's memoirs, as the gay man's speeding journey
      across the deserts is punctuated by haunting brief (non-sexual) encounters,
      reflections on the elusiveness of belonging, and his lover's abiding
      refrain: 'trust only movement'. Rechy's novels – especially *City of Night*
      – are also obvious examples of an explicitly queer reworking of the
      Beats' coast-to-coast journeys.

113. Of course, this 'ruggedness' was also – at least in his early years – a
      means of survival.

114. Wojnarowicz, *In the Shadow of the American Dream*, p. 128.

115. Wojnarowicz, *Close to the Knives*, p. 15.

116. Ibid., p. 16.

117. Wojnarowicz, 'Biographical dateline', p. 117.

118. Wojnarowicz, *Close to the Knives*, p. 183.
119. Rechy, *Numbers*, p. 111.
120. Ibid., p. 182.
121. Wojnarowicz, *Close to the Knives*, p. 54.
122. Wojnarowicz, *Waterfront Journals*, p. 122.
123. Scholder, Editor's Preface to Wojnarowicz, *Waterfront Journals*, p. x.
124. Wojnarowicz, *Waterfront Journals*, p. 109.
125. Ibid., pp. 112–13.
126. Ibid., p. 113.
127. Wojnarowicz, *Close to the Knives*, p. 79.
128. 'Romance' entry, *The American Heritage Dictionary of the English Language*. Citing, amongst others, Derek Jarman's romantic description of cruising on Hampstead Heath in *Modern Nature*, David Bell has similarly observed that 'texts written by advocates of public (homo)sex . . . do allude to romanticism and to fulfilments beyond the purely bodily.' (Bell, 'Perverse dynamics', p. 314.) Bell argues, as I do here and in the previous chapter, that such 'public' sexual encounters can be experienced as 'moments in love' (p. 313).
129. Wojnarowicz, *Close to the Knives*, p. 54.
130. Snitow, 'Mass market romance', p. 261.
131. Radway, 'Women read the romance', p. 208. This article is expanded upon in Radway's *Reading the Romance*.
132. Snitow, 'Mass market romance', p. 255. Snitow is paraphrasing Parisi's unpublished paper.
133. Kath Weston has emphasised that 'the gay imaginary is spatialized, just as the nation is territorialized. The result is a sexual geography in which the city represents a beacon of tolerance and gay community, the country a locus of persecution and gay absence. . . . In story after story, a symbolics of urban/rural relations locates gay subjects in the city while putting their presence in the countryside under erasure.' (Weston, 'Get thee to a big city,' p. 262.) As in life, the draw of the city as a source of possibly – if not necessarily – enabling anonymity and diversity is obviously a central trope of gay (and lesbian) fiction, beyond the central examples in this study. In the definitively urban *Dancer from the Dance*, for instance, the unnamed New Yorker who has decided 'to make a clean break with my former life' by relocating to 'the Deep South' (p. 9) with his lover becomes increasingly disillusioned with his initially idyllic new life after he reads *Wild Swans*, a novel centred on Manhattan gay sex and love sent to him by a friend back in the city: 'The novel is more *vivid* than I had expected, and frankly brought back things that are a little too close to me still. I had to leave New York, you know, not for any practical reason but for a purely emotional one: I simply couldn't stand to have it cease to be enchanted to me' (p. 240).
134. However, a substantial number of these men will not be gay-identified, or will even be hostile to the very notion of gayness in their sexual partners; what George Chauncey observes in relation to early twentieth-century male New Yorkers using 'tearooms' for sex is also applicable in this context: 'Pervasive anti-homosexual social attitudes kept many men who were interested in other men from fully acknowledging that interest to themselves, and many of them sought sexual encounters in spaces, such as public washrooms, that seemed to minimize the implications of the experiences by making them easy to isolate from the rest of their lives and identities. The same association of tearooms with the most primal

of bodily functions reinforced men's sense that the sexual experiences they had were simply another form of release, a bodily function that implied nothing more about a man's character than those normally associated with the setting.' (Chauncey, 'Privacy could only be had in public', p. 253.) But as I suggested in my comments about trucker sex earlier, straight-identified men are unlikely to constitute the majority in these environments.

135. Knopp, 'Sexuality and urban space', p. 152.
136. Ibid., p. 160, n. 7.
137. Weston, 'Get thee to a big city', pp. 263 and 262.
138. On the other hand, as is evidenced by Wojnarowicz's distance from the gay scene, many urban commercial social venues cater primarily, or only, for relatively wealthy white gay men, limiting the number of available options for other queers.
139. Wojnarowicz, *Close to the Knives*, pp. 54–5.
140. Chauncey, 'Privacy', p. 249. Chauncey's phrase refers to men cruising in early twentieth-century New York.
141. Ibid., p. 224.
142. de Certeau, 'Walking in the city', p. 152.
143. Wojnarowicz, *Close to the Knives*, p. 65.
144. Tucker, 'Our right to the world', p. 32.
145. Ibid.
146. Ibid.
147. Wojnarowicz, *Close to the Knives*, p. 32.
148. Chauncey notes that in early twentieth-century New York, the fact that many straight couples, like their queer counterparts, 'met in unsupervised public places and even had sex there was . . . shocking . . . to middle-class reformers, in part because it challenged the careful delineation between public and private spaces that was so central to bourgeois conceptions of public order.' Chauncey, *Gay New York*, p. 203.
149. Yablonskaya, 'Covering the slaughterfront', p. 81.
150. Wojnarowicz, *In the Shadow of the American Dream*, p. 206.
151. Rechy, *Sexual Outlaw*, p. 25.
152. Ibid., p. 27.
153. Ibid., p. 299.

Glancing Back

True to the progressively faster postmodern recycling of cultural history, the late 1990s in America have been partly moulded in the image of the 1970s and 1980s. A few years after the phenomenon had taken hold in Britain during the early to mid-1990s, American popular culture began to cite the iconography of both preceding decades, with a particular emphasis on the retrospective laughs to be had from 1970s fashion flamboyance and disco glitz. The fashion industry increasingly reworked 1970s styles, making bellbottoms commonplace again on the streets; retro club nights spread across the country; VH1 music television aired numerous 1970s (and 1980s) specials; *Saturday Night Fever* – the ultimate mass market symbol of 1970s nightlife – and *Grease* were re-released; and two film recreations of New York's legendary Studio 54 club, *The Last Days of Disco* and *54*, appeared in 1998.

Of course, this was mostly a resurrection of those aspects of popular culture that had already been appropriated from marginalised cultural groups (most obviously, black people and gay men) during the 1970s and early 1980s. This resurrection therefore perpetuated the usually airbrushed mainstream images of pleasure and liberation disseminated back in the day. However, just as any citation of the past tells us as much about the present, so the parodic or mocking reworking of that earlier popular imagery spoke in part of the comparative sexual conservatism, and loss of radicalism and idealism, in the more resolutely main-streamed 1990s. The insipidly heterocentric versions of Studio 54's polymorphous perversity served up in *The Last Days of Disco* and *54*, along with finger-wagging cinematic morality tales like *Boogie Nights* and *The Ice Storm*, were perhaps the most blatant signs of this narrow look back at recent American histories of sociosexual pleasure.

Nevertheless, as if in answer to its limp cinematic representation, Studio 54 promptly reopened its doors in 1998 to house Sam Mendes' appropriately polymorphously perverse Broadway revival of *Cabaret* –

itself a reminder of yet another earlier era of queer nightlife. Meanwhile, the mass market 1970s and 1980s revivals have also been shadowed by a number of generally more probing gay male glances back at the 'Age of Promiscuity' through the lens of autobiographical fiction. Twenty years after works like *Dancer from the Dance*, *Faggots* and *The Sexual Outlaw* – and Wojnarowicz's then-unpublished journals – had reflected on the gains and losses attending the newly invigorated promiscuous gay sexuality, several gay novels (of varying degrees of declared auto-biographical origin) appeared in 1996–7, reflecting on that earlier era from the more painful perspective of the end of the century, when so many of those earlier sexual adventurers were no longer there to share in reminiscing: Brad Gooch's *The Golden Age of Promiscuity*, Allan Gurganus's *Plays Well With Others*, Andrew Holleran's *The Beauty of Men* and Edmund White's *The Farewell Symphony*.

In many ways, these novels echo the range of contrasting and self-conflicting observations on gay promiscuity seen across those earlier works. *The Golden Age of Promiscuity*, for instance, depicts its young filmmaking protagonist, Sean, hedonistically immersing himself in the bars and underground artistic world of 1970s gay New York. Somewhat like Rechy's cruising studs, the less wholeheartedly 'masculine' Sean veers between mocking the macho exclusivity of the bar where he is a regular ('MINE SHAFT Dress Code . . . NO Cologne or Perfume or DESIGNER sweaters. . . . NO RUGBY STYLED shirts or DISCO DRAG'[1]) and defending the intricacies of this world: 'in the club Sean never actually observed the uniformity ascribed to it by people's gossip or even by its own dress code.'[2]

Yet while the narrative portrays Sean's pleasure in multiple individual and group sexual encounters, it ultimately has a more conventional trajectory that reaches a monogamous closure partly reminiscent of *Faggots*. Hints of this outcome occur earlier on, when Sean's youthful promiscuity is linked to irresponsibility – he tells a friend that once he arrives at his regular bar, 'I don't take any responsibility for anything I do'[3] – and to a rejection of maturity: 'Sean didn't really want to mature yet. He didn't really want satisfaction yet. Satisfaction is counterproductive, he thought smugly.'[4]

Absolving responsibility within a circumscribed, pre-AIDS-awareness sexual context or avoiding normative adult 'maturity' are not, of course, in themselves pejorative characteristics. Nor should the exploration of these characteristics, or the representation of a promiscuous gay man finding happiness in monogamy, necessarily be criticised in a novel. But the use of 'smug' to describe Sean's thoughts on deferring satisfaction tallies with the narrative's subsequent punishment of his promiscuous pleasure in sexual passivity and masochism by placing him in a near-death situation with a non-consensually sadistic master. Suitably chastised, Sean is then steered away from all the sexual 'pantings that had swirled him down into so much trouble'[5] and into the arms of monogamous love, seen as a more solidly (if still initially 'uncomfortable') 'condensed rather than scattered loving,'[6] which he experiences as an epiphany that will change him forever: 'when he allowed [his boyfriend] Willie the weakness of his love he felt a door open in himself. He was suddenly in a new room, and there was never any going back.'[7] Rather like in *Faggots*, then, the deferral of socially expected monogamous adult 'satisfaction' throughout the promiscuous main body of this text – a deferral that, unlike in *Faggots*, is consciously upheld by the protagonist for most of the novel – reaches a conventionally monogamy-centred goal. (This conclusion also recalls promiscuous Petra's resignation to eventually marrying 'the miller's son' in *A Little Night Music*.) Unlike Fred in *Faggots*, though, here the hero also gets his man in the end.

Allan Gurganus's *Plays Well With Others* articulates the overlapping attraction and ambivalence towards promiscuity voiced by many pro-promiscuous gay men themselves, as in Rechy's and Wojnarowicz's writings; although here, as in Rechy, that ambivalence is specifically shaped by the influence of religious guilt. The novel is its narrator Hartley Mims's memoir of his life in New York, where he arrived in the early 1980s in search of a successful writing career, seen from the present perspective of his North Carolina home in the mid-1990s, where he continues to mourn the loss of all of his close friends from that era to AIDS. 'A busy bee erotically'[8] during his New York years, who rejected the message that 'PROMISCUITY POLLUTES'[9] blaring from a poster in a VD clinic he visited soon after moving there, Hartley tells us that 'I had got to fuck my brains out'[10] for most of the 1980s, and warns us against some other, more judgemental retrospective accounts of that era: 'The prigs won't tell you how sweet and rollicking the peasant dance was. Before such accurate lightning struck us.'[11]

As with *City of Night*'s narrator, though, Hartley's religious upbringing – 'I'd grown up Presbyterian, okay?'[12] – also makes him 'sure that any pleasure would exact a tax far greater,'[13] echoing Kramer's (not explicitly religious) 1997 declaration that 'nature always extracts a price for sexual promiscuity.'[14] This moral framework informs Hartley's eventual visit to the St. Mark's baths, which he compares to a joyless 'Purgatorio',[15] in a subsection of the novel punitively entitled '*On Being Overly Active Sexually*'[16]:

I had been memorizing Blake's epigraphs. Now the scent of steam, poppers, rubber soles brought one to mind. 'Fun I love, but too much fun is of all things the most loathsome. Mirth is better than fun, and happiness is better than mirth.'[17]

Hartley ends up seeking escape from a sexually aggressive encounter in the baths on the roof of the building, where he nevertheless enjoys an orgasmic jacuzzi with a 'nice guy . . . who seems to hail from a large affable Maryland Catholic family,'[18] and who therefore provides a sort of happy medium between Hartley's vying decorum and desire. This ambivalent combination of a religiously moulded anxiety about 'too much fun' and an otherwise highly enjoyable promiscuous sexuality recurs at the broader narrational level as well, in the novel's general aversion to incorporating details of Hartley's allegedly prodigious sex life into its otherwise very detailed recreation of his New York years.

Andrew Holleran's *The Beauty of Men* similarly focuses on a middle-aged white gay man glancing back at his promiscuous past in New York from a temporal and geographical distance. In this case, it is Gainesville, Florida in the mid-1990s, where the protagonist, Lark, moved to in 1983 to care for his bedridden mother, and where, in his loneliness, he now ponders the absence of his dead New York friends and melancholically yearns for and shadows Becker, a gorgeous younger man he had sex with once, who finally bluntly rejects him.

The doubt and negativity concerning promiscuity that we have seen at various levels of intensity in other gay male literature is frequently at its most pessimistic here. We saw a brief connection in Chapter 2 between Kramer's rejection of promiscuity and Holleran's occasional representation of gay male promiscuous culture as a doomed ghetto, closed off from an idyllically viewed heterosexual family world, in *Dancer from the Dance*. In *The Beauty of Men*, that vision of gay promiscuity as lack is more pronounced: 'There is a cost to this. There is a constant, cumulative cost. Slutty is as slutty does',[19] Lark tells himself as he circles the local baths listlessly.

The partial origin of this attitude in a yearning for a romanticised family life and parenthood is made explicit in two conversations that Lark remembers having with his closest New York friend, Sutcliffe. The pair once observed a man chastising his daughter for losing her glove, prompting Sutcliffe to momentarily envy the girl for her father's concern:

'Nobody asks me where *my* glove is. They ask me if I've come yet or if I'm into scat, but nobody ever asks me where I lost my glove.'
 'You see?"' said Lark. 'That's why gay romances don't last.'[20]

And more pointedly, in another conversation:

'you're a pessimist, dear,' said Sutcliffe . . . 'You think the future is provided by kids, and we didn't have any. No kids, no future. For you it's that simple.'
 'But then – what am I supposed to do? Cruise for the rest of my life?'

'Yes,' he said. 'That's *exactly* what you have to do. Cruise for the rest of your life.'[21]

Having been unable to secure the long-term partner he craves, Lark, 'racked with guilt for my failure to have children,'[22] now finds little comfort in the memory of Sutcliffe's advice to just keep cruising: 'Oh God, thinks Lark as he passes yet another glistening shirtless runner, do you never acquire the object? Do you never get to rest?'[23]

But like all of Holleran's writing, the novel is more than a simplistic dramatisation of this morose point of view on promiscuity, which relies heavily on a disavowal of the lovelessness, isolation and betrayal that can also characterise monogamy and family life. In the first flash-back conversation above, for example, Sutcliffe goes on to stress the possibility of enjoying love within promiscuity, or within friendships that arise from passing sexual connections:

'You see?' said Lark. 'That's why gay romances don't last.'

'Speak for yourself,' said Sutcliffe. 'I'm still in love with all my boyfriends.'[24]

Here, Sutcliffe takes on the role of Sutherland, the witty socialite in *Dancer from the Dance* (the similarity in names is clearly intentional), whom we saw in the introduction similarly espousing the pleasures of promiscuity, and declaring the culturally idealised state of monoga-mous love to be as intrinsically fantasmatic as any other form of desire – to be, 'after all, my dears, all anticipation and imagination.'[25] Indeed, Lark himself momentarily echoes this sentiment – albeit less confidently – when he pragmatically tells himself: 'Forget Love; that was much too dicey, quite possibly a myth.'[26]

The novel also complicates Lark's mostly jaundiced view of promis-cuity by presenting his multiple and unresolved thoughts on the motivations behind it:

('Why are gay men so promiscuous?' his cousin had asked him one evening as they sat watching a segment about AIDS on the evening news. 'Because,' he said, – thinking, Because sex is wonderful, and who wouldn't want to do it as much as possible? Because sex is ecstasy, and there's no ecstasy left in this civilization anymore. Because we thought penicillin would cure every-thing. Because people are looking for Love. Because in this society we can't find support for stable partnerships. Because we're ashamed, and seek out sex with strangers we don't have to say hello to in the street the next day, much less mention at our funerals. Because, because, because, he thought, and then he turned to her and said, 'Why do you smoke?')[27]

Rather than implicitly comparing gay promiscuity to a potentially fatal addiction, a better rejoinder here might have been, 'Why are hetero-sexuals, or any group, so promiscuous?' This response would have highlighted his cousin's normative heterosexual fascination with gay male promiscuity to the exclusion of heterosexuality's own diverse promiscuities (which we have seen similarly discounted by the patriarch Abe in *Faggots*, or by conservative or liberal anti-promiscuous gay male writers like Kramer). Nevertheless, as in Holleran's suitably contradic-tory 1980s 'Notes on promiscuity', Lark reiterates the impossibility of essentialising the meanings or effects of promiscuity for one gay man, let alone for gay men or any other group in general, as he moves rapidly between thoughts of the benefits and constraints of promiscuity: its status as a goal for some and a means to a monogamous end for others; its perception by some as a source of abundant sexual pleasure unin-flected by moralism, and by others as a symptom of social oppression; and its negotiation of disease.

Yet as with Wojnarowicz's openness to contemplating his promiscuous experiences without a pre-determined political stance, Lark's general sexual despair, as when he asks, 'Oh God, . . . do you never acquire the object? Do you never get to rest?,' can be seen to mirror the occasion-ally exhausted and nihilistic cruising thoughts of Wojnarowicz's journals, which are, of course, mainly far more sexually optimistic:

I step away from myself for a moment and watch myself climbing around [the piers] and I wonder, what keeps me going? Why is it these motions con-tinue over and over, animal sexual energy? . . . Deep in the back of my head I wish it would all burn down, exploding in some screaming torrent of wind and flame.[28]

To be precise, though, *The Beauty of Men* is primarily concerned with the cumulative effects of two major factors on its protagonist's attitudes to sex: AIDS, and the compromises and losses brought on by ageing, which Lark feels guilty for bemoaning in the face of his friends' early deaths, but cannot of course avoid confronting. The effects of AIDS are articulated throughout in Lark's depressive thought processes, as he hedges around finding out his own HIV status. The loss of friends makes New York feel like 'a vast cemetery'[29] when he visits, and he is constantly pulled between a plague-fuelled increase in his sex drive – 'The more friends dead, the more he wishes to have sex; to do what he imagines they could do;'[30] 'Everyone he knows with HIV is tricking like mad'[31] – and a frequent mournful alienation from sexual contact when it is finally offered. His predicament recalls Eric Rofes' observation that, 'whether HIV positive, HIV negative, or unaware of anti-body status, significant numbers of gay men in America appear to

be experiencing confusion, dysfunction, impotency, and deep ambivalence about sexuality and intimacy between men.'[32]

At the same time, though, Lark's sexual misery is due to his changing desires in middle age, when 'I can no longer pretend that brief
ecstasy is adequate. Because I grow old.'[33] Of course, middle age need
not necessarily produce such a desire for longer-term relationships.
Nevertheless, the novel is a breathtakingly clear-eyed corrective to the
prevalent youth-oriented accounts of gay sexual life, raising the issue
of older gay men's relationship to promiscuous gay culture, and also the
issue of how older gay men are excluded from that world. Generali-
sations about age and desirability are problematic, given that many
middle-aged men fit into the widespread pan-generational gay male
erotic fascination with 'daddy/boy' fantasies. Similarly, the embodiment
of dominant codes of masculinity and muscularity is prized in most
age ranges. However, increasing age in later life does of course decrease
sexual currency, and despite going to the gym regularly, Lark feels
himself being placed progressively at the edges of desirability when he
visits the local boat ramp cruising ground or goes to the bars. In one of
the novel's many self-consciously provocative expressions of otherwise secret private thoughts, Lark thinks angrily to himself: 'Who cares
about politics and interest groups? – I'm not getting laid.'[34]

Despite only being forty-seven, for Lark, as for many gay men, ageing
brings him closer to the bleaker aspects of gay promiscuity, which he
had also encountered at times in his New York youth: the common
boredom of repetition in cruising and tricking, 'the sense, sitting in the
park at three a.m., that you were wasting your life,'[35] and the rejection,
all of which are now intensified by his depleted desirability:

He used to go to the baths because it cut through all the games and affectations,
the pretense, the tedious peregrinations of seduction. Now he goes because
he has no place else to go.[36]

The novel indicates that this growing dissatisfaction with promiscuity
is shared by other ageing gay men by, for example, offsetting Sutcliffe's
dictum, 'Cruise for the rest of your life', with his posthumously
remembered remark that 'after twenty years, meaningless sex becomes,
well . . . meaningless.'[37]

However, even if Lark's paralysed and widowed mother has evaded
what he calls 'the homosexual nightmare: No child to wipe your fevered
brow,'[38] her complete dependence on her son's nursing home visits until
she dies at the end of the narrative acts as a continuous counterpoint
to Lark's partial idealisation of married or otherwise monogamous
coupledom, indirectly illustrating the compromises and losses of the
ageing process for everyone. Or in Sutcliffe's words: 'We *all* see the

bone beneath the flesh, we *all* know we're getting older and our breasts have fallen, . . . straight and gay [and monogamous and promiscuous].'[39] Nor, of course, was a lot of the promiscuous pleasure of his and Sutcliffe's past merely 'meaningless.'

Rather, Lark's sexual and general pessimism is presented throughout the novel as a complex result of the overlapping 'effects of . . . age and AIDS. Both tended to produce withdrawal'[40]; internalised homophobia ('I'm ashamed of being gay'[41]); 'geographical isolation'[42]; and – as with Rechy's and Gurganus's texts – a long-standing un/conscious moralism that Sutcliffe saw as being religiously informed: 'No! Don't moralize! . . . You're always trying to find the moral! You were like this before the plague! . . . Because you're a Calvinist! A puritan!'[43] And this complex state of pessimism leads Lark to experience the ephemerality of (in Sondheim's words) 'what passes by' as crushing, almost unbearable, given that the universal transience of experience, youth and desire has been doubly impressed on him by the untimely loss of his friends. His predicament recalls Edmund White's 1983 observation on the dominant cult of 'permanence' which, White argued, needs to be contested by a wider sociosexual validation of 'what passes by':

In conventional, straight America, people honor only the permanent and dismiss, even forget (or at least forget to mention) the transitory. Only what lasts is good. This prejudice in favor of what endures is unfortunate, I'd say, a concession to social institutions rather than a recognition of human experiences.[44]

The Beauty of Men represents Lark's lonely embrace of these dominant values. Yet equally, its representation of the predicament of many gay men who are dealing with AIDS-related loss, together with the adjustments of ageing, in the 1990s, clarifies the potentially (but not necessarily) strong lure of some form of sexual/emotional consistency in the face of overwhelming loss and vulnerability.

White's novel *The Farewell Symphony* offers a similarly ambivalent perspective on this predicament. In a sense, the novel attempts to come to terms with the changed connotations of its author's 1983 comment on the pervasiveness of transience, after living with the effects of AIDS for the better part of two decades. Like Gurganus's and Holleran's novels, it provides a retrospective appraisal of a promiscuous past in 1970s–80s New York (and Paris, Rome and Venice) by an older gay man who is one of the only survivors he knows from that time – and who has, in this instance, also 'been seropositive for a decade.'[45] Unlike these other novels, though, White's text is as openly autobiographical as those examined in the preceding chapters, albeit still fictionalised, 'not a literal transcription of my experiences.'[46]

The novel's celebration of promiscuity is implicit in its narrational preoccupations and structure. Whereas Lark's thoughts mostly draw him back to his present isolation, and Hartley rarely elaborates on his youthful sex life, this narrator mainly enjoys recounting the interweaving fleeting details of his promiscuous sexual encounters, both one-off and longer-term. In formal terms as well, the numerous digressional fragmentations and considerable length of the text (as in *City of Night*, *Faggots* or Wojnarowicz's journals) mirror the promiscuity of its subject matter. Rejecting the frequently linear determinism of narratives of 'official history – elections, battles, legal reforms', the narrator remarks that he 'didn't want to be a historian but rather an archaeologist of gossip'[47] – hence his gossipingly intimate and semi-fictionalised unfurling of story after story, sometimes seeking to promiscuously seduce a wide audience with tales of sexual variations and famous personalities (whose names are often teasingly withheld), and sometimes simply taking pleasure in the details of the tale without any conventional narrational goal. (These qualities also characterise Gore Vidal's supremely gossipy 1995 memoir, *Palimpsest*, although Vidal never withholds his parade of famous names.) In one sense, then, the narrator's retelling of these memories to his readers functions as the kind of public recognition and respect of 'the transitory' that gossip enacts (with dramatic embellishments), and that White encouraged in his 1983 essay. (However, the narrator explains that his disinterest in 'official history' also stems from the fact that he has generally 'felt no connection to society'[48] or politics beyond his sexual pursuits and immediate friendships.)

In another related sense, the narrator constructs from the web of these promiscuous tales a version of Freud's fantasmatic psychical nature reserve, to compensate for the changed fortunes of his present life, which is (like Lark's) informed by escalating grief and declining desirability. He begins his narrative in Paris six months after the death of his lover, Brice, and admits that he is likely to omit the telling of this particular part of his sexual and romantic history:

I met Brice five years before he died – but I wonder whether I'll have the courage to tell his story in this book. The French call a love affair a 'story,' *une histoire*, and I see getting to it, putting it down, exploring it, *narrating* it as a challenge I may well fail.[49]

Indeed, the long-flowing narrative eventually breaks down during his description of the end of Brice's life: 'I can't go on. I can't tell this story, neither its happy beginning nor its tragic end.'[50] Brief fragments of their life together appear during the course of the narrative, but for the most part, the promiscuous profusion of earlier memories of sex and friendship serves to hold at bay this most recent loss. At the same time, the novel's detailed resurrection of the narrator's sexual past is also an attempt to make sense of the deaths of his friends from that time – a resurrection whose sexual charge arises not only from the sexual content of many of those memories, but also from the erotics of loss itself, as in the narrator's private masturbatory communion with those lost loves[51]:

My fantasies are memories as accurate as I can make them of past lovers and what they did to me. These days I find myself fucking the dead most of the time.[52]

Alongside its promiscuous structure and focus, *The Farewell Symphony* also pays homage to the pleasures of 1970s and 1980s gay promiscuity by reminiscing about the range of beneficial psychical effects that accompanied the physical sexual satisfaction of those years. Central to these effects for the narrator was a post-coital intimacy, the ephemerality of which made it no less significant or memorable than that shared between more lasting lovers:

For those who never lived through that period (and most of those who did are dead), the phrase 'anonymous sex' might suggest unfeeling sex, devoid of emotion. And yet, as I can attest, to hole up in a room at the baths with a body after having opened it up and wrung it dry, to lie, head propped on a guy's stomach just where the tan line bisects it, smoke a cigarette and talk to him late into the night and early into the morning about your childhood, his unhappiness in love, your money worries, his plans for the future – well, nothing is more personal, more emotional. The best thing of all were [sic] the random, floating thoughts we shared.[53]

Sometimes the profound intimacy of those shared moments or hours, because of their concentrated brevity and the presence of someone who listened to your story without any complicating familiarity with your day-to-day life, made them in fact all the more intensely memorable over time:

Just the other day a black opera singer, who's famous now, sent me one of his recordings and a note that said, 'In memory of that night at the baths twenty-five years ago.'[54]

The narrator goes on to recall the occasional romance of this intense brief intimacy, which in one case surpassed anything he experienced in his longer-term relationships, with the same poetic detail that Wojnaro-wicz uses to commemorate the sometimes romantic heightening of sensations in his brief encounters:

The most romantic night of my life I spent with an older man on the dunes of Fire Island, kissing him until my face burned with his beard stubble, treasuring the beauty of his skin and skin warmth and every flaw as though it were an adornment. When he walked me home through the salt mist floating in off the sea and the sudden coldness of dawn, we strolled arm in arm as though we'd been lovers before the war, say, any war, and were reunited only now.[55]

As with Wojnarowicz, the psychical pleasure of fantasy interlaces with the narrator's physical pleasure; and at the same time, presents an alternative view of promiscuous sexual intimacy on Fire Island in the 1970s to Fred's denunciation of the 'misguided masses' on the beach at the end of *Faggots*.

The Farewell Symphony glances back with similar fondness at the revolutionary optimism of much of post-Stonewall 1970s urban gay life, with its conviction that promiscuity could provide, in Douglas Crimp's later words, 'a positive model of how sexual pleasures might be pursued by and granted to everyone if those pleasures were not confined within the narrow limits of institutionalized sexuality.'[56] Central to this evolving model of erotic intimacy was an attempt to draw together the conventionally polarised areas of friendship and relationship, in order to reject the normative equation of sex and ownership within traditional coupledom and marriage, and also to place more emphasis on the frequently communal focus of friendship, which is devalued as secondary to the privatised monogamous couple within the dominant social model:

We wanted sexual friends, loving comrades, multiple husbands in a whole polyandry of desire. Exclusivity was a form of death – worse, old hat. If love was suspect, jealousy was foul. We were intent on dismantling all the old marital values and the worse thing we could be accused of by one of our own was aping the heterosexual world.[57]

However, the narrator's partial gentle mockery here of his own previous radical wholesale rejection of all manifestations of monogamy is magnified at other points in the narrative, as he repeatedly questions aspects of his promiscuous past. On the one hand, he qualifies his earlier 'revolutionary' enthusiasm by clarifying that, contrary to those post-Stonewall gay men and lesbians who were seriously intent on bringing about revolutionary change in dominant straight sociosexual arrangements, and linking these changes to gender, class and racial struggles, 'I belonged to that group of gay men who lost all interest in the others the minute he left the club, the trucks or the baths.'[58] Like Kramer's and others' warning against a fight for rights that is purely sex-based, the narrator now acknowledges that his particular subgroup of promiscuous gay men 'equated sexual freedom with freedom itself.'[59]

On the other hand, the narrator points to the common disparity between his avowed sexual politics and his sexual practices and desires back then. Although he 'responded in any abstract discussion to the concept of the couple with implacable hostility'[60] while upholding the sanctity of promiscuity, the un/conscious complications inherent in all forms of sexuality continued to surface in various guises. Like Johnny Rio nervously keeping score of his conquests in *Numbers*, the narrator experienced conventionally 'masculine' sexual competitiveness with other gay men, which troubled the new ideal of promiscuity as unrepressed plenitude with a lived reality of perceived deprivation:

The funny thing is that I always felt deprived, as though all the other fellows must be getting laid more often. A gay shrink once told me that that was the single most common complaint he heard from his patients, even from the real satyrs: they weren't getting as much tail as the next guy.[61]

Looking back at this predicament, the narrator goes so far as to say that, in some respects, his anxious embodiment of the putatively liberatory 'freedom' of promiscuity made him an addicted 'prisoner to sex'.[62]

At the same time, this competitive anxiety need not only be traced to the influence of normative masculine gendering. Like Rechy's and Wojnarowicz's acknowledgement of how their familial past had some formative impact on their promiscuity, this narrator hints that his eagerness to please and be accepted within the newly open gay promiscuous culture is somewhat informed by his childhood experience: 'I'd been the son of a [supposedly] wicked divorcee who'd moved from city to city every year and I, like she, longed to make an impression even on strangers – *especially* on strangers;'[63] 'she made me spend my eighth, ninth and tenth birthdays in a nightclub with her while she cruised men at the bar.'[64]

The narrator also re-evaluates his old belief that 'the couple would disappear and be replaced by new, polyvalent molecules of affection'[65] by recalling his strong craving for coupledom at many points during that promiscuous era:

Of course the sermons I preached against love and jealousy were all the more absurd because I was so besotted with Kevin [whom he lived with, mostly platonically, for some time]. I wanted to be his wife in the most straitlaced of marriages. I wanted to cook his breakfast and bear his babies.[66]

As the reference to bearing babies confirms, the heavy influence of dominant heterosexual monogamous/marital fantasies partly accounts for this yearning for an intimate arrangement that would, in reality, be unpleasurably constraining for him. But as in all the other texts explored so far, this repeated eruption of monogamous desires within the highly promiscuous subject illustrates once again the perpetual interdependence and mutability of conflicting sexual and emotional desires in any subject or group, regardless of the desires and sociosexual arrangement that they most vehemently subscribe to.

These various critical reconsiderations of the meanings and experiences of promiscuity during the 1970s and early 1980s also need to be viewed within the context of the narrator's current life. His attention to the ambivalences of 'that druggy promiscuity of love and friendship, jealousy and envy',[67] is heightened in the present by his changing priorities in late middle age, by being 'the survivor of a dead generation',[68] and by the love and subsequent AIDS-related death of his partner, Brice: 'After all my years of defending promiscuity, I'd become a fierce champion of the couple.'[69] However, unlike the normatively monogamous ending of *The Golden Age of Promiscuity*, this narrator rejects any sense of monogamy providing narrative resolution by continuing to dwell on the contradictions in his desires. He speculates, with a frank promiscuous logic, that he may have finally found a mutually loving long-term relationship with Brice 'because I knew he was dying, . . . for I'd always been more afraid of being overwhelmed by what I possessed than of being abandoned by someone who'd never belonged to me.'[70] And equally, he points out the frustrating sexual paradox of his later life, when 'no one ever looks at me on the street and my dreams become more and more erotic.'[71]

So although *The Farewell Symphony* repeatedly calls into question a single-mindedly positive celebration of promiscuity, it also distinguishes itself from other recent gay male fictional reappraisals of the promiscuous past by producing a more sustained understanding throughout of the many contradictory potential experiences of promiscuous sexuality during the sexually experimental 1970s and early 1980s. At the same time, the novel's detailed recreation of the physical and psychical dimensions of numerous sexual adventures serves as an appropriately irreverent memorial to the diverse transitory encounters of that period, and demonstrates their often profound psychical longevity, both as personal memories and as a complex communal history of promiscuous pleasures, friendships and relationships that, as Eric Rofes notes, is now being widely swept aside by monogamy-centred accounts of that era:

A view has been put forward and become dominant that indicts gay male culture for pushing the limits of biology. We are told that the 1970s were a time of selfishness, excesses, decadence, and self-abuse. With perspectives imbibed through recovery movements focused on drug addiction, alcoholism, incest, sexual compulsion, and child abuse, we look back at this period and see only three features: drugs, attitude, and kinky sex. We pathologize the men and the culture of the 1970s from what we consider the superior morality of the 1990s. Huge numbers of men who participated most intensely in gay culture in the 1970s are dead and thus unable to provide voices that would broaden recollections and perspectives on those years. Many men died ugly and painful deaths, yet never stopped valuing the erotic experiences of those years and died with no regrets.[72]

While White realistically draws attention to the intermittent selfishness, excess and attitude of that era – qualities which can, of course, be unearthed in various forms in any period of history – his novel partly functions as a corrective to such smug justifications of an anti-promiscuous agenda for the present with a simplistically anti-promiscuous reading of the past. Indeed, *The Farewell Symphony*'s implicit defence of gay promiscuity, in all its difficult complexity, against this prevalent gay and straight cultural marriage-and-monogamy mandate became explicit when Kramer attacked White in his 1997 'Sex and sensibility' article for writing a novel that 'parades before the reader what seems to be every trick he's ever sucked, fucked, rimmed, tied up, pissed on, or been sucked by, fucked by, rimmed by, tied up by – you get the idea. There are so many faceless, indistinguishable pieces of flesh that litter these 500 pages that reading them becomes, for any reasonably sentient human being, at first a heartless experience and finally a boring one.'[73] In response to Kramer's wilfully selective account of the novel's detailed psychology and characterisation, and his hysteria over its unapologetically abundant sexual content (rather hypocritical coming from the author of the similarly sexually prodigious *Faggots*), White wrote an article for *Out* magazine on 'The joy of gay lit', where he challenged 'one of our prominent gay prudes'[74] with his own rationale for writing fiction about sex – a rationale that reiterates the ubiquity of promiscuous fantasy, and the unbounded promiscuousness of all sexual fantasy:

What has always been my guiding principle is that: (1) Every male thinks about sex once every 30 seconds, a frequency seriously underrepresented in serious fiction; (2) thoughts of sex are never neatly cloistered away but rather tincture every other thought and one goes seamlessly from Kant to cunt, from pianist to penis; (3) every time sex occurs it's a brand-new, virtually unclassifiable experience, and the novelist's job is to capture the novelty and the nuance.[75]

However, at the broader social level, the drive towards gay monogamy in America at the end of the twentieth century has been partly defended with references to the widely publicised practice of 'bareback' sex. In the July 1997 issue of *Out* magazine, prominent gay cultural journalist and author Michelangelo Signorile contributed an article entitled 'Bareback and reckless', in which he drew attention to this 'growing, alarming phenomenon'[76]: 'Also known as "skin-to-skin" or "raw," among several other terms, "going bareback" quite simply means having anal sex without condoms.'[77] During his investigations, Signorile had found that there were 'more than 250 users who have the word *bareback* in their America Online profiles',[78] leading him to speculate that 'if this sudden prevalence in cyberspace is any indication, these men are just the tip of a larger, dangerous iceberg.'[79]

While 'going bareback' is 'a choice HIV-positive men have faced for years'[80] with one another, Signorile's 'two dozen' interviewees who engage in bareback sex all 'either say they are negative or are unsure of their status.'[81] Disturbingly, a number of these men 'spoke of HIV infection as now being a minor inconvenience'[82] since the advent of protease inhibitor drugs – which, while promising, have currently in no way been proven to cure HIV, and have extreme side effects.

More startling, though, are Signorile's findings on what he calls a 'parallel new trend toward eroticizing the virus, where men actually talk about *desiring* both to infect others (if they are positive) or to become infected (if they are negative)' – an extreme example of coming to desire what is most frightening, and destructive, to oneself, perhaps as an attempt to override the widespread fatalism amongst American gay men, faced with the relentless presence of AIDS. He observes that 'on a Web site called XtremeSex, gay men in fact talk of "gift-giving" and receiving "that hot poz load." '[83] Although a number of these men might be playing out therapeutic, or less easily explained, fantasies, the seriousness of some of their comments suggests an actual desire to seroconvert: 'Some men lament their difficulties in getting infected: "Guess I haven't gotten the right virulent strain yet." '[84]

At the most immediate level, Signorile's findings on HIV-negative or unsure bareback men illustrate once again the ongoing risks and anxieties for promiscuous gay men in the age of AIDS. These particular bareback men have decided to embrace those risks, and forego those anxieties as much as possible, because sex is the primary priority in their lives. It would certainly be too simplistic to dismiss their frustration with sustaining safer sex practices year after year. Moreover, in Michael Warner's analysis of his own reasons for having had an *unplanned* unsafe sexual encounter, he underlines the attraction of prohibition and risk in unsafe sex, as he reflects that:

shame and fear had not been enough to keep me safe. Suddenly I had to think about why I wanted risky sex, knowing that the danger was part of the attraction. In the vast industry of AIDS education and prevention, I knew of nothing that would help me answer this question.[85]

But complex and varied as the un/conscious motivations of those particular 'barebackers' may be, their normalisation, and in some cases romanticisation, of unsafe sex does partly bring to mind Kramer's (and other critics') questioning of the prioritisation of sexual freedom over all other cultural and personal factors in many areas of mainstream gay male culture.

At another level, though, Signorile's interpretation of the bareback men's sexual practices echoes the most blaming and anti-promiscuous aspects of Kramer's texts. For beyond its straightforward recording of interviewees' comments, 'Bareback and reckless' also argues that the HIV-negative/unsure bareback men's sexual behaviour 'could have a devastating effect on efforts to contain the AIDS epidemic, and ultimately on the entire lesbian and gay community.'[86] Yet although Signorile cites one 'barebacker' who wrote online about infecting his boyfriend without warning him of his positive status,[87] the rest of the article suggests that self-declared bareback men generally have *consensual* unsafe sex (hence the Web site chat room exchanges), be they HIV-positive, negative or unsure. With this apparent consensuality in mind, Signorile's warning of the potentially 'devastating effect' of bareback sex on 'the entire lesbian and gay community' can be seen more precisely to serve a broader pro-monogamous liberal gay male scapegoating of promiscuous sex *per se* – an ideology shared by the activist organisation GALPHA (Gay and Lesbian HIV Prevention Activists), of which Signorile is a member. (As Alison Redick has noted, GALPHA targets 'public' sex in particular by asserting that 'a sharp increase in HIV transmission . . . can only be prevented by eliminating public, promiscuous sex,' thereby making 'regulation *appear to be* prevention activism while relying upon a false equation that links public sex with higher rates of seroconversion.'[88]) This anti-promiscuous agenda is underscored by the article's final collapsing together of a (possibly) 'growing group of people within our own community [who] are behaving recklessly and selfishly' in the late 1990s, and the supposed stubbornness of promiscuous gay men at the start of the AIDS epidemic:

Over 15 years ago, when AIDS first surfaced, many of us stuck our heads in the sand and – along with the government and the media – allowed the situation to get out of control. Will we not learn from our own past?[89]

In specific terms, Signorile's closing comments here wrongly recast as merely stubborn avoidance tactics the genuine confusion, uncertainty and sense of threat that gay men experienced in the early 1980s in response to mixed messages about how they should change their sexual practices. In more general terms, however, this normative image of 'reckless' and 'selfish' promiscuous men who 'allowed the situation to get out of control' serves to demonstrate once again that a rigidly anti-promiscuous and pro-monogamous/marital perspective always needs to construct an oversimplifed target group to blame for actual and perceived cultural problems (in this case, HIV/AIDS and promiscuous sexual pleasures respectively).

Equally, as we have repeatedly seen, such a rigid perspective invariably disavows the more complicated connections between avowedly monogamous and promiscuous groups/individuals. Hence, Signorile's article further avoids the fact that consensual unsafe sex is unlikely to have as widely devastating an effect on contemporary culture as the seroconversions that are enabled by those who strive to embody the dominant monogamous cultural ideal by having unprotected sex with a primary partner, while secretly having unprotected promiscuous sex outside the relationship, or else remaining monogamous but having unsafe sex with the assumption that they are HIV-negative. To requote Redick:

the problem of maintaining safer sex practices in the context of monogamous relationships is one of the greatest obstacles that prevention research has encountered. . . . Indeed, current research indicates that the pressures to engage in unprotected anal sex are much higher in the context of a long-term relationship than at a [sex] club, because sex without latex barriers tends to operate symbolically as a measure of trust and commitment.[90]

Apart from re-emphasising that monogamous sex is no guarantee against HIV unless it is safe (or unless one has had no other sexual partners), such research findings might be used to support the argument – implicit throughout this book – for a greater social acknowledgement and integration of promiscuous sexual desires and practices, which would, amongst other things, reduce the high degree of secrecy and shame surrounding non-monogamous needs within an unevenly monogamous dominant culture – a culture that is always already intrinsically informed by promiscuous desires.

Such an argument for the potentially beneficial effects of socially accommodating promiscuity has been most publicly put forward in late 1990s queer America by Sex Panic!, a New York City pro-sexual diversity activist organisation responding to crackdowns on 'public' and non-monogamous sex venues and practices in the city, and to the monopolisation of queer and straight media by anti-promiscuous voices. Work carried out by the group includes pressuring gay bars, the New York City Health Department and Gay Men's Health Crisis to provide adequate information and facilities towards HIV prevention/harm reduction; holding 'Queer-Ins' to assert an organised queer presence in public spaces used for sex; and disseminating information for men who cruise in the Ramble in Central Park concerning police arrest tactics and park users' legal rights.[91] At the 1997 National Sex Panic! Summit in San Diego, a Declaration of Sexual Rights was adopted that stressed the group's broad coalitional framework for tackling the widespread censorship and restriction of sexual rights:

The LGBT [lesbian/gay/bisexual/transgender] movement, feminism, and AIDS activism all include long histories of advocating the principles of sexual self-determinism. These principles are under attack. In the name of 'mainstream' acceptance, many are increasingly willing to embrace regulation and stigma for more marginal groups. And in the name of fighting AIDS, many deny that effective HIV prevention must emphasize pleasure and the complexity of sex. Increasingly forgotten are the diverse pleasures, intimacies, meanings and relations that sex enables. Those with fewer resources and least access to power – including those marginalized by race, class and gender – suffer disproportionately from denial of sexual rights.[92]

The document goes on to assert sexual and reproductive self-determination for all, without government intervention, and makes a number of general demands, including 'an end to the prohibition and stigmatization of public sex', 'HIV-prevention efforts built upon the right to be sexual and the need to sustain shared sexual cultures' and 'an end to state preference for traditional households and relationships.' Perhaps most importantly, given the general political rejection of progressive sex/uality-related policies, the Declaration seeks to link its concerns about diverse sexual rights to the (inter)national political landscape in material terms by demanding 'advocacy for the above principles and demands by all progressive and civil rights organizations.'

While clearly grounded in defending various forms of promiscuous sexuality against increasing prohibitions, the emphasis in Sex Panic!'s statement on promoting an extensive social accommodation of the 'complexity of sex' in numerous contexts – from youths to sex workers – also avoids creating a reverse discourse that would merely idealise promiscuity in the same way that dominant discourses and practices fantasise monogamy and/or marriage as the solution to myriad complex social problems. For as we have seen, the primary rejection of normative notions of promiscuity in Rechy's or White's or Wojnarowicz's texts repeatedly collides with the general unstable promiscuousness of desire itself, whether at the conscious, subconscious or unconscious level.

On the one hand, then, in cruising culture, we have seen that cruising cultures exist – consciously or otherwise – throughout self-declared monogamous and promiscuous groups alike, regardless of their sexuality, sex, gender, class, ethnicity or race, and despite hypocritical dominant projections of promiscuous desires onto various marginalised groups. On the other hand, in Rechy's and Kramer's often anxiously pessimistic cruising characters, or in Wojnarowicz's monogamous romantic fantasies, or in his deeply ambivalent relationship to the Manhattan piers where he pursued dangerous-looking men, we are reminded of the interdependence of monogamous and promiscuous desires within all cultures and individuals alike, to greater or lesser degrees of consciousness. And in engaging with these texts, we are also reminded of the substantially *unsocialisable* disruptiveness of desire, which can never be fully resolved within avowedly monogamous or promiscuous sexual identities. After all, when we glance back at someone who catches our eye on the street, in a club, or in any other eroticised public space, we are also glancing back internally, psychically, activating memories and fantasies that are continuously – and unpredictably – at work in the endless flux of our desires.

Notes

1. Gooch, *The Golden Age of Promiscuity*, p. 171.
2. Ibid., p. 158.
3. Ibid., p. 169.
4. Ibid., pp. 125–6.
5. Ibid., p. 260.
6. Ibid., p. 297.
7. Ibid., p. 282.
8. Gurganus, *Plays Well With Others*, p. 230.
9. Ibid., p. 49.
10. Ibid., p. 280.
11. Ibid., p. 83.
12. Ibid., p. 78.
13. Ibid., p. 124.
14. Kramer, 'Sex and sensibility', p. 59.
15. Gurganus, *Plays Well With Others*, p. 81.
16. Ibid., p. 76.
17. Ibid., p. 77.
18. Ibid., p. 83.
19. Holleran, *The Beauty of Men*, p. 223.
20. Ibid., p. 29.
21. Ibid., p. 235.
22. Ibid., p. 59.

192   CRUISING CULTURE

23. Ibid., p. 234.
24. Ibid., p. 29.
25. Holleran, *Dancer*, p. 210.
26. Holleran, *The Beauty of Men*, p. 79.
27. Ibid., p. 196.
28. Wojnarowicz, *Close to the Knives*, p. 187.
29. Holleran, *The Beauty of Men*, p. 153.
30. Ibid., p. 74.
31. Ibid.
32. Rofes, *Reviving the Tribe*, p. 98.
33. Holleran, *The Beauty of Men*, pp. 222–3.
34. Ibid., p. 75.
35. Ibid., p. 78.
36. Ibid., p. 213.
37. Ibid., p. 186.
38. Ibid., p. 55.
39. Ibid., p. 249.
40. Ibid., p. 35.
41. Ibid., p. 230.
42. Ibid., p. 270.
43. Ibid., p. 250.
44. White, 'Paradise found', p. 153.
45. White, *The Farewell Symphony*, p. 21.
46. Ibid., prefatory statement.
47. Ibid., p. 431.
48. Ibid.
49. Ibid., p. 2.
50. Ibid., p. 502.
51. We saw another eroticisation of loss, in a different context, in Rechy and Wojnarowicz's retrospective promiscuous eroticisation of their fathers' ambiguous withholding and enforcement of their affections.
52. White, *The Farewell Symphony*, p. 21.
53. Ibid., p. 300.
54. Ibid.
55. Ibid., pp. 300–1.
56. Crimp, 'How to have promiscuity', p. 253.
57. White, *The Farewell Symphony*, pp. 298–9.
58. Ibid., p. 181.
59. Ibid., p. 299.
60. Ibid., p. 384.
61. Ibid., p. 300.
62. Ibid., p. 200.
63. Ibid., p. 409.
64. Ibid., p. 193.
65. Ibid., p. 414.
66. Ibid., p. 301.
67. Ibid., p. 420.
68. Ibid., p. 495.
69. Ibid., p. 421.
70. Ibid., p. 501.
71. Ibid., p. 21.
72. Rofes, *Reviving the Tribe*, pp. 104–5.

73. Kramer, 'Sex and sensibility', p. 64.
74. White, 'The joy of gay lit', p. 112.
75. Ibid., p. 114.
76. Signorile, 'Bareback and reckless', p. 38.
77. Ibid., p. 36.
78. Ibid.
79. Ibid.
80. Ibid., p. 38.
81. Ibid., p. 36.
82. Ibid., p. 39.
83. Ibid., p. 38.
84. Ibid.
85. Warner, 'Why gay men are having unsafe sex', p. 33.
86. Signorile, 'Bareback and reckless', p. 36.
87. '"[O]ne thing led to another. We fucked some, talked some. 'So are you infecting me?' he asked, real quiet. 'Yeah, I am.'"' Ibid., p. 38.
88. Redick, 'Dangerous practices', p. 92.
89. Signorile, 'Bareback and reckless', p. 39.
90. Redick, 'Dangerous practices', p. 97.
91. My thanks to Bill Dobbs of Sex Panic! for providing me with details of the group's work.
92. 'A Declaration of sexual rights', reproduced at: http://www.cruisingfor-sex.com/manifesto.html

Bibliography

Adams, Stephen (1980), *The Homosexual as Hero in Contemporary Fiction*, New York: Barnes & Noble.

Advocate Men (1984), June.

Altman, Dennis (1983), *The Homosexualization of America*, Boston: Beacon Press.

Angier, Natalie (1999), *Woman: An Intimate Geography*, London: Virago.

Aperture (1994), special issue: 'David Wojnarowicz: brushfires in the social landscape', Fall.

Baldwin, James (1993), *Another Country*, New York: Vintage.

Barrett, Michèle and Mary McIntosh (1991), *The Anti-Social Family*, 2nd edn, London and New York: Verso.

Bell, Alan P. and Martin S. Weinberg (1978), *Homosexualities: A Study of Diversity Among Men and Women*, New York: Simon & Schuster.

Bell, David (1995), 'Perverse dynamics, sexual citizenship and the transformation of intimacy', in Bell and Valentine (eds), *Mapping Desire: Geographies of Sexualities*, London and New York: Routledge.

Berlant, Lauren and Michael Warner (1998), 'Sex in Public', *Critical Inquiry*, vol. 24, no. 2, Winter.

Bersani, Leo (1995), *Homos*, Cambridge, MA and London: Harvard University Press.

Bersani, Leo (1987), 'Is the rectum a grave?' in Crimp (ed.), *AIDS: Cultural Analysis, Cultural Activism*, Cambridge, MA and London: MIT Press.

Bérubé, Allan (1991), 'Marching to a different drummer: Lesbian and gay GIs in World War II', in Duberman et al. (eds), *Hidden from History: Reclaiming the Gay and Lesbian Past*, Harmondsworth: Penguin.

Blinderman, Barry (1990), 'The compression of time: an interview with David Wojnarowicz', in Blinderman (ed.), *David Wojnarowicz: Tongues of Flame*, New York and Normal, IL: DAP/Illinois State University.

Boswell, John (1980), *Christianity, Social Tolerance, and Homosexuality: Gay People in Western Europe from the Beginning of the Christian Era to the Fourteenth Century*, Chicago and London: University of Chicago Press.

Bredbeck, Gregory W. (1995), 'The new queer narrative: intervention and critique', *Textual Practice*, vol. 9, no. 3.

Bronski, Michael (1993), 'How sweet (and sticky) it was', in Preston (ed.), *Flesh and the Word 2: An Anthology of Erotic Writing*, New York: Plume.

Brown, Rita Mae (1988), *Rubyfruit Jungle*, New York and Toronto: Bantam.

Burgin, Victor (1992), 'Fantasy' entry in Wright, Elizabeth (ed.), *Feminism and Psychoanalysis: A Critical Dictionary*, Cambridge, MA and Oxford: Blackwell.

Burton, Peter (1991), *Talking To . . .*, Exeter: Third House.

Burton, Peter (1996), 'Tearoom trade', *Rouge*, no. 20.

Butler, Judith (1993), *Bodies That Matter: On the Discursive Limits of 'Sex'*, New York and London: Routledge.

Butler, Judith (1990), *Gender Trouble: Feminism and the Subversion of Identity*, New York and London: Routledge.

Butterick, Brian (1982), Foreword to D. Wojnarowicz, *Sounds in the Distance*, London: Aloes Books.

Cagle, Chris (1996), 'Rough trade: sexual taxonomy in postwar America', in Hall and Pramaggiore (eds), *RePresenting Bisexualities: Subjects and Cultures of Fluid Desire*, New York and London: New York University Press.

Califia, Pat (1994), *Public Sex: The Culture of Radical Sex*, Pittsburgh and San Francisco: Cleis Press.

Califia, Pat (1993), *Sapphistry: The Book of Lesbian Sexuality*, 3rd edn, Tallahassee, FL: The Naiad Press.

Califia, Pat (1992), 'Slipping', in Cooper (ed.), *Discontents: New Queer Writers*, New York: Amethyst Press.

Callen, Michael and Bob Caviano (1992), 'Sex after AIDS', *NYQ*, 19 April.

Carr, C (1993), *On Edge: Performance at the End of the Twentieth Century*, Hanover, NH and London: Wesleyan University Press/University Press of New England.

Chauncey, George (1994), *Gay New York: Gender, Urban Culture, and the Making of the Modern Gay World 1890–1940*, New York: Basic Books.

Chauncey, George (1996), '"Privacy could only be had in public": gay uses of the street', in Sanders (ed.), *Stud: Architectures of Masculinity*, New York: Princeton Architectural Press.

Chesebro, James W. and Kenneth L. Klenk (1981), 'Gay masculinity in the gay disco', in Chesebro (ed.), *GaySpeak: Gay Male and Lesbian Communication*, New York: The Pilgrim Press.

Chua, Lawrence (1995), 'Lyons at the Gate', *Out*, July–August.

Collard, James (1994), 'Wanna be in my gang?' *Attitude*, November.

Cooper, Dennis (1985), 'The East Village and its new gay ways', *The Advocate*, 19 March.

Cowie, Elizabeth (1984), 'Fantasia', *m/f*, no. 9.

Creed, Barbara (1989), 'Horror and the monstrous-feminine: an imaginary abjection', in Donald (ed.), *Fantasy and the Cinema*, London: British Film Institute.

Crenson, Matt (1997), 'Chimpanzees sleep around, study says', *The Morning Call* (Allentown, PA), 22 May.

Crimp, Douglas (1987), 'How to have promiscuity in an epidemic', in Crimp (ed.), *AIDS: Cultural Analysis, Cultural Activism*, Cambridge, MA and London: MIT Press.

Crimp, Douglas (1993), 'Mourning and melancholia,' in Ferguson et al. (eds), *Out There: Marginalization and Contemporary Cultures*, New York, Cambridge, MA and London: The New Museum of Contemporary Art/MIT Press.

Dangerous Bedfellows (eds) (1996), *Policing Public Sex: Queer Politics and the Future of AIDS Activism*, Boston: South End Press.

Davies, Peter M. et al. (1993), *Sex, Gay Men and AIDS*, London and Bristol, PA: Falmer Press.

de Certeau, Michel (1984), 'Walking in the city', in *The Practice of Everyday Life*, Berkeley: University of California Press; rpt. in During (ed.) (1993), *The Cultural Studies Reader*, London and New York: Routledge.

Deitcher, David (1989), 'Ideas and emotions', *Artforum*, May.

Delany, Samuel R. (1990), *The Motion of Light in Water: East Village Sex and Science Fiction Writing: 1960–1965*, London: Paladin.

de Lauretis, Teresa (ed.) (1991), *differences*: 'Queer theory: lesbian and gay sexualities' issue, vol. 3, no. 2.

DeLynn, Jane (1991), *Don Juan in the Village*, London: Serpent's Tail.

D'Emilio, John (1983), 'Capitalism and gay identity', in Snitow (eds), *Powers of Desire: The Politics of Sexuality*, New York: Monthly Review Press.

D'Emilio, John and Estelle B. Freedman (1988), *Intimate Matters: A History of Sexuality in America*, New York: Perennial/Harper & Row.

Dollimore, Jonathan (1991), *Sexual Dissidence: Augustine to Wilde, Freud to Foucault*, Oxford: Clarendon Press.

Douglas, Susan J. (1995), *Where the Girls Are: Growing Up Female with the Mass Media*, New York: Times Books.

Dyer, Richard (1992), 'Don't look now: the instabilities of the male pin-up', in *Only Entertainment*, London and New York: Routledge.

Dyer, Richard (1990), *Now You See It: Studies on Lesbian and Gay Film*, London and New York: Routledge.

Eighner, Lars (1994), *Travels with Lizbeth: Three Years on the Road and on the Streets*, New York: Fawcett Books.

Ehrenreich, Barbara et al. (1987), *Re-Making Love: The Feminization of Sex*, London: Fontana/Collins.

Fain, Nathan (1982), 'Is our "lifestyle" hazardous to our health? Part II', *The Advocate*, 1 April; cited in Jeffrey Weeks (1986), *Sexuality and its Discontents: Meanings, Myths and Modern Sexualities*, London and New York: Routledge & Kegan Paul.

Fisher, Gary (1996), *Gary in Your Pocket*. See Kosofsky Sedgwick.

Foucault, Michel (1984), *The History of Sexuality: An Introduction*, Harmondsworth: Penguin/Peregrine.

Freud, Sigmund (1991), 'General theory of the neuroses', *Introductory Lectures on Psychoanalysis*, Penguin Freud Library, vol. 1, Harmondsworth: Penguin.

Freud, Sigmund (1977), 'On the universal tendency to debasement in the sphere of love (Contributions to the Psychology of Love II)', *On Sexuality*, Penguin Freud Library, vol. 7, Harmondsworth: Penguin.

Garber, Eric (1991), 'A spectacle in color: The lesbian and gay subculture of jazz age harlem', in Duberman et al. (eds), *Hidden from History: Reclaiming the Gay and Lesbian Past*, Harmondsworth: Penguin.

Getlin, Josh (1978), 'Kramer vs. Kramer', *The Los Angeles Times*, 10 December.

Gibson, Colin S. (1994), *Dissolving Wedlock*, London and New York: Routledge.

Gillings, Andrew (1997), 'B-boy blues', *The Village Voice*, August 26.

Ginsberg, Allen (1987), *Collected Poems 1947–1980*, Harmondsworth: Penguin.

Giteck, Lenny (1979), 'Larry Kramer: Mad about faggots', *The Advocate*, 8 February.

Goldberg, Jonathan (1992), *Sodometries: Renaissance Texts, Modern Sexualities*, Stanford: Stanford University Press.

Gooch, Brad (1997), *The Golden Age of Promiscuity*, New York: Hard Candy Books.

Gottfried, Martin (1993), *Sondheim*, New York: Harry N. Abrams, Inc.

Gough, Jamie (1989), 'Theories of sexual identity and the masculinization of the gay man', in Shepherd and Wallis (eds), *Coming On Strong: Gay Politics and Culture*, London: Unwin Hyman.

Gurganus, Allan (1999), *Plays Well With Others*, London: Faber and Faber.

Hemphill, Essex (1991), Introduction to Hemphill (ed.), conceived by Beam, *Brother to Brother: New Writings by Black Gay Men*, Boston: Alyson.

Hess, Elizabeth (1996), 'Last action hero', *The Village Voice*, 14 May.

Hess, Elizabeth (1990), 'Queer in normal', *The Village Voice*, 13 February.

Hirsh, David (1989), 'Speed at all costs: an interview with David Wojnarowicz', *New York Native*, 6 March.

Hobsbawm, Eric (1995), *Age of Extremes: The Short Twentieth Century 1914–1991*, London: Abacus.

Holleran, Andrew (1997), *The Beauty of Men*, New York: Plume.

Holleran, Andrew (1990), *Dancer from the Dance*, Harmondsworth: Penguin.

Holleran, Andrew (1988), *Ground Zero*, New York: New American Library/ Plume.

Holleran, Andrew (1992), 'Steam, soap, and sex', *The Advocate*, 6 October.

Howes, Keith (1979), 'Where love has gone', *Gay News* (London), 26 July– 22 August.

Isenberg, Barbara (1977), 'Defiance, despair of a "sexual outlaw"', *The Los Angeles Times*, 31 March.

Isherwood, Charles (1996), 'Beyond the night', *The Advocate*, 15 October.

Jay, Karla (1975), 'The spirit is liberationist but the flesh is . . ., or, you can't always get into bed with your dogma', in Jay and Young (eds), *After You're Out: Personal Experiences of Gay Men and Lesbian Women*, New York and London: Links.

Julien, Isaac and Kobena Mercer (1988), 'Race, sexual politics and black masculinity: A dossier', in Chapman and Rutherford (eds), *Male Order: Unwrapping Masculinity*, London: Lawrence & Wishart.

Julien, Isaac and Kobena Mercer (1991), 'True confessions: A discourse on images of black male sexuality', in Hemphill (ed.), conceived by Beam, *Brother to Brother: New Writings by Black Gay Men*, Boston: Alyson.

Katz, Jonathan Ned (1996), *The Invention of Heterosexuality*, New York: Plume.

Kerouac, Jack (1982), *On the Road*, New York: Signet.

King, Edward (1993), *Safety in Numbers: Safer Sex and Gay Men*, London and New York: Cassell.

Kleinberg, Seymour (1980), *Alienated Affections: Being Gay in America*, New York: St. Martin's Press.

Knopp, Lawrence (1995), 'Sexuality and urban space: A framework for analysis', in Bell and Valentine (eds), *Mapping Desire: Geographies of Sexualities*, London and New York: Routledge.

Koehler, Robert (1985), '"Normal Heart": An AIDS theme on upbeat scale', *The Los Angeles Times*, 5 December.

Kosofsky Sedgwick, Eve (1996), *Gary in Your Pocket: Stories and Notebooks of Gary Fisher*, Durham, NC and London: Duke University Press.

Krafft-Ebing, Richard von (1893), *Psychopathia Sexualis, with Especial Reference to Contrary Sexual Instinct: A Medico-Legal Study*, Philadelphia: F. A. Davis.

Kramer, Larry (1986), *Faggots*, London: Methuen.

Kramer, Larry (1985), *The Normal Heart*, New York and Scarborough, Ontario: Plume.

Kramer, Larry (1995), *Reports from the Holocaust: The Story of an AIDS Activist*, revised edition, London: Cassell.

Kramer, Larry (1997), 'Sex and sensibility', *The Advocate*, 27 May.

Kristeva, Julia (1982), *Powers of Horror: An Essay on Abjection*, New York: Columbia University Press.

Kuby, Adam (1992), 'The art of David Wojnarowicz', *Out/Look*, Spring.

Laermer, Richard (1986), 'The real John Rechy', *New York Native*, 3 November.

Laermer, Richard (1986), 'Rechy on AIDS: stop, live, change', *New York Native*, 3 November.

Laplanche, Jean and Jean-Bertrand Pontalis (1988), *The Language of Psychoanalysis*, London: The Institute of Psychoanalysis/Karnac Books.

Legman, Gershon (1941), 'The language of homosexuality: An American glossary', in Henry, *Sex Variants: A Study of Homosexual Patterns*, vol. 2, New York: Paul B. Hoeber.

Lippard, Lucy R. (1990), 'Out of the safety zone', *Art in America*, December.

Lippard, Lucy R. (1994), 'Passenger on the shadows', *Aperture*, Fall.

Lorde, Audre (1994), *Zami: A New Spelling of My Name*, Freedom, CA: The Crossing Press.

Martin, Biddy (1994), 'Sexualities without genders and other queer utopias', *diacritics*, vol. 24, nos. 2–3.

Mass, Lawrence D. (1997), 'Larry versus Larry: the making of a writer/activist', in Mass (ed.), *We Must Love One Another or Die: The Life and Legacies of Larry Kramer*, London: Cassell.

Maves, Karl (1979), review of *Faggots*, *The Advocate*, 8 February.

McCormick, Carlo (1990), 'Fables, facts, riddles, and reasons in Wojnarowicz's mythopoetica', in Blinderman (ed.), *David Wojnarowicz: Tongues of Flame*, New York and Normal, IL: DAP/Illinois State University.

Merck, Mandy (1998), 'Savage nights', in Merck et al. (eds), *Lesbian and Gay Studies: Coming Out of Feminism?*, Oxford: Blackwell.

Millet, Kate (1977), *Sexual Politics*, London: Virago.

Moon, Michael (1993), 'Outlaw sex and the "Search for America": Representing male prostitution and perverse desire in sixties film (*My Hustler* and *Midnight Cowboy*)', *Quarterly Review of Film and Video*, vol. 15, no. 1.

Morris, William (ed.) (1980), *The American Heritage Dictionary of the English Language*, Boston: Houghton Mifflin Company.

Morrison, Toni (1992), *Playing in the Dark: Whiteness and the Literary Imagination*, Cambridge, MA and London: Harvard University Press.

Morrisroe, Patricia (1995), *Mapplethorpe: A Biography*, London: Macmillan.

Munt, Sally (1995), 'The lesbian *flâneur*', in D. Bell and G. Valentine (eds), *Mapping Desire: Geographies of Sexualities*, London and New York: Routledge.

Nagle, Dean (1977), 'Sisyphus as outlaw: crimes against nature, an interview with John Rechy', *The Advocate*, 1 June.

Odets, Walt (1995), *In the Shadow of the Epidemic: Being HIV-Negative in the Age of AIDS*, Durham, NC and London: Duke University Press and Cassell.

O'Hara, Scott (1997), 'Safety first?' *The Advocate*, 8 July.

Oppenheimer, Joshua (1997), 'Unforgiving errors', *Gay Community News*, Summer.

Orr, Deborah (1995), 'Say grace', *The Guardian*, 22 July.

The Oxford English Dictionary (1989), 2nd edn, vol. XII, Oxford: Clarendon Press.

Pally, Marcia (1986), 'A visit with author John Rechy: caught between worlds in the American landscape', *The Advocate*, 23 December.

Parkes, James Cary (1996), 'Silences and Secrets', *Gay Times*, February.

Patton, Cindy (1990), *Inventing AIDS*, New York and London: Routledge.

Patton, Cindy (1985), *Sex and Germs: The Politics of AIDS*, Boston: South End Press.

Phillips, Adam (1996), *Monogamy*, London and Boston: Faber and Faber.

Preston, John (1993), *My Life as a Pornographer and Other Indecent Acts*, New York: Richard Kasak.

Radway, Janice (1983), 'Women read the romance: the interaction of text and context', *Feminist Studies*, vol. 9, no. 1; rpt. in Dines and Humez (eds) (1995), *Gender, Race and Class in Media: A Text-Reader*, Thousand Oaks, CA and London: Sage Publications.

Rechy, John (1964), *City of Night*, London: MacGibbon & Kee.

Rechy, John (1994), Introduction to *City of Night*, New York: Quality Paperback Book Club.

Rechy, John (1990), *Numbers*, New York: Grove Weidenfeld.

Rechy, John (1981), *Rushes*, New York: Grove Press.

Rechy, John (1978), *The Sexual Outlaw: A Documentary*, London: W. H. Allen.

Redick, Alison (1996), 'Dangerous practices: ideological uses of the "second wave"', in Dangerous Bedfellows (eds), *Policing Public Sex: Queer Politics and the Future of AIDS Activism*, Boston: South End Press.

Rofes, Eric (1996), *Reviving the Tribe: Regenerating Gay Men's Sexuality and Culture in the Ongoing Epidemic*, New York and London: Harrington Park Press.

Rose, Jacqueline (1986), *Sexuality in the Field of Vision*, London and New York: Verso.

Rotello, Gabriel (1997), *Sexual Ecology: AIDS and the Destiny of Gay Men*, New York: Dutton.

Rubin, Gayle (1992), 'Thinking sex: notes for a radical theory of the politics of sexuality', in Vance (ed.), *Pleasure and Danger: Exploring Female Sexuality*, London: Pandora.

Sadownick, Douglas (1996), *Sex Between Men: An Intimate History of the Sex Lives of Gay Men Postwar to Present*, San Francisco: Harper-SanFrancisco.

Schofield, Michael (1976), *Promiscuity*, London: Victor Gollancz.

Scholder, Amy (1996), Editor's Preface to Wojnarowicz, *The Waterfront Journals*, New York: Grove Press.

Scholder, Amy (1999), *Fever: The Art of David Wojnarowicz*, New York: Rizzoli.

Schulman, Sarah (1994), *My American History: Lesbian and Gay Life During the Reagan/Bush Years*, New York: Routledge.

Segal, Lynne (1990), *Slow Motion: Changing Masculinities, Changing Men*, London: Virago.

Seidman, Steven (1992), *Embattled Eros: Sexual Politics and Ethics in Contemporary America*, New York and London: Routledge.

Seidman, Steven (1991), *Romantic Longings: Love in America, 1830–1980*, New York and London: Routledge.

Signorile, Michelangelo (1997), 'Bareback and restless', *Out*, July.

Simpson, Mark (1994), *Male Impersonators: Men Performing Masculinities*, New York: Routledge.

Sinfield, Alan (1994), *The Wilde Century: Effeminacy, Oscar Wilde and the Queer Moment*, London: Cassell.

Smiley, Jane (1992), *A Thousand Acres*, New York: Fawcett Columbine.

Snitow, Ann Barr (1983), 'Mass market romance: pornography for women is different', in Snitow et al. (eds), *Powers of Desire: The Politics of Sexuality*, New York: Monthly Review Press.

Sondheim, Stephen and Hugh Wheeler (1995), *A Little Night Music*, London: Nick Hern Books.

Stallybrass, Peter and Allon White (1986), *The Politics and Poetics of Transgression*, London: Methuen.

Straayer, Chris (1996), *Deviant Eyes, Deviant Bodies: Sexual Re-orientations in Film and Video*, New York: Columbia University Press.

Straight to Hell (1973), no. 3.

Sullivan, Andrew (1995), 'Larry Kramer, with sugar on top', *POZ*, April–May.

Tennyson, Alfred (1989), *Tennyson: A Selected Edition*, ed. Christopher Ricks.

Tucker, Scott (1979), 'Ivory towers and barricades: why we need better books', *The Body Politic*, June.

Tucker, Scott (1989), 'Larry Kramer's ghetto of illusions', *Lambda Rising Book Report*, April–May.

Tucker, Scott (1982), 'Our right to the world', *The Body Politic*, July–August.

Vidal, Gore (1994), *The City and the Pillar*, revised edn, London: Andre Deutsch.

Vidal, Gore (1996), *Palimpsest: A Memoir*, London: Abacus.

Warner, Michael (1997), 'Media gays: a new stone wall', *The Nation*, July 14.

Warner, Michael (1995), 'Why gay men are having unsafe sex', *The Village Voice*, January 31.

Watney, Simon (1995), Foreword to L. Kramer, *Reports from the Holocaust: The Story of an AIDS Activist*, revised edition, London: Cassell.

Watney, Simon (1989), *Policing Desire: Pornography, AIDS and the Media*, 2nd edn, Minneapolis: University of Minnesota Press.

Watney, Simon (1994), *Practices of Freedom: Selected Writings on HIV/AIDS*, London: Rivers Oram Press.

Weeks, Jeffrey (1986), *Sexuality and its Discontents: Meanings, Myths & Modern Sexualities*, London and New York: Routledge & Kegan Paul.

Weir, John (1996), 'Is there life after sex?' in Mark Simpson (ed.), *Anti-Gay*, London and New York: Freedom Editions.

Weston, Kath (1995), 'Get thee to a big city: sexual imaginary and the great gay migration', *GLQ*, vol. 2, no. 3.

Weston, Kath (1991), *Families We Choose: Lesbians, Gays, Kinship*, New York: Columbia University Press.

'When park sex is not public' (1994), *The Pink Paper*, 18 November.

White, Edmund (1995), 'Paradise found', in *The Burning Library: Writing on Art, Politics and Sexuality 1969–1993*, London: Picador.

White, Edmund (1997), *The Farewell Symphony*, London: Vintage.

White, Edmund (1997), 'The joy of gay lit', *Out*, September.

Whitmore, George (1978), 'Beer, baloney and champagne', *The Body Politic*, September.

Wilton, Tamsin (1996), *Finger-Licking Good: The Ins and Outs of Lesbian Sex*, London and New York: Cassell.

Wojnarowicz, David (1990), 'Biographical dateline', in Blinderman (ed.), *David Wojnarowicz: Tongues of Flame*, New York and Normal, IL: DAP/Illinois State University.

Wojnarowicz, David (1992), *Close to the Knives: A Memoir of Disintegration*, London: Serpent's Tail.

Wojnarowicz, David (1999), *In the Shadow of the American Dream: The Diaries of David Wojnarowicz*, New York: Grove Press.

Wojnarowicz, David (1992), *Memories That Smell Like Gasoline*, San Francisco: Artspace Books.

Wojnarowicz, David (1982), *Sounds in the Distance*, London: Aloes Books.

Wojnarowicz, David (1996), *The Waterfront Journals*, New York: Grove Press.

Wolf, Naomi (1997), *Promiscuities: The Secret Struggle for Womanhood*, New York: Random House.
Wood, Robin (1989), *Hitchcock's Films Revisited*, New York: Columbia University Press.
Wright, Elizabeth (ed.) (1992), *Feminism and Psychoanalysis: A Critical Dictionary*, Oxford and Cambridge, MA: Blackwell.
Yablonskaya, Linda (1991), 'Covering the slaughterfront', *Outweek*, 3 July.
Young, Elizabeth and Graham Caveney (1992), *Shopping in Space: Essays on American 'Blank Generation' Fiction*, London: Serpent's Tail.
Zonana, Victor (1992), 'Kramer vs. the world', *The Advocate*, 1 December.

Index

abjection, 54–5, 70–1, 96, 97–8, 100, 115

Adams, Stephen, 44, 45, 48, 58, 74n

Adventures of Priscilla, Queen of the Desert, The, 50

AIDS/HIV, 13, 30–3, 81–5, 87–8, 115–23, 133, 148–50, 162, 168n, 174, 175, 178–82, 185, 187–90

Altman, Dennis, 14, 41, 91, 92, 99, 102

Andros, Phil, 5

autobiography, 5, 30, 42, 44, 46, 50, 69, 74n, 75n, 78n, 81, 83, 86, 100, 116, 127n, 130n, 135–6, 164n, 166n, 174, 180

auto-eroticism, 146

Baldwin, James, 77n

'bareback' sex, 186–9

Barrett, Michèle, 94, 95

Bell, David, 171n

Berlant, Lauren, 16

Bersani, Leo, 18, 37n, 62, 79n, 126n

Bérubé, Allan, 24

Bredbeck, Gregory W., 165–6n

Bronski, Michael, 27

Brown, Rita Mae, 128n

Burgin, Victor, 146

Burroughs, William, 168n

Burton, Peter, 142

Cagle, Chris, 46, 74n

Califia, Pat, 32, 88, 102, 137

Callen, Michael, 85, 131n

celibacy, 91

Chauncey, George, 22–3, 25, 38n, 45, 65, 67–8, 129n, 161, 171–2n

Chesebro, James W., 75–6n

Cole, David, 138

Cowie, Elizabeth, 17, 113

Creed, Barbara, 96, 97–8, 115

Crimp, Douglas, 14, 92, 116, 117, 130n

cruising, 22, 24, 27–9, 33, 107–10, 111–12, 129n, 140–6, 160–3, 179, 190

Davies, Peter M. et al., 120

de Certeau, Michel, 161

Delany, Samuel R., 14, 36n

DeLynn, Jane, 107

D'Emilio, John, 10, 22, 28, 95

Dollimore, Jonathan, 79n

Douglas, Susan J., 11

Duffy, Maureen, 107

Dyer, Richard, 78n

Ehrenreich, Barbara et al., 9